The Manga Jesus
Book Three

SIKU

H
HODDER

To my three girls, Khreeo, Petra and Talitha

The Manga Jesus: Book Three
Copyright © 2009 by Siku

First published in Great Britain in 2009 by Hodder & Stoughton
An Hachette UK company

1

A CIP catalogue record for this title is available from the British Library

ISBN 978 0 340 96407 1

Printed and bound in Italy by Legoprint S.P.A

Hodder & Stoughton policy is to use papers that are natural, renewable and
recyclable products and made from wood grown in sustainable forests. The logging
and manufacturing processes are expected to conform to the environmental
regulations of the country of origin.

Hodder & Stoughton Ltd
338 Euston Road
London NW1 3BH

www.hodderfaith.com

Ding ding ding! Jesus... fiction... comic book... superhero. Alarm bells!

I'm a historian. My PhD thesis compared the work of St Luke with the best of the Greek and Roman historians. This project flashed twenty different kinds of red lights in my head.

OK, I knew Siku. He did an undergraduate degree in theology where I work, The London School of Theology, formerly known as London Bible College. He's a great student. I worked with him on the New Testament portion of *The Manga Bible*, which illustrates the text of Scripture in manga form. It is most excellent.

But this?! To fill in gaps that the Bible leaves blank?
To employ a medium we associate with ludicrous and outrageous fantasies to portray what I think is truth? Ding ding ding!

I was approached to be the 'theological consultant'. Ummm. Thought I'd have to say no. Decline gracefully. This might be going too far.

Then I saw the material. Whoa! He's done his homework! He knows the ancient sources; he's sensitive to the ancient culture. Whoa!

Then I saw the drawings. Wow! He's totally captured John the Baptist; his gap-filling is helpful rather than distracting. And, I'm sorry, for me that IS the Temple.

And then, beyond wow! This is not only filled with learning about the ancient world. It's also so clearly filled with sympathy for the characters and, better still, filled with love for the Scriptures and for the Lord.

You look at these pages — or through these pages — a man pushes the hood back from his head and turns to you. A wry smile. And with

the suggestion of a twinkle in his eye, he says to you — to you —
'Oh. By the way... They call me Yeshua — Jesus.'

Gulp.

Yeah, ok, maybe manga comics seemed inappropriate. A worldly
medium. An earthen vessel. Just like any of us.

No more alarms; sound the 'all clear'. For some people in today's
culture — all very, very clear.

Dr Conrad Gempf, London School of Theology

N.D.O.A. (Not Dead, Only Asleep)

I was concluding Jesus' Passion Week chapter in *The Manga Jesus Book Three*, in the week leading to Easter Sunday. The original deadline was January, but the marketing boys had redrawn the battle plans, so I needn't push the boat out. If you tell an artist there are no serious time constraints... well, don't ever tell an artist that there are no serious time constraints. They'll just think you mean they have ten years to do the work. With all that extra time the marketing boys gave this artist (a no no!), I had a bright idea... 'Why don't I just re-write the second half of the book?' And so I did! It added another couple of months to the schedule but why quibble about little things like schedules when an artist is at work, huh?

And so, out go chapters like 'Montage', where Yeshua's followers reminisce about the Saviour after his death; in comes 'Auf Wiedersehen'. Judas gets to talk to us while hanging on a noose from a tree! Out goes the chapter 'Road to Emmaus' and in comes 'N.D.O.A. (Not Dead, Only Asleep)'. Here, I would like to introduce you to what my mate, Paul Kercal, calls 'Zombies'. They come alive from the dead after Jesus is resurrected and decide, 'Hey, why don't we go into town to visit the faithful before we make our way to heaven?' Eliminating the Nicodemus story in 'Montage' meant my fantasia segment (the Gospel of Matthew's dark clouds over the whole land) had room to breathe. Like all epic stories, you've got to have that cosmos-shaking climactic... um, bit.

Now, I have gone astray, haven't I? As Easter week begins, I am more mindful of it than at any time of my life. I write, read, re-read, research, design and draw and all the time I am getting closer to the Saviour and suddenly, Easter is a practical, as well as a spiritual, landmark.

From Palm Sunday, I had been listening to Andrae Crouch while I worked. By Wednesday, John Debney's The Passion of the Christ was my guide. It replicated my emotions and mood for the strip exactly. I wish I could have listened to Peter Gabriel's Passion on Spotify, but it wasn't available. Nonetheless, the moody 'The Olive Garden' from John Debney's soundtrack perfectly matched the mood I was creating with Yeshua sweating blood as he wrestled with his destiny in Gethsemane – that sense of being alone in the cosmos with absolutely nothing except The Dark creeping in on you. You know this is a reality to be borne out in only a few hours. Then the second track picks up at two minutes thirty-eight seconds. The haunting bassline heralds the crescendo of the drums and then it's perfect... played over and over again, that was *TMJ3* summarised! This was the music that inspired Book Three.

WORK IT, LIKE MIKE LEIGH

So, how do I work? I start with a reading of the gospels. At this stage I know I'll be using the Gospel of John as the spine of my narrative. Next up is a reading of the Talmud commentaries and then some research of historical material and papers by ancient and contemporary historians and scholars. Jewish scholars have a somewhat different (more certain) view of obscure parts of their history. I use this as the basis for historical reconstruction. Now I write a synopsis, then move on to the art. I do not write full scripts (unless specifically required by the publisher). It's sort of the way Mike Leigh works – the actors get on set without a full script and ad lib. My characters arrive and interact with each other. I know what the beginning, middle and end of any given chapter feels like and I 'work it'. As I draw, I write sketchy dialogue alongside the drawings. After the drawings are inked, I begin full dialogue. Manga is cinematic – image-driven, so text only serves to do what can't be done by images alone. Hence, many pages here will be without words. If you listen carefully, you'll hear the sounds of 1st century Palestine.

Siku
N.D.O.A.
(Not Dead, Only Alive)

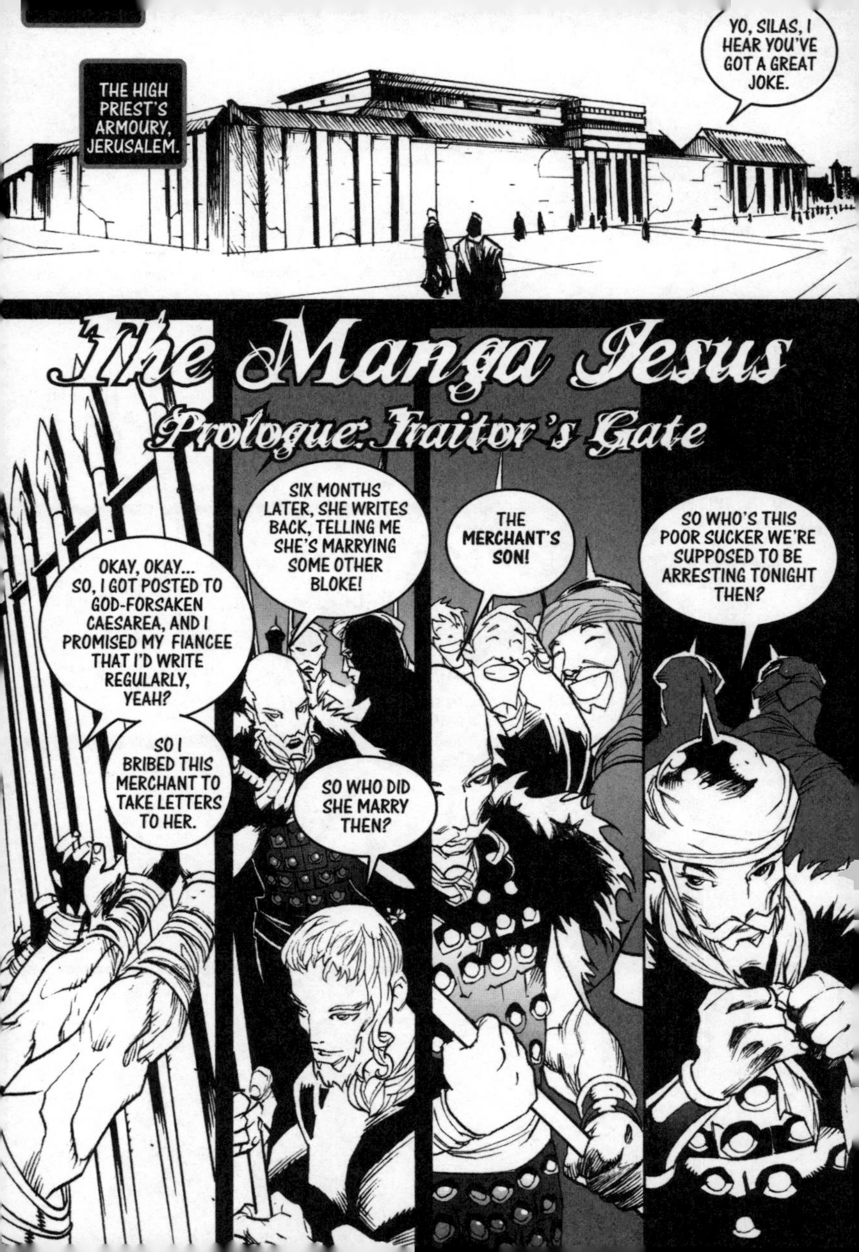
THE HIGH PRIEST'S ARMOURY, JERUSALEM.
YO, SILAS, I HEAR YOU'VE GOT A GREAT JOKE.
The Manga Jesus
Prologue: Traitor's Gate
OKAY, OKAY... SO, I GOT POSTED TO GOD-FORSAKEN CAESAREA, AND I PROMISED MY FIANCEE THAT I'D WRITE REGULARLY, YEAH?
SO I BRIBED THIS MERCHANT TO TAKE LETTERS TO HER.
SIX MONTHS LATER, SHE WRITES BACK, TELLING ME SHE'S MARRYING SOME OTHER BLOKE!
SO WHO DID SHE MARRY THEN?
THE MERCHANT'S SON!
SO WHO'S THIS POOR SUCKER WE'RE SUPPOSED TO BE ARRESTING TONIGHT THEN?

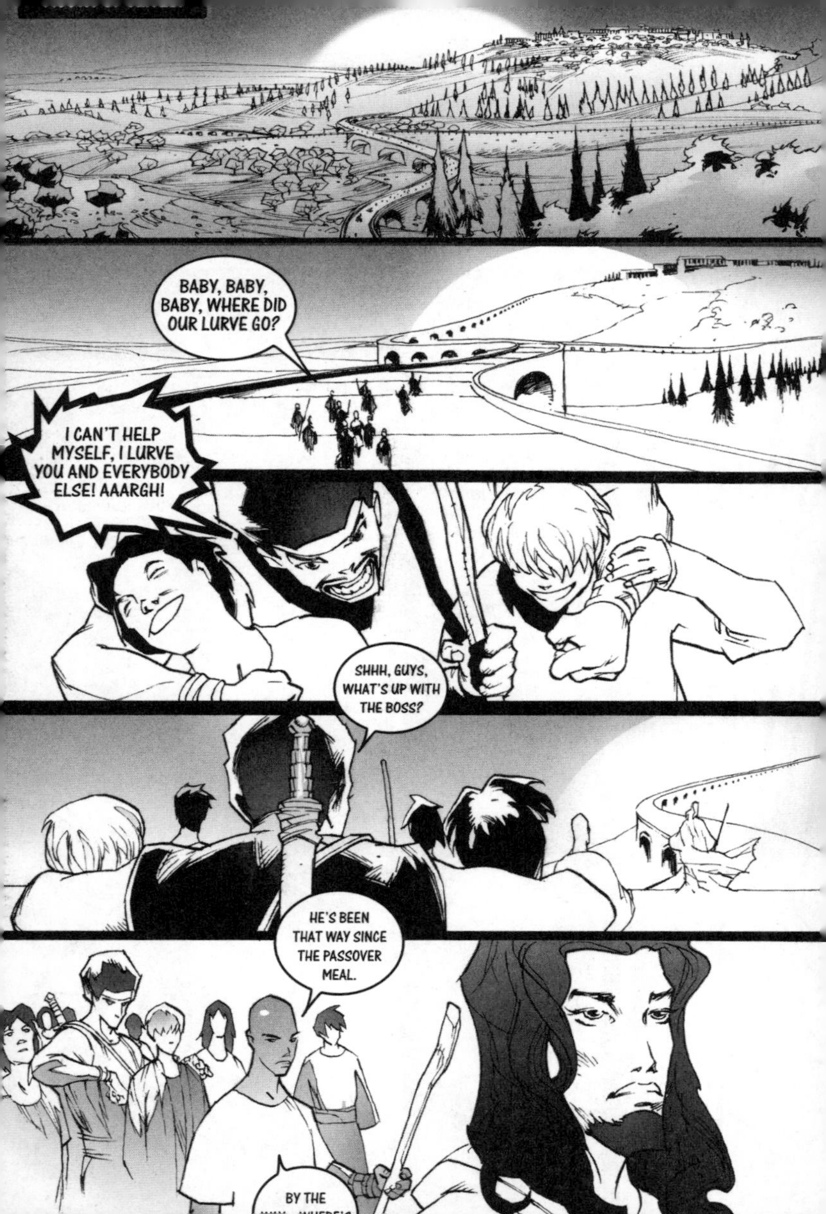

BABY, BABY, BABY, WHERE DID OUR LURVE GO?
I CAN'T HELP MYSELF, I LURVE YOU AND EVERYBODY ELSE! AAARGH!
SHHH, GUYS, WHAT'S UP WITH THE BOSS?
HE'S BEEN THAT WAY SINCE THE PASSOVER MEAL.
BY THE

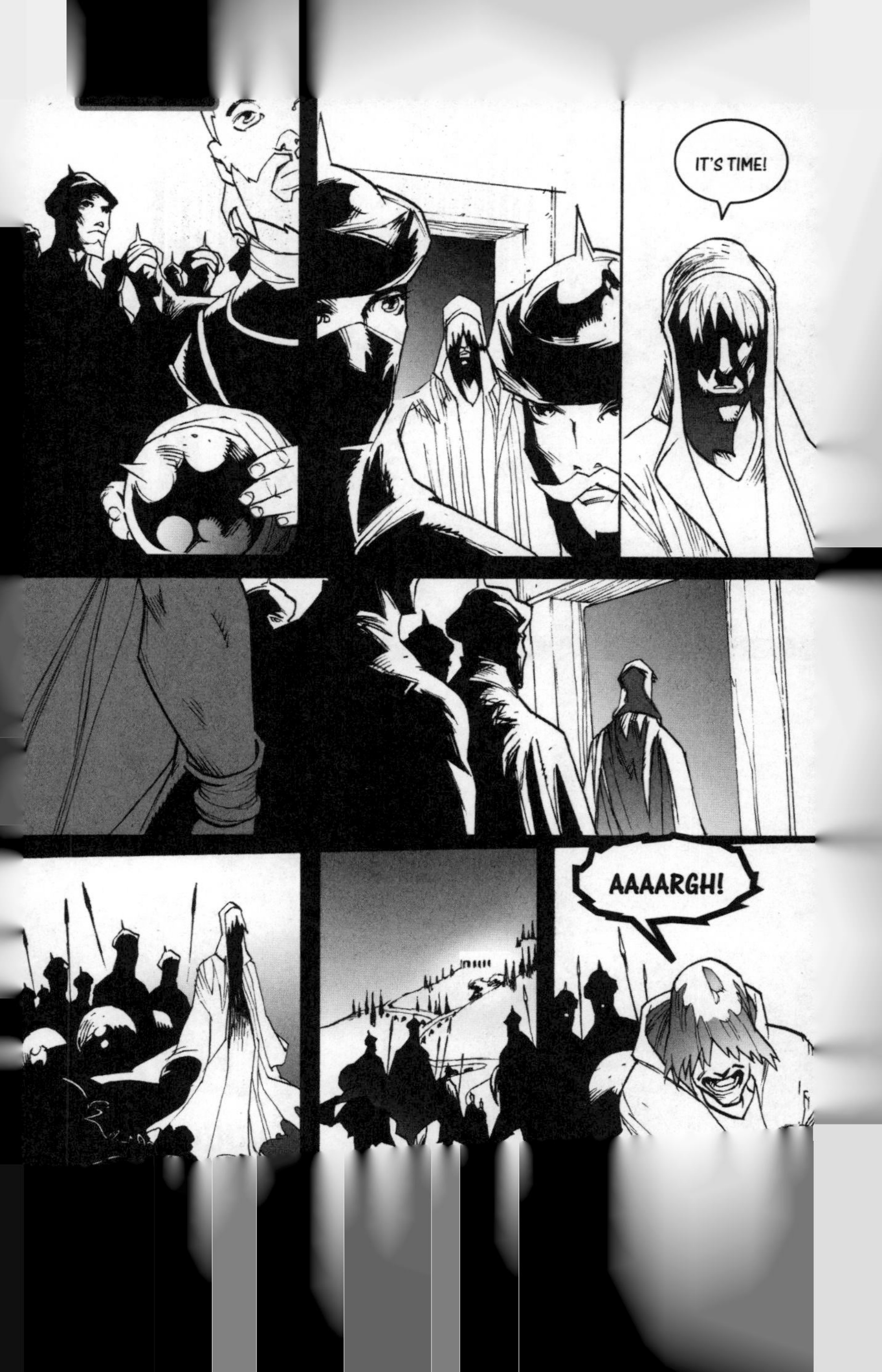
IT'S TIME!
AAAARGH!

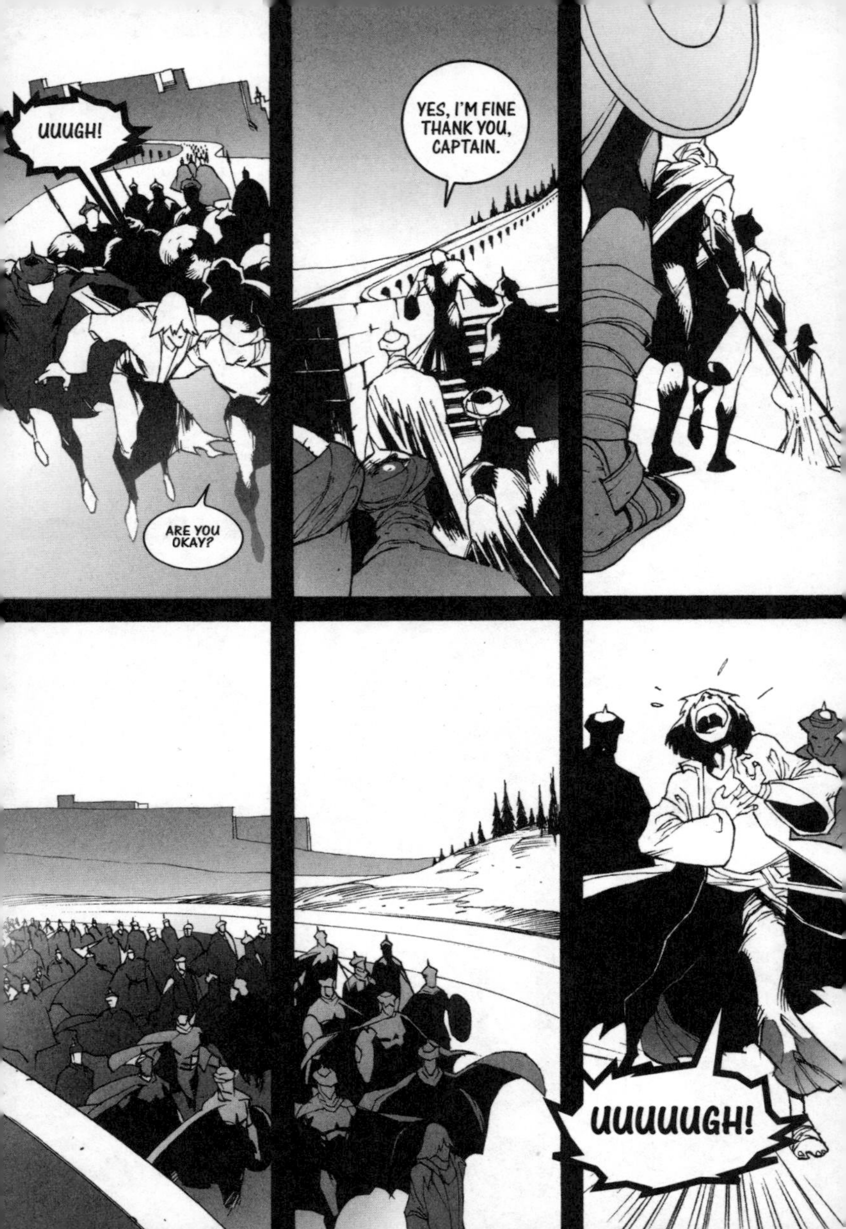
UUUGH!
ARE YOU OKAY?
YES, I'M FINE THANK YOU, CAPTAIN.
UUUUUGH!

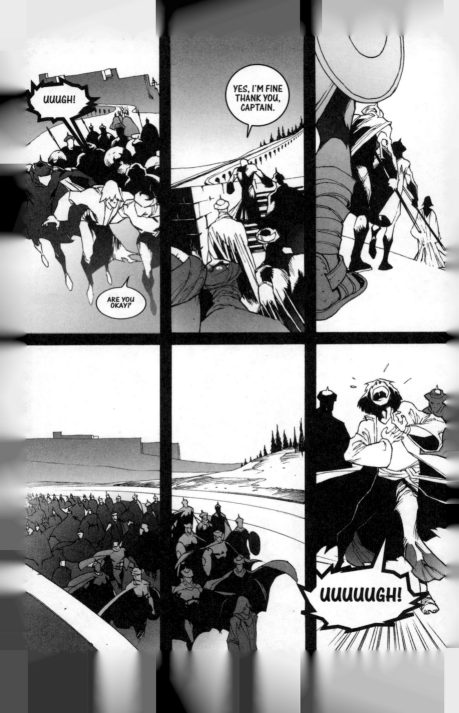

12.00 PM.
THE GARDEN OF GETHSEMANE.
DO WE JUST WAIT HERE FOR THE BOSS THEN?
THAT'S WHY IT'S CALLED A PRAYER VIGIL ... AND LOOK, ANDREW'S ALREADY IN LALA LAND.
ZZZZ
uuurr...
AAAAAAAAAA!

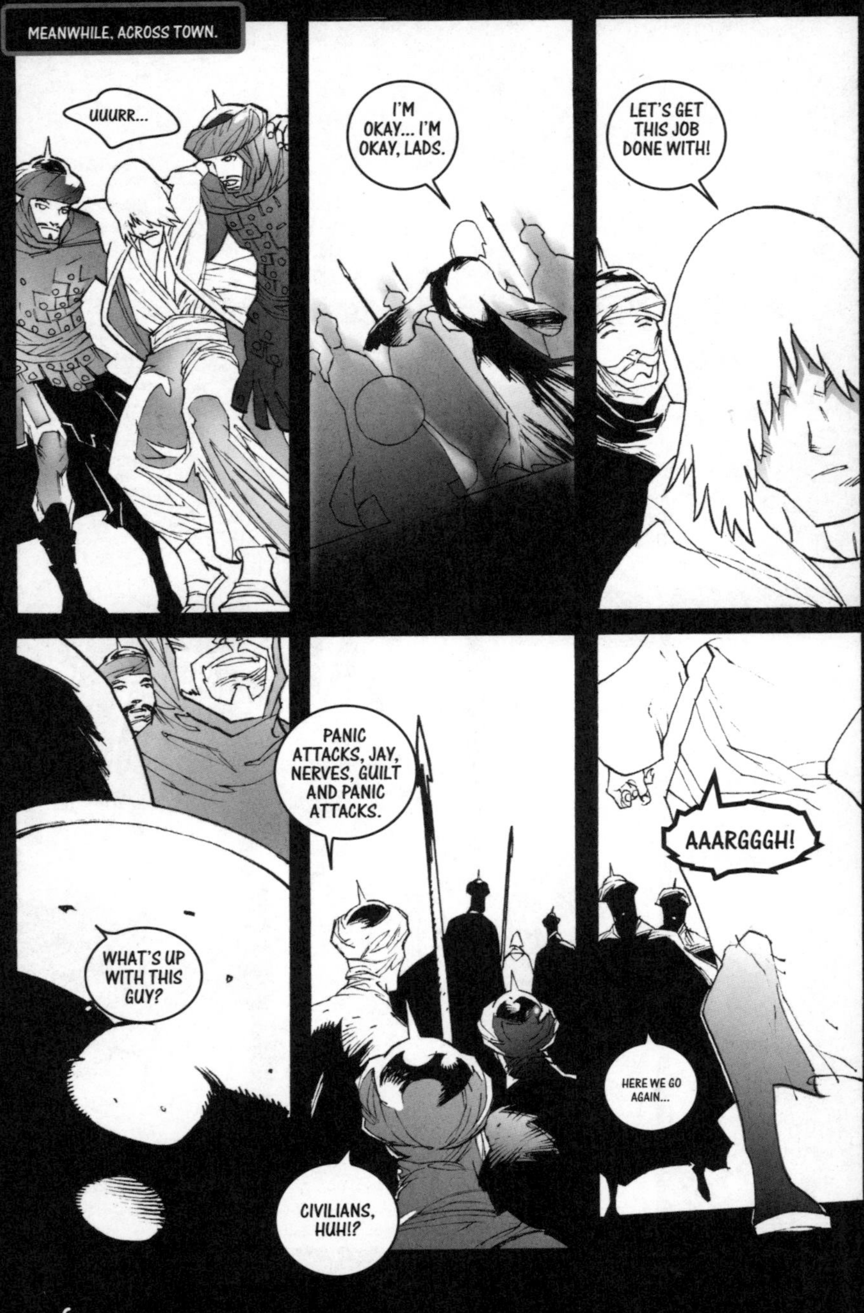
MEANWHILE, ACROSS TOWN.
UUURR...
I'M OKAY... I'M OKAY, LADS.
LET'S GET THIS JOB DONE WITH!
WHAT'S UP WITH THIS GUY?
PANIC ATTACKS, JAY, NERVES, GUILT AND PANIC ATTACKS.
CIVILIANS, HUH!?
AAARGGGH!
HERE WE GO AGAIN...

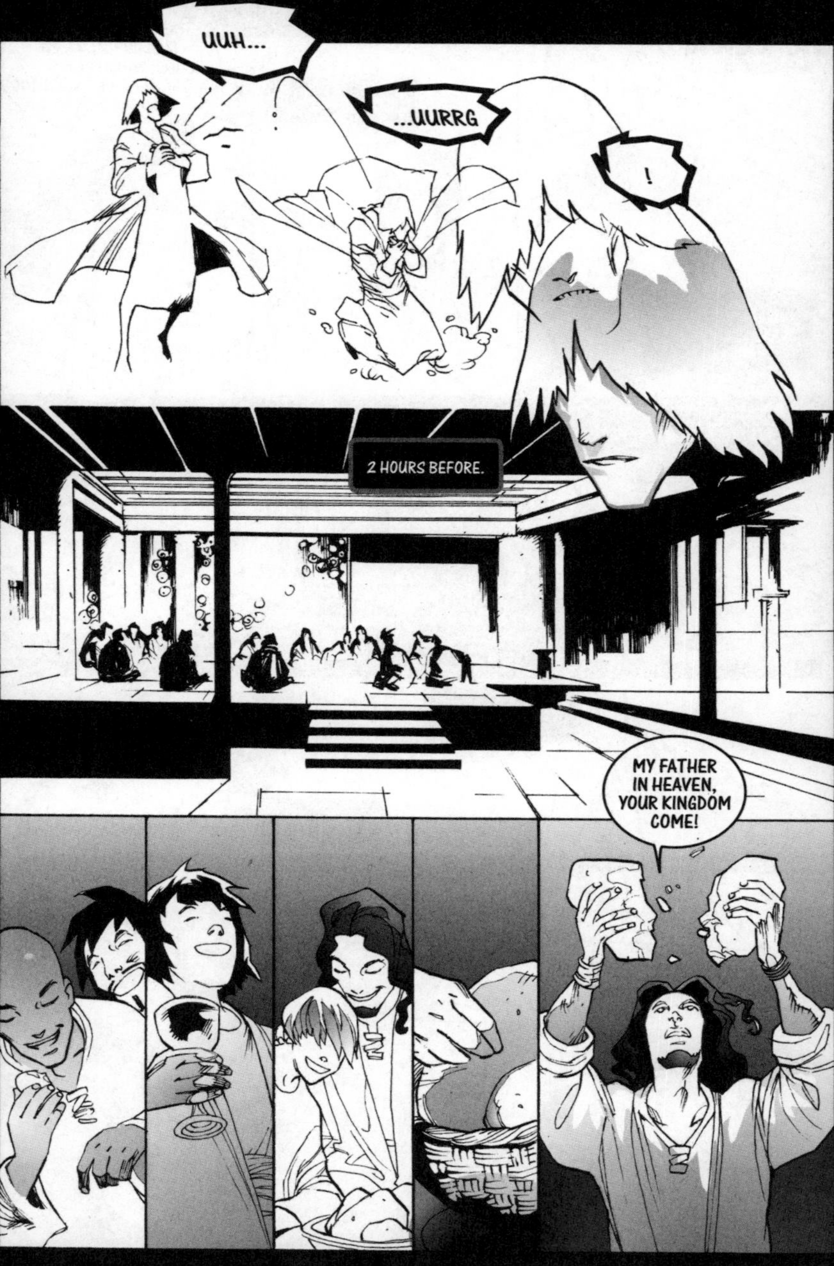
UUH...
...UURRG
!
2 HOURS BEFORE.
MY FATHER IN HEAVEN, YOUR KINGDOM COME!

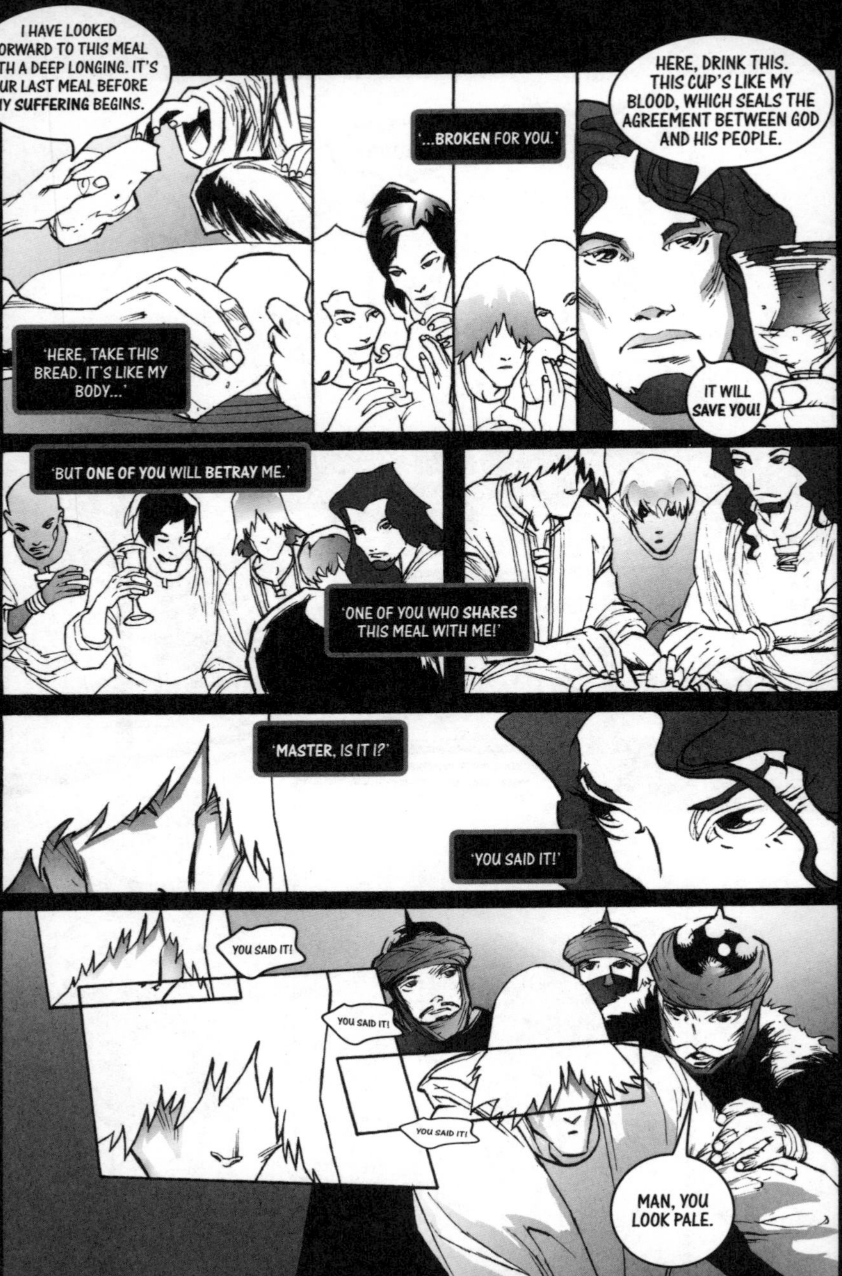
I HAVE LOOKED FORWARD TO THIS MEAL WITH A DEEP LONGING. IT'S OUR LAST MEAL BEFORE MY SUFFERING BEGINS.
'HERE, TAKE THIS BREAD. IT'S LIKE MY BODY...'
'...BROKEN FOR YOU.'
HERE, DRINK THIS. THIS CUP'S LIKE MY BLOOD, WHICH SEALS THE AGREEMENT BETWEEN GOD AND HIS PEOPLE.
IT WILL SAVE YOU!
'BUT ONE OF YOU WILL BETRAY ME.'
'ONE OF YOU WHO SHARES THIS MEAL WITH ME!'
'MASTER, IS IT I?'
'YOU SAID IT!'
YOU SAID IT!
YOU SAID IT!
YOU SAID IT!
MAN, YOU LOOK PALE.

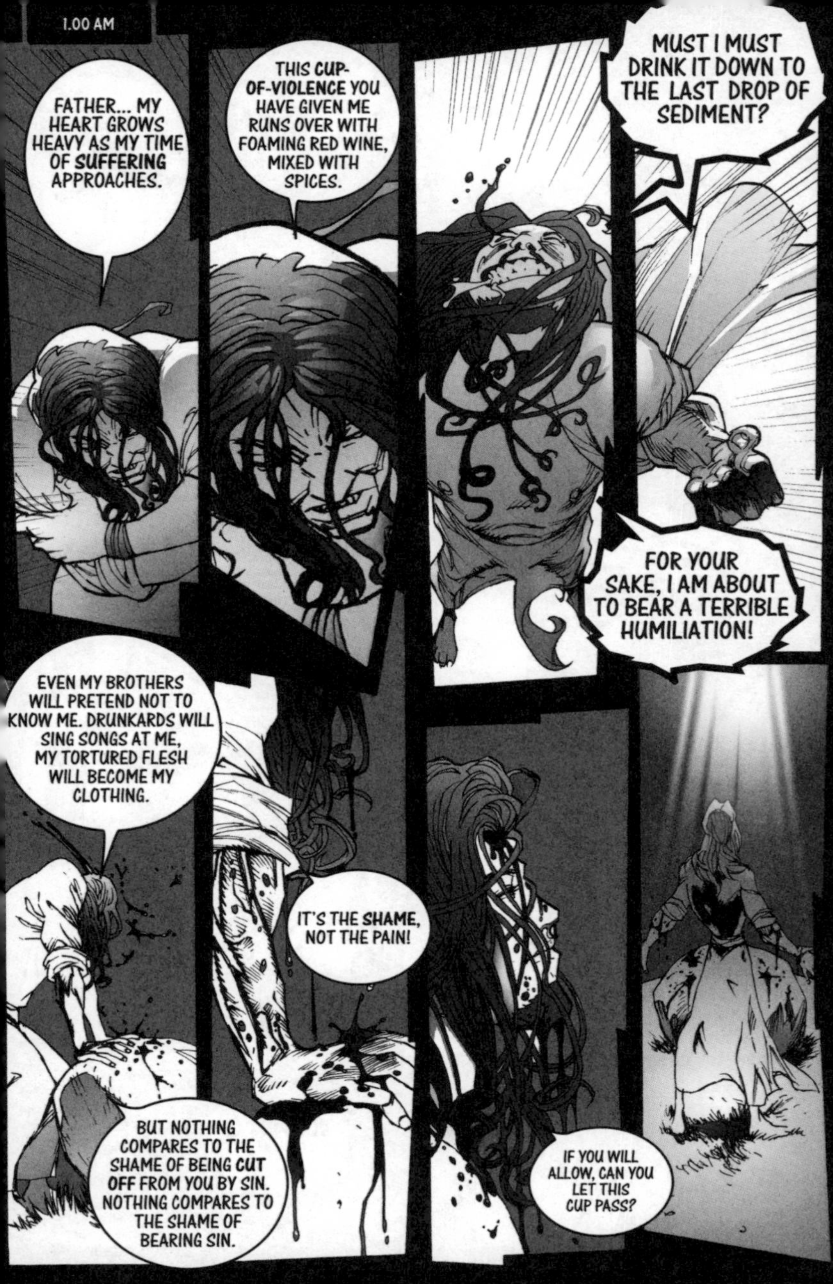
1.00 AM
FATHER... MY HEART GROWS HEAVY AS MY TIME OF SUFFERING APPROACHES.
THIS CUP-OF-VIOLENCE YOU HAVE GIVEN ME RUNS OVER WITH FOAMING RED WINE, MIXED WITH SPICES.
MUST I MUST DRINK IT DOWN TO THE LAST DROP OF SEDIMENT?
FOR YOUR SAKE, I AM ABOUT TO BEAR A TERRIBLE HUMILIATION!
EVEN MY BROTHERS WILL PRETEND NOT TO KNOW ME. DRUNKARDS WILL SING SONGS AT ME, MY TORTURED FLESH WILL BECOME MY CLOTHING.
IT'S THE SHAME, NOT THE PAIN!
BUT NOTHING COMPARES TO THE SHAME OF BEING CUT OFF FROM YOU BY SIN. NOTHING COMPARES TO THE SHAME OF BEARING SIN.
IF YOU WILL ALLOW, CAN YOU LET THIS CUP PASS?

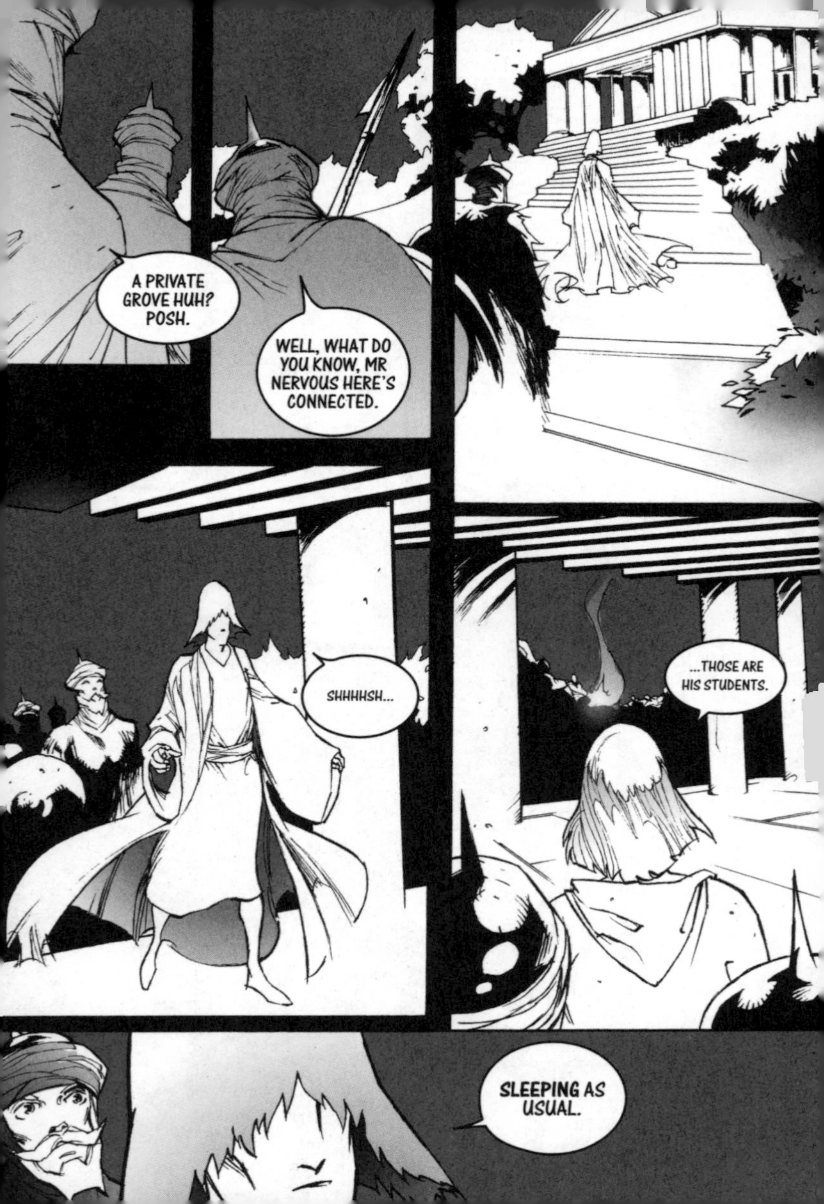
A PRIVATE GROVE HUH? POSH.
WELL, WHAT DO YOU KNOW, MR NERVOUS HERE'S CONNECTED.
SHHHHSH...
...THOSE ARE HIS STUDENTS.
SLEEPING AS USUAL.

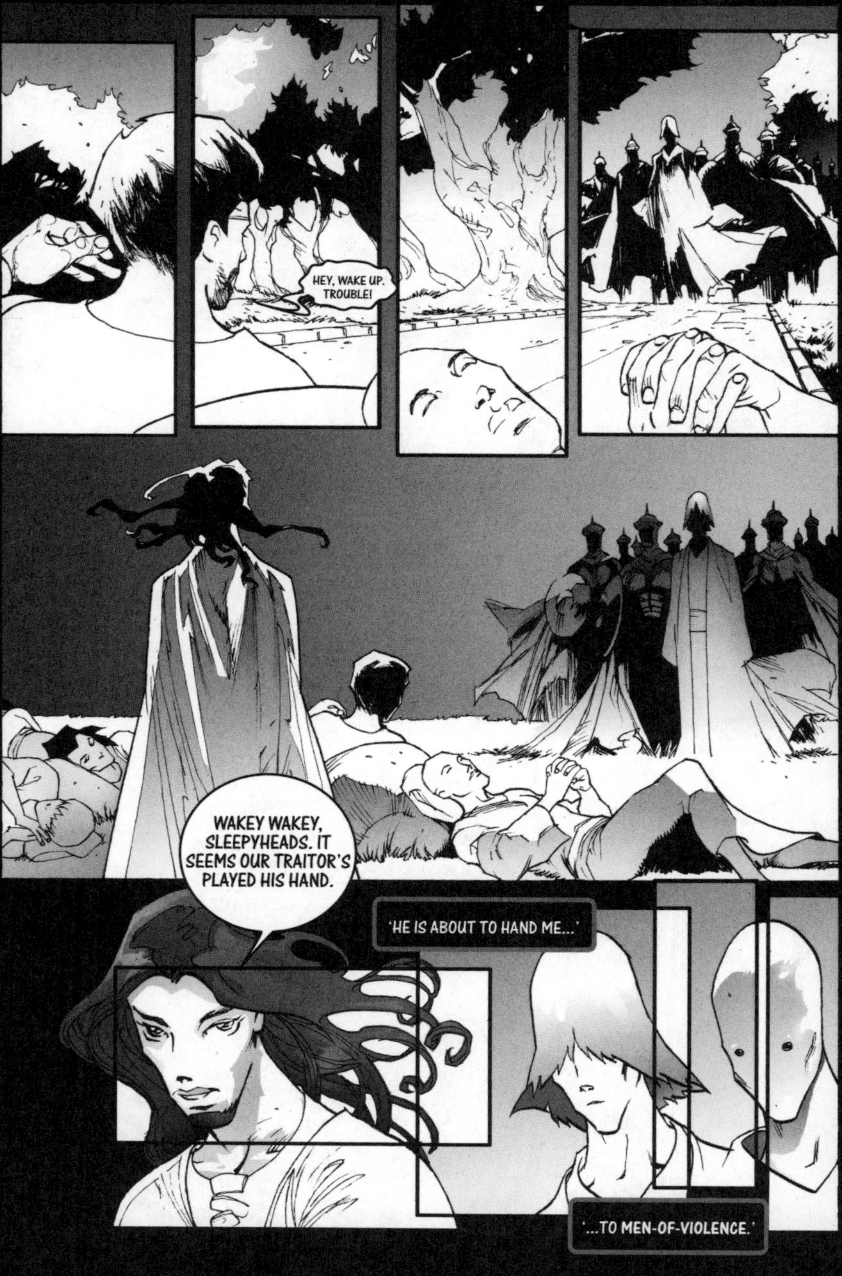
HEY, WAKE UP. TROUBLE!
WAKEY WAKEY, SLEEPYHEADS. IT SEEMS OUR TRAITOR'S PLAYED HIS HAND.
'HE IS ABOUT TO HAND ME...'
'...TO MEN-OF-VIOLENCE.'

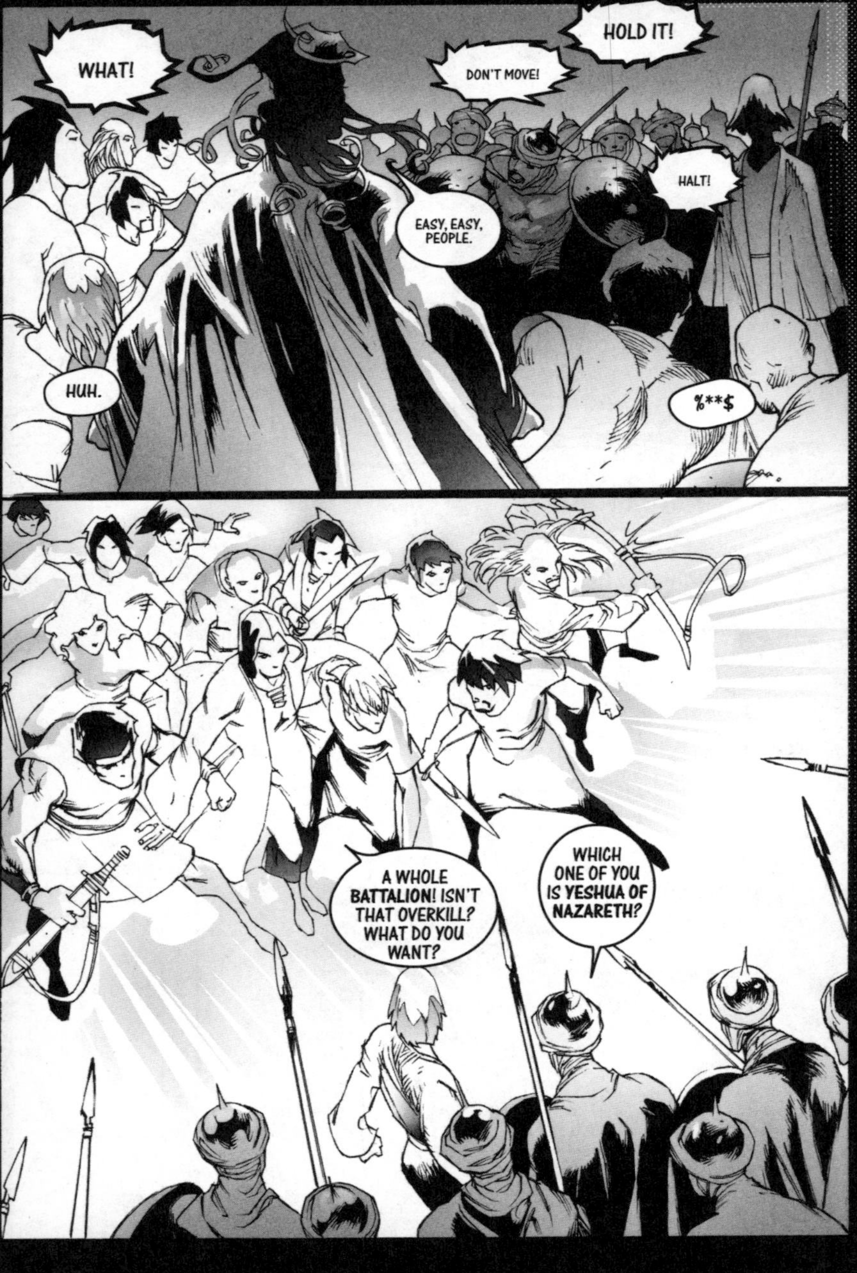
WHAT!
DON'T MOVE!
HOLD IT!
EASY, EASY, PEOPLE.
HALT!
HUH.
%**$
A WHOLE BATTALION! ISN'T THAT OVERKILL? WHAT DO YOU WANT?
WHICH ONE OF YOU IS YESHUA OF NAZARETH?

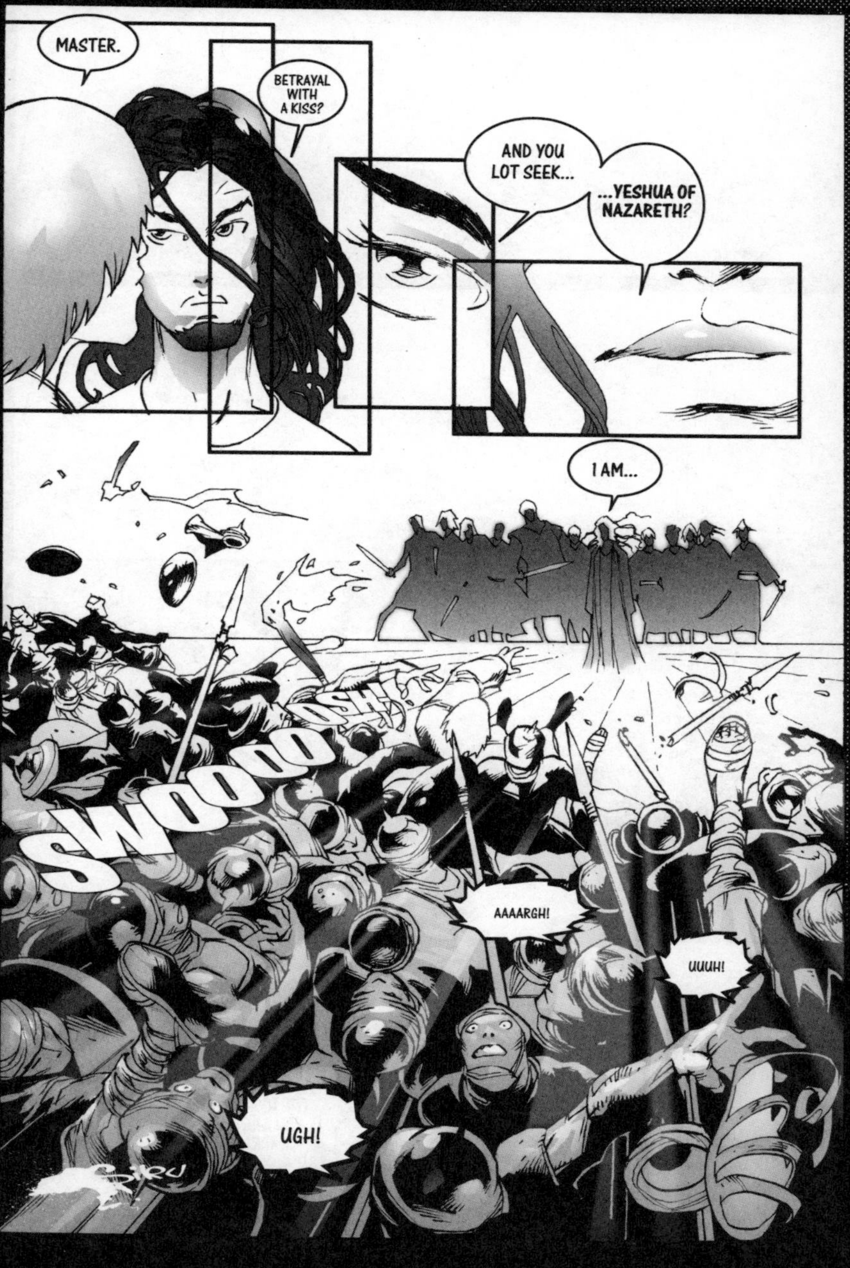
MASTER.
BETRAYAL WITH A KISS?
AND YOU LOT SEEK...
...YESHUA OF NAZARETH?
I AM...
SWOOOOSH
AAAARGH!
UUUH!
UGH!

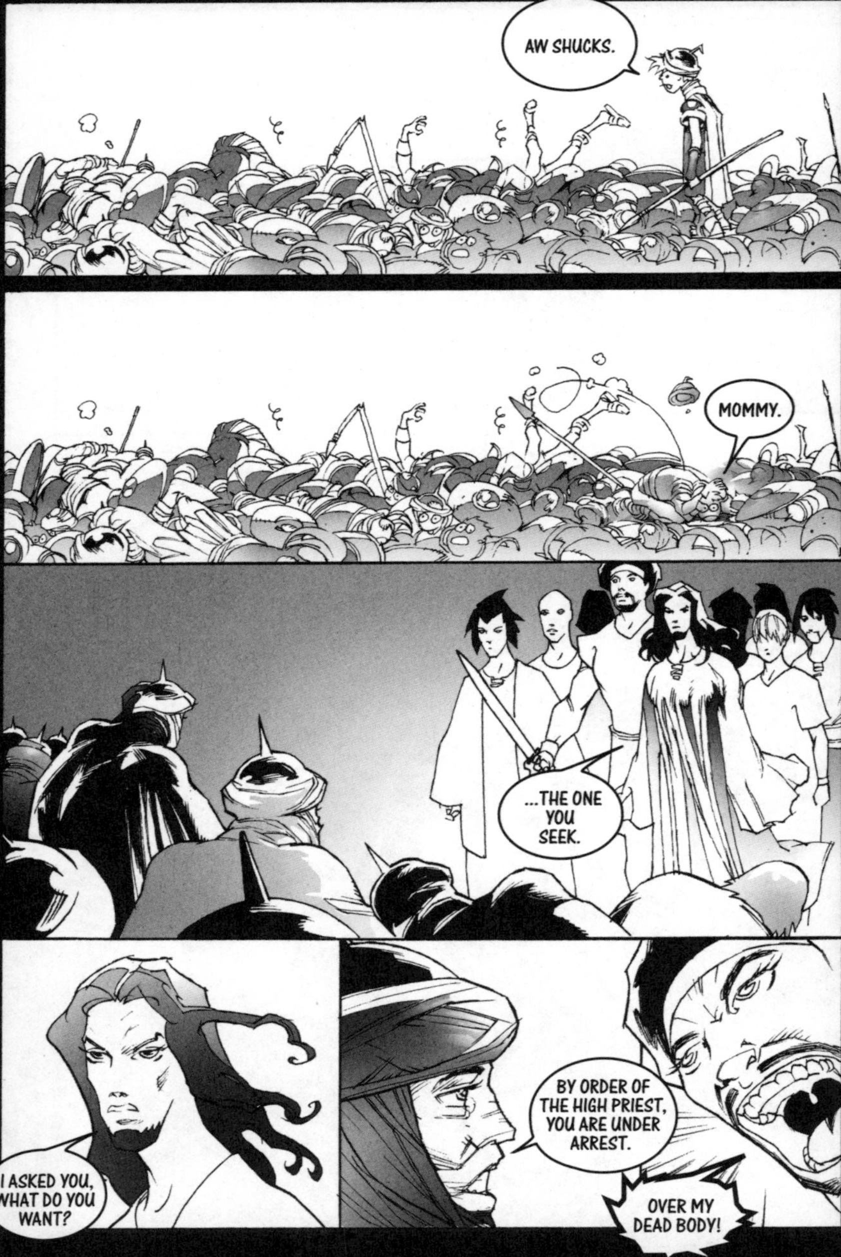
AW SHUCKS.
MOMMY.
...THE ONE YOU SEEK.
I ASKED YOU, WHAT DO YOU WANT?
BY ORDER OF THE HIGH PRIEST, YOU ARE UNDER ARREST.
OVER MY DEAD BODY!

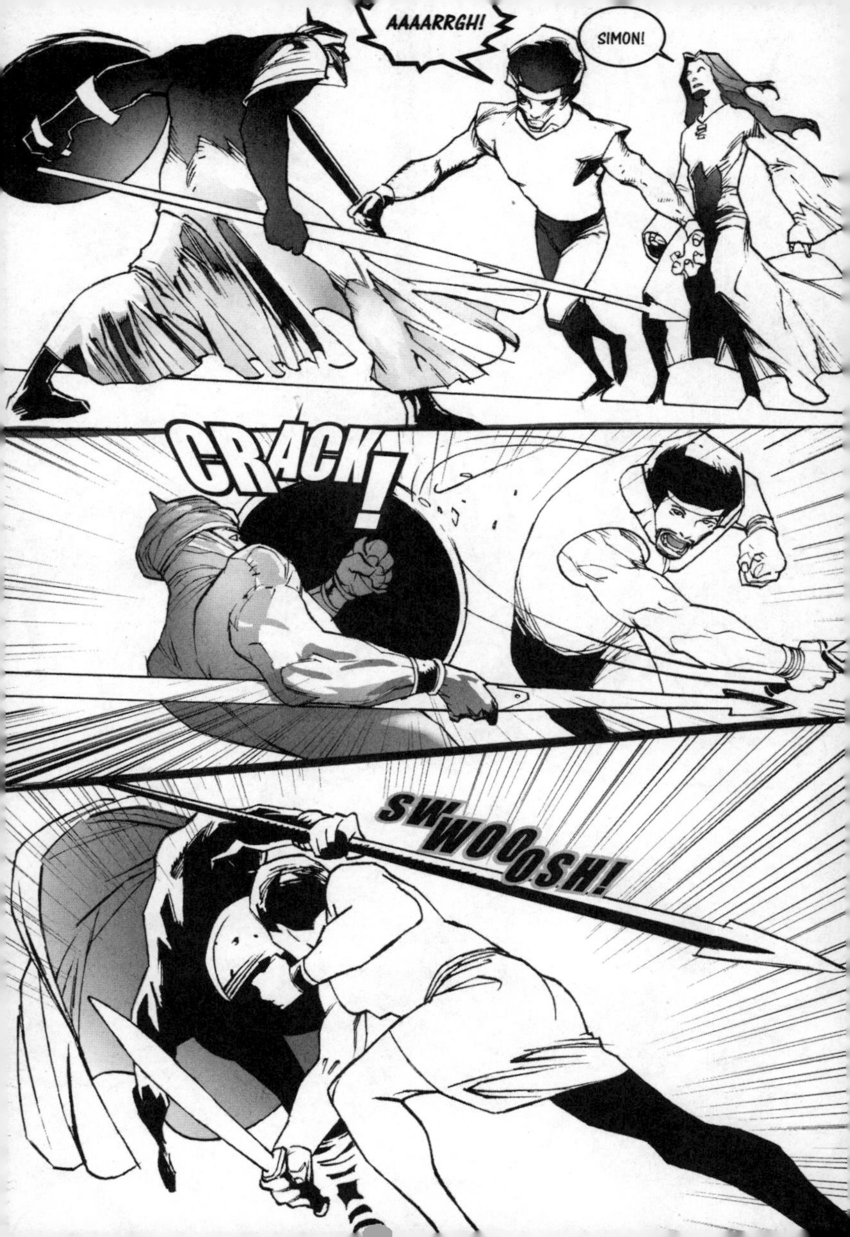
AAAARRGH!
SIMON!
CRACK!
SWWOOOOSH!

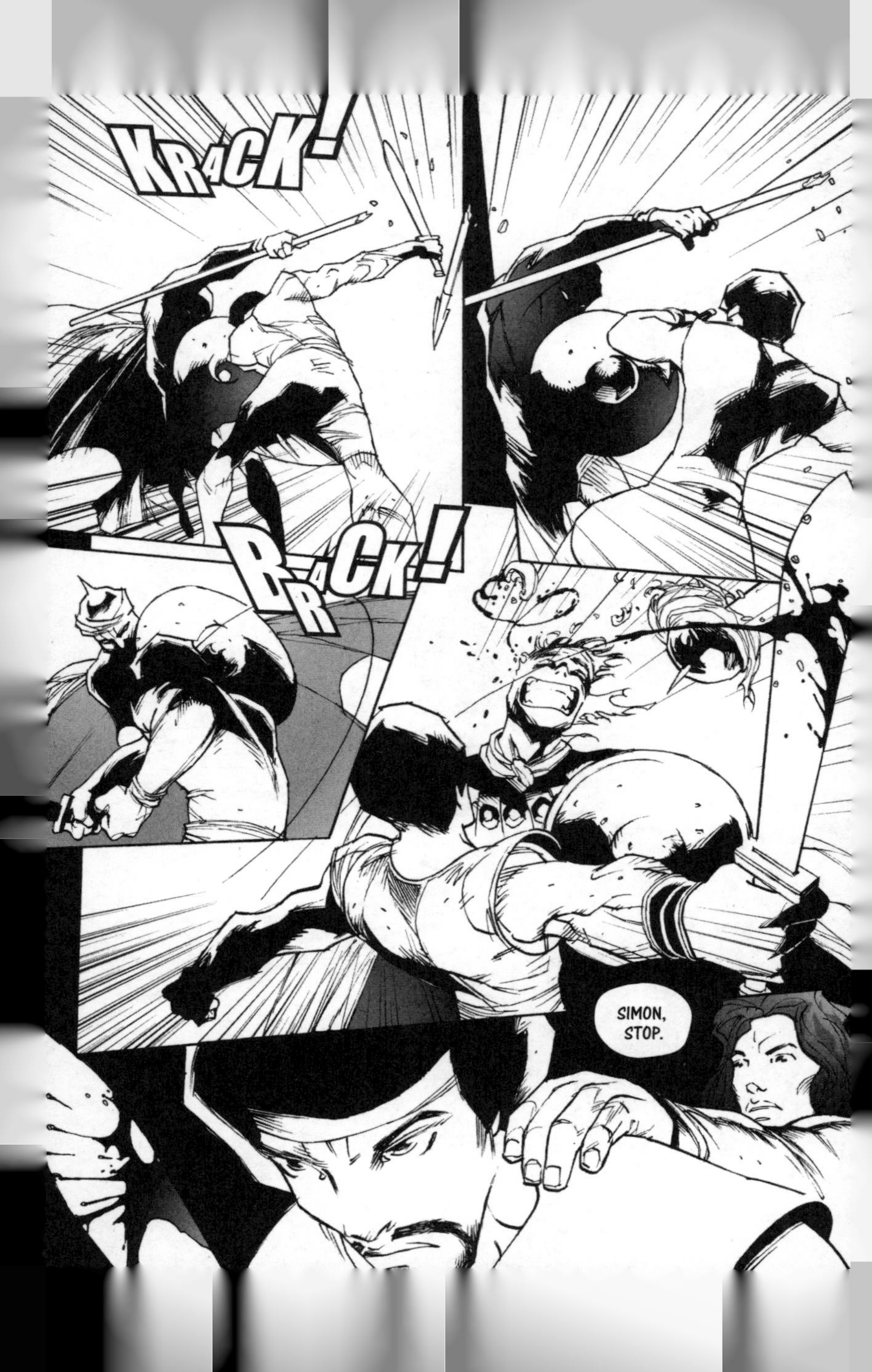
KRACK!
BRACK!
SIMON, STOP.

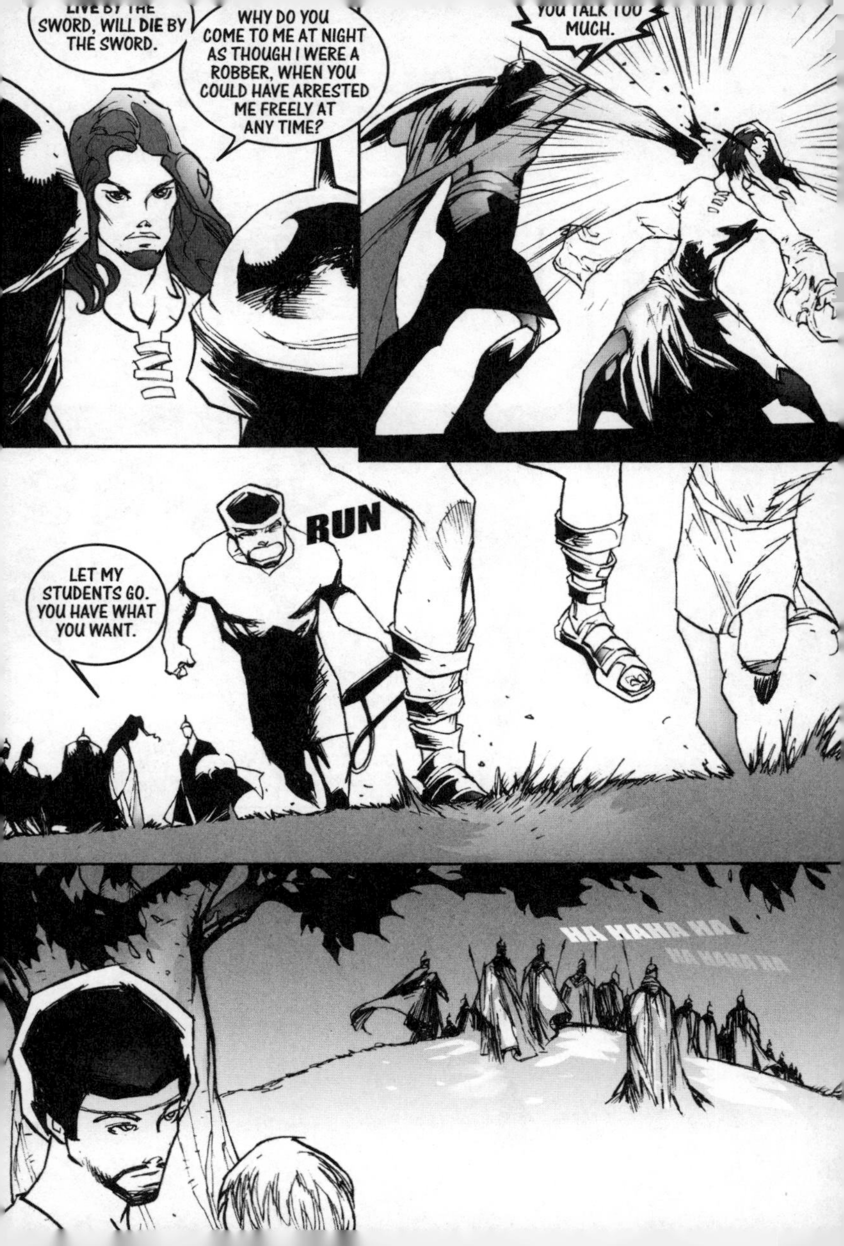
LIVE BY THE SWORD, WILL DIE BY THE SWORD.
WHY DO YOU COME TO ME AT NIGHT AS THOUGH I WERE A ROBBER, WHEN YOU COULD HAVE ARRESTED ME FREELY AT ANY TIME?
YOU TALK TOO MUCH.
RUN
LET MY STUDENTS GO. YOU HAVE WHAT YOU WANT.
HA HAHA HA
HA HAHA HA

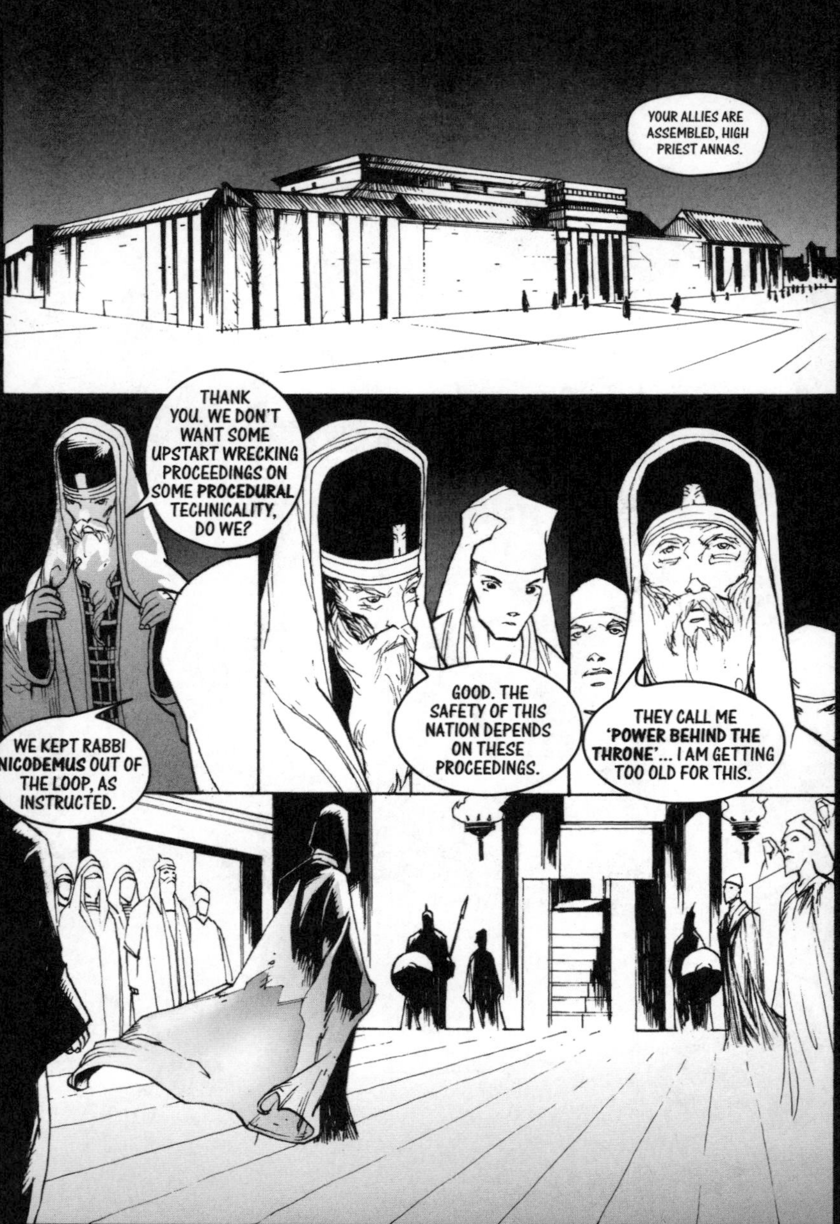
YOUR ALLIES ARE ASSEMBLED, HIGH PRIEST ANNAS.
THANK YOU. WE DON'T WANT SOME UPSTART WRECKING PROCEEDINGS ON SOME **PROCEDURAL** TECHNICALITY, DO WE?
WE KEPT RABBI **NICODEMUS** OUT OF THE LOOP, AS INSTRUCTED.
GOOD. THE SAFETY OF THIS NATION DEPENDS ON THESE PROCEEDINGS.
THEY CALL ME **'POWER BEHIND THE THRONE'**... I AM GETTING TOO OLD FOR THIS.

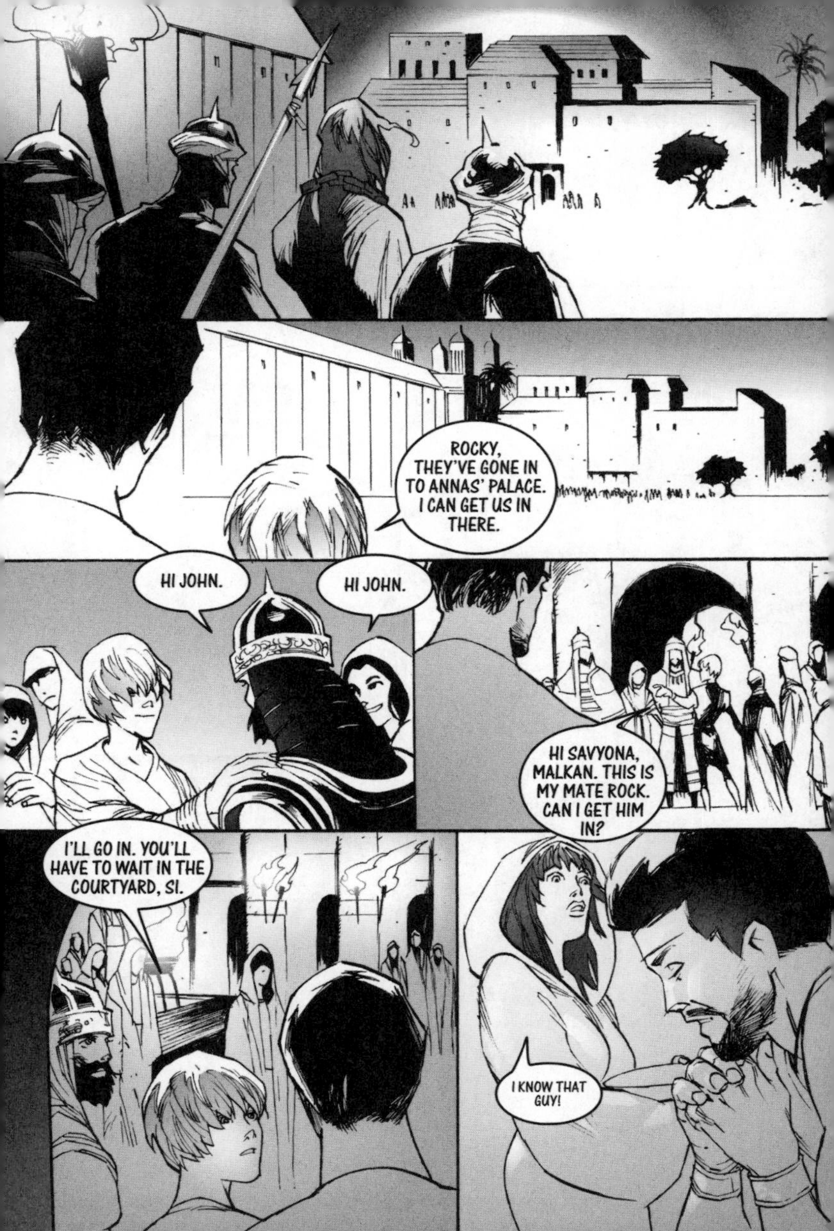
ROCKY, THEY'VE GONE IN TO ANNAS' PALACE. I CAN GET US IN THERE.
HI JOHN.
HI JOHN.
HI SAVYONA, MALKAN. THIS IS MY MATE ROCK. CAN I GET HIM IN?
I'LL GO IN. YOU'LL HAVE TO WAIT IN THE COURTYARD, SI.
I KNOW THAT GUY!

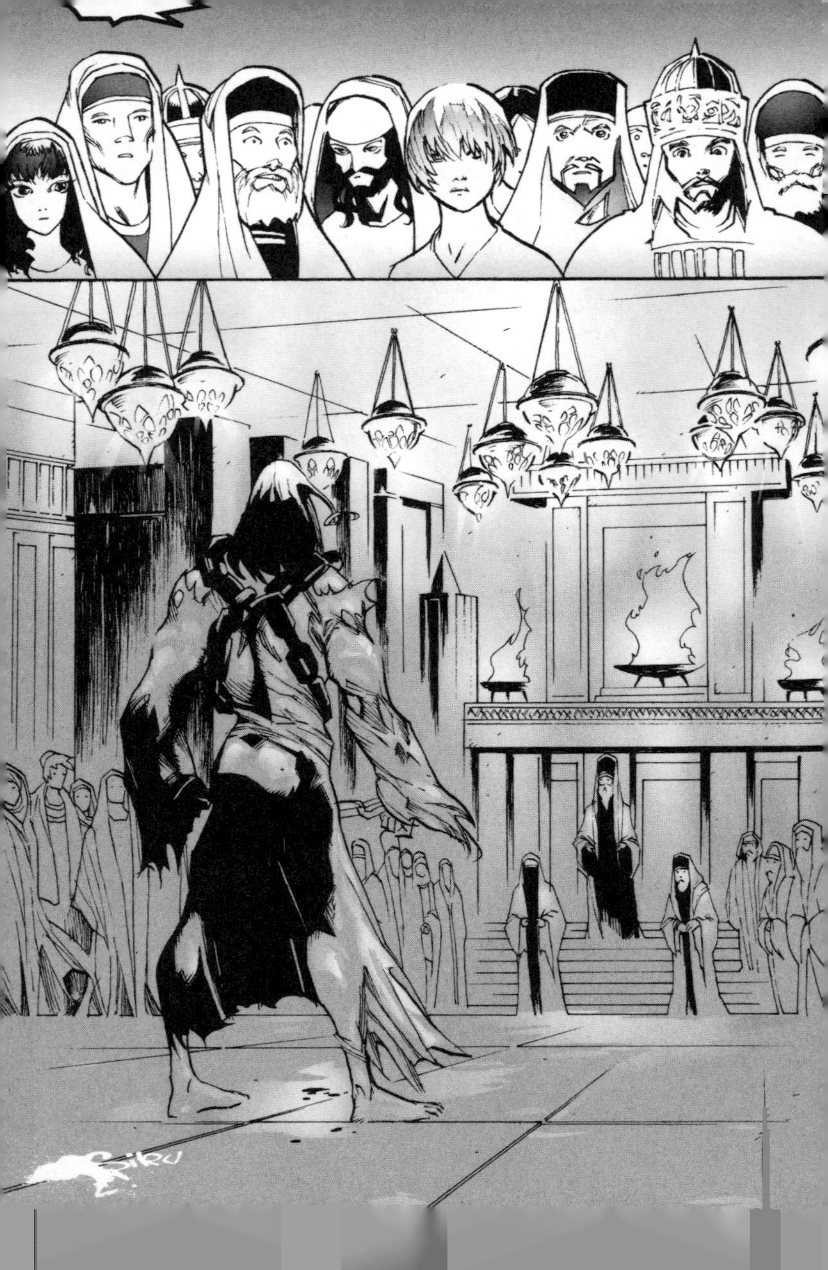
Siku

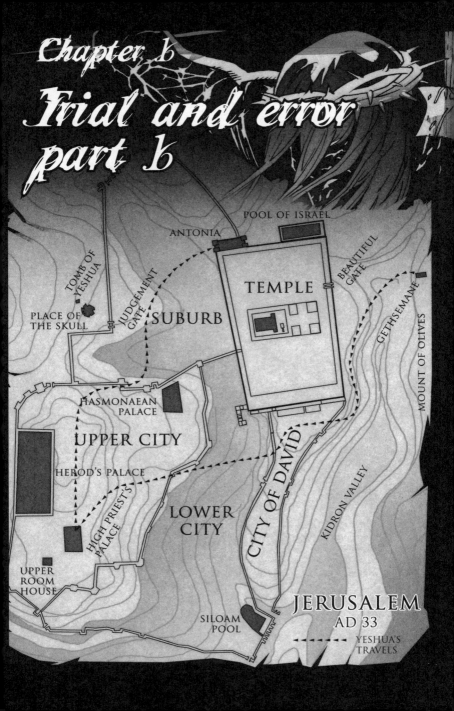

Chapter 6
Trial and error part 6

POOL OF ISRAEL

ANTONIA

TOMB OF YESHUA

PLACE OF THE SKULL

JUDGEMENT GATE

SUBURB

TEMPLE

BEAUTIFUL GATE

GETHSEMANE

MOUNT OF OLIVES

HASMONAEAN PALACE

UPPER CITY

HEROD'S PALACE

HIGH PRIEST'S PALACE

LOWER CITY

CITY OF DAVID

KIDRON VALLEY

UPPER ROOM HOUSE

SILOAM POOL

JERUSALEM
AD 33

◄---- YESHUA'S TRAVELS

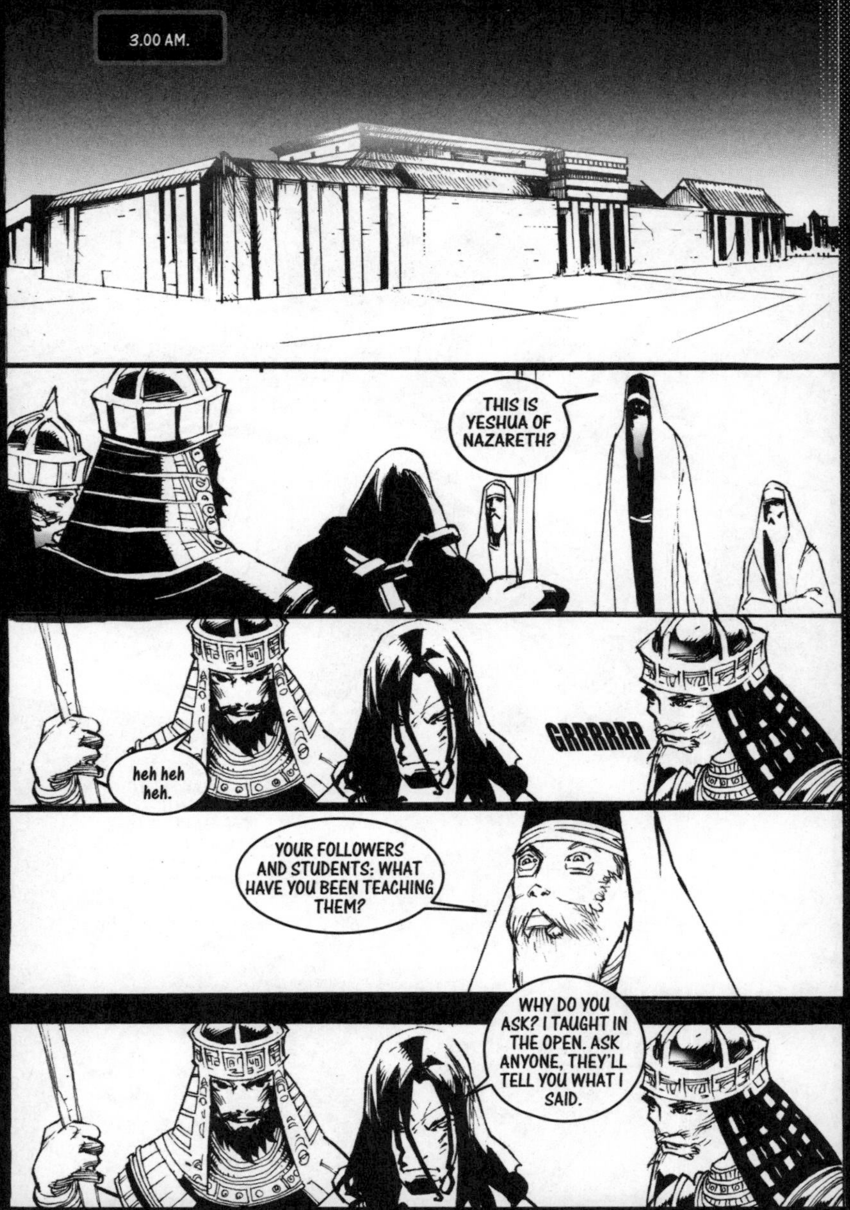
3.00 AM.
THIS IS YESHUA OF NAZARETH?
heh heh heh.
GRRRRRR
YOUR FOLLOWERS AND STUDENTS: WHAT HAVE YOU BEEN TEACHING THEM?
WHY DO YOU ASK? I TAUGHT IN THE OPEN. ASK ANYONE, THEY'LL TELL YOU WHAT I SAID.

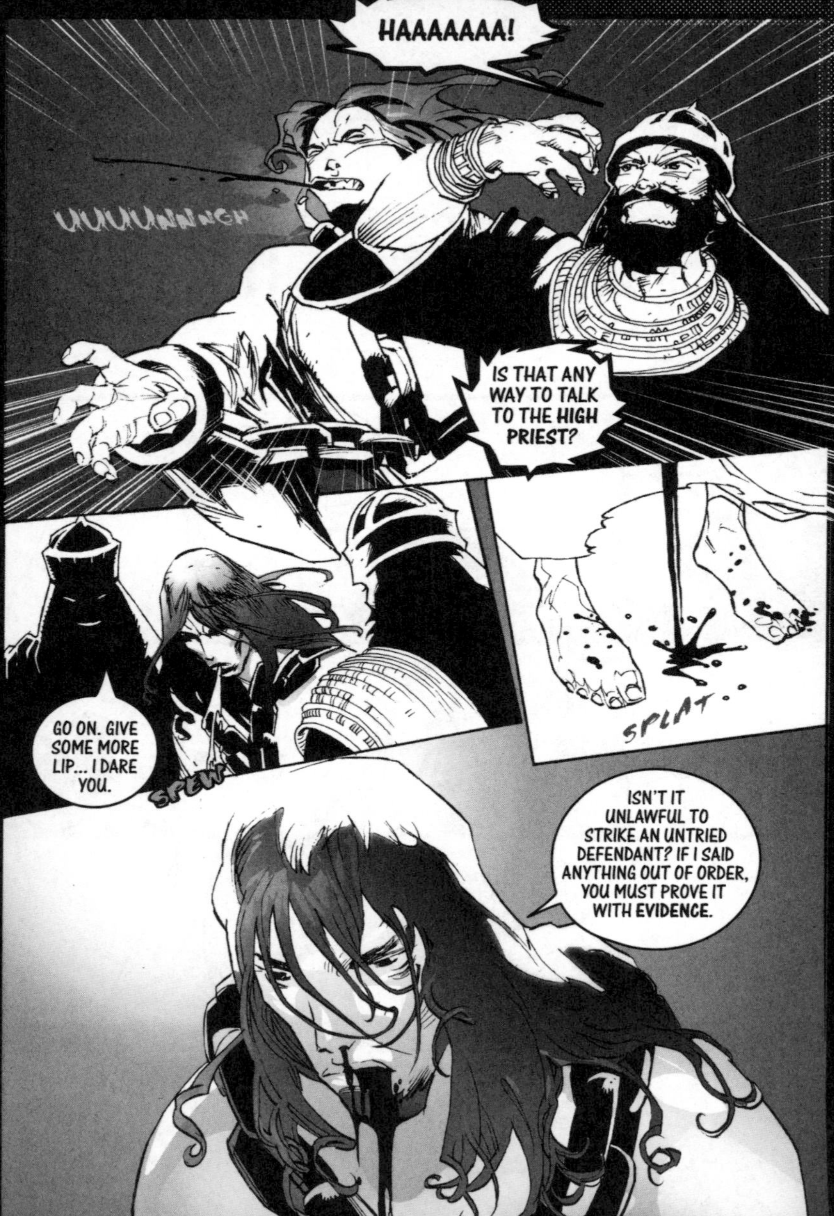
HAAAAAAA!
UUUUNNNGH
IS THAT ANY WAY TO TALK TO THE HIGH PRIEST?
SPLAT
GO ON. GIVE SOME MORE LIP... I DARE YOU.
SPEW
ISN'T IT UNLAWFUL TO STRIKE AN UNTRIED DEFENDANT? IF I SAID ANYTHING OUT OF ORDER, YOU MUST PROVE IT WITH EVIDENCE.

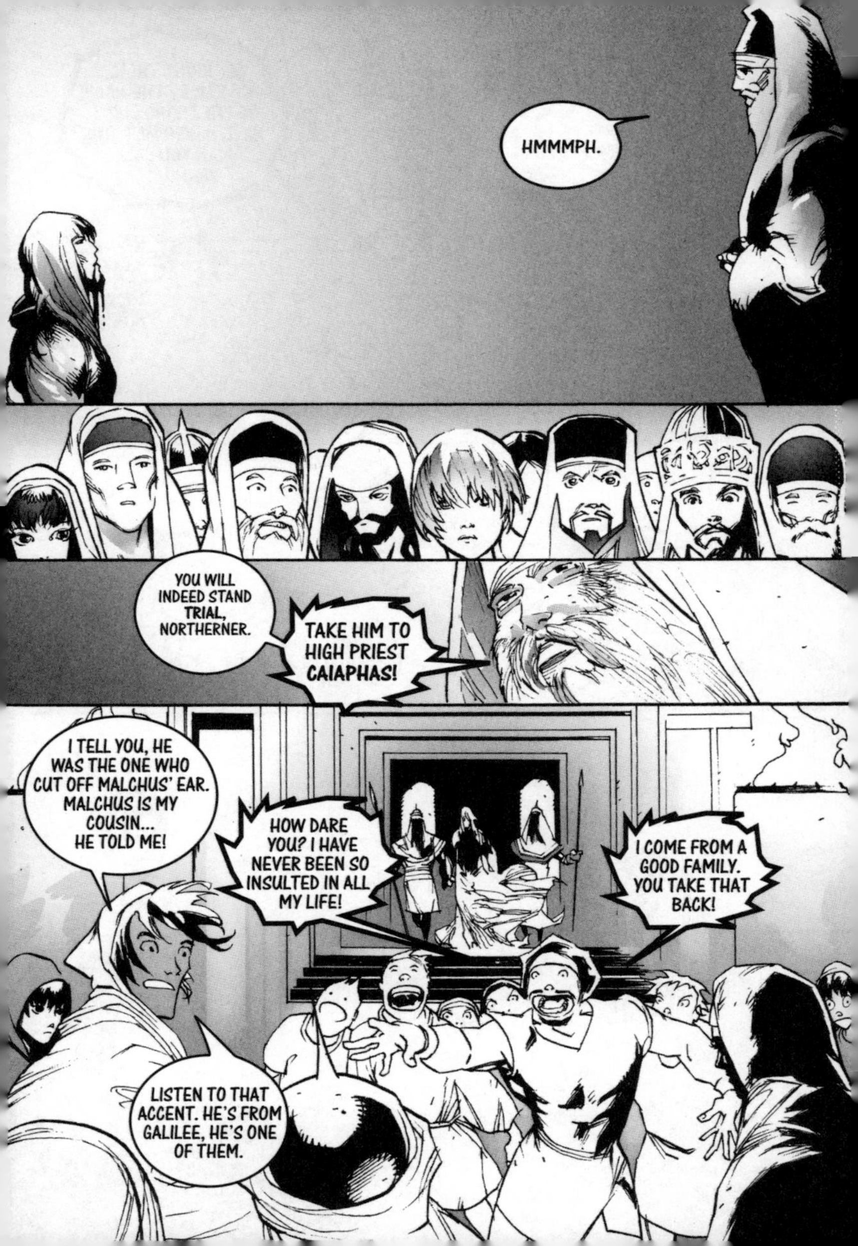
HMMMPH.
YOU WILL INDEED STAND TRIAL, NORTHERNER.
TAKE HIM TO HIGH PRIEST CAIAPHAS!
I TELL YOU, HE WAS THE ONE WHO CUT OFF MALCHUS' EAR. MALCHUS IS MY COUSIN... HE TOLD ME!
HOW DARE YOU? I HAVE NEVER BEEN SO INSULTED IN ALL MY LIFE!
I COME FROM A GOOD FAMILY. YOU TAKE THAT BACK!
LISTEN TO THAT ACCENT. HE'S FROM GALILEE, HE'S ONE OF THEM.

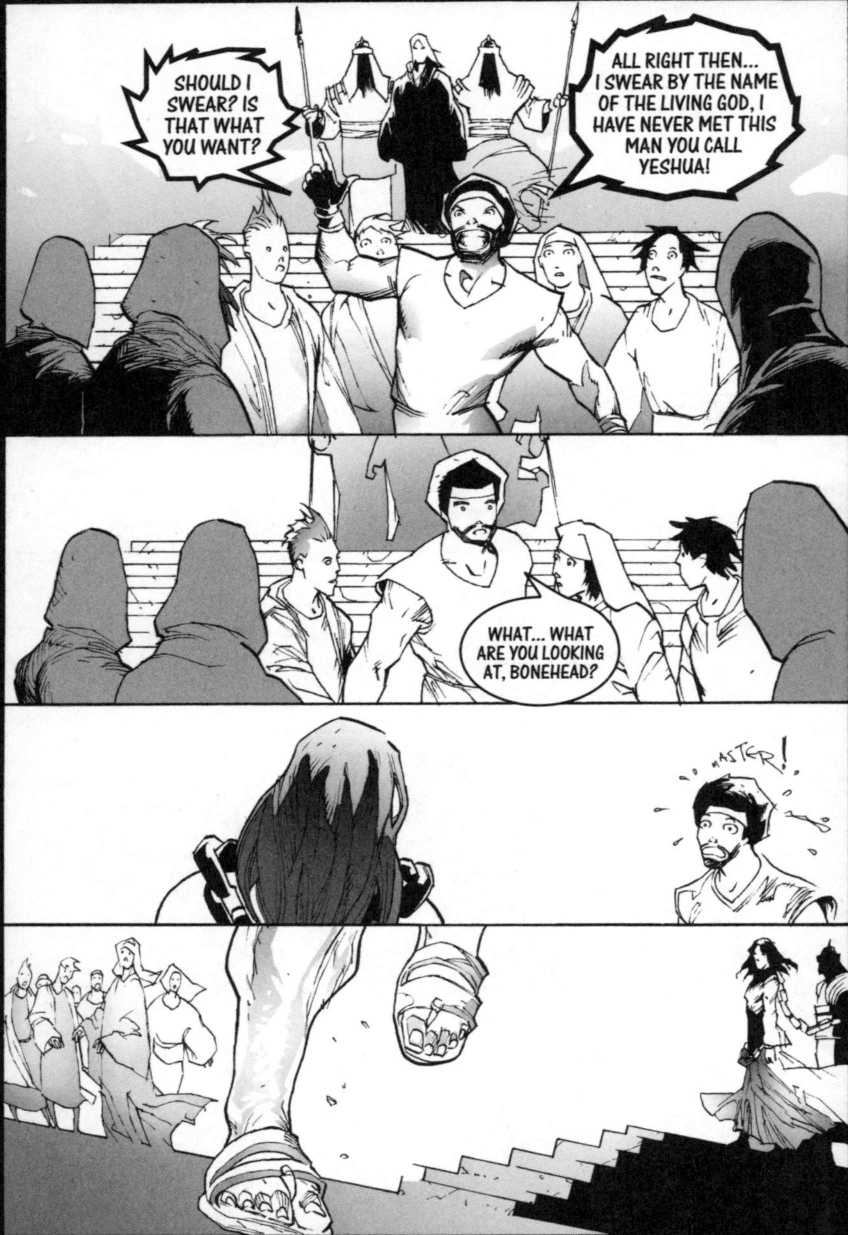
SHOULD I SWEAR? IS THAT WHAT YOU WANT?
ALL RIGHT THEN... I SWEAR BY THE NAME OF THE LIVING GOD, I HAVE NEVER MET THIS MAN YOU CALL YESHUA!
WHAT... WHAT ARE YOU LOOKING AT, BONEHEAD?
MASTER!

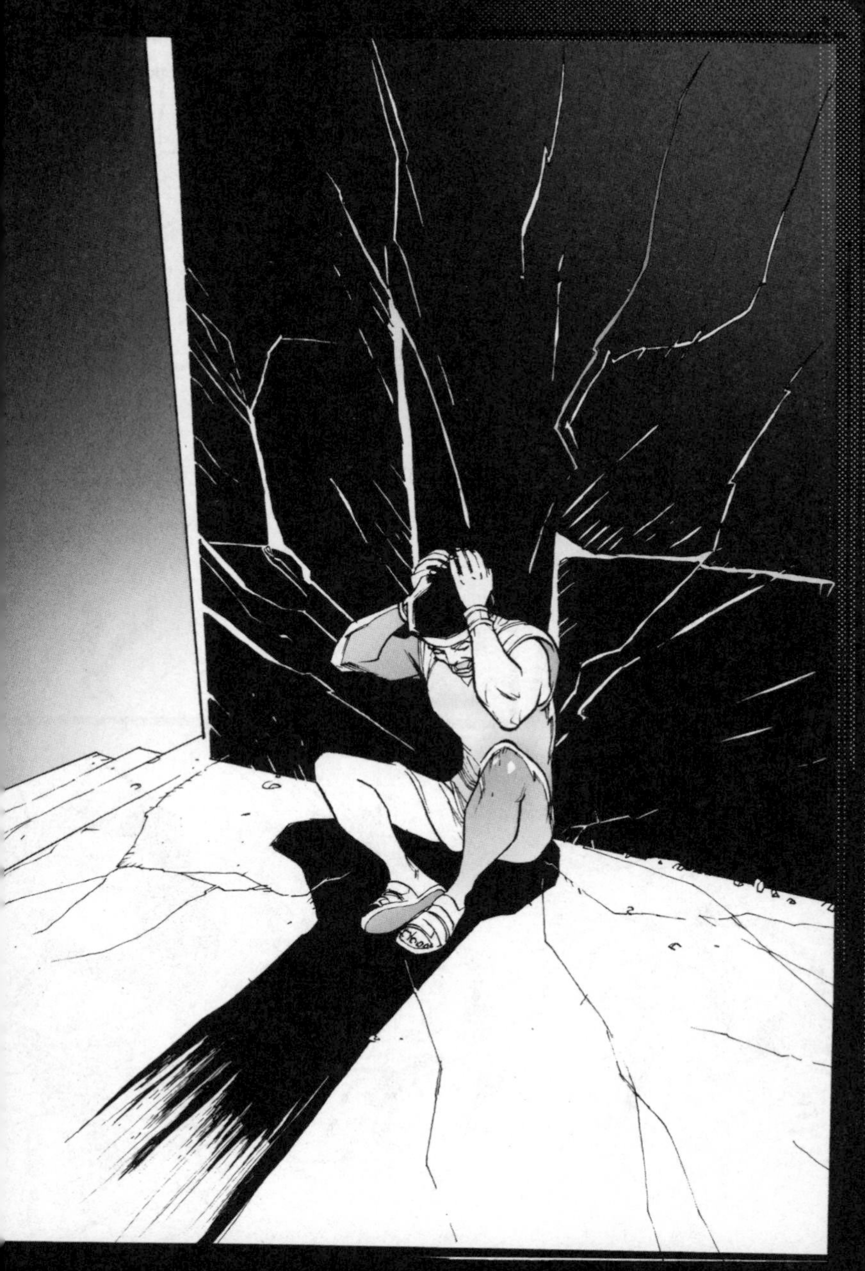

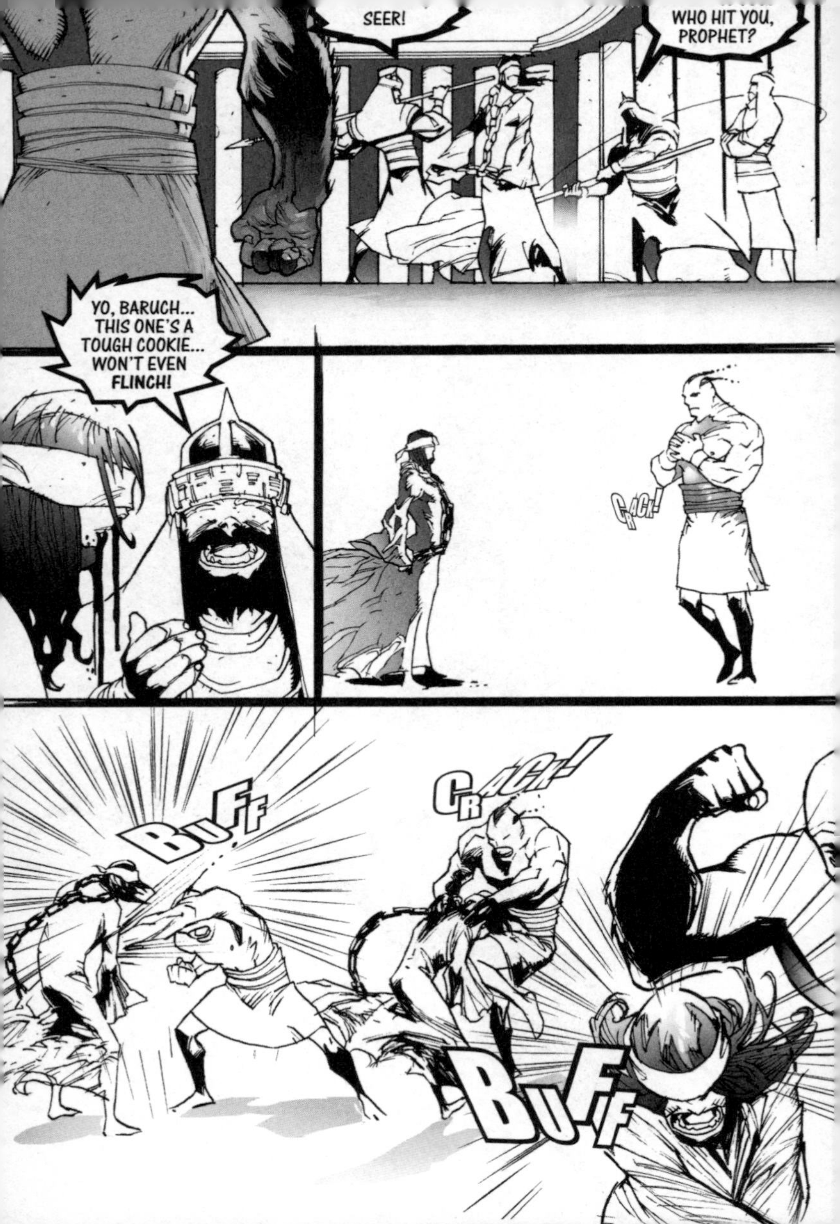
SEER!
WHO HIT YOU, PROPHET?
YO, BARUCH... THIS ONE'S A TOUGH COOKIE... WON'T EVEN FLINCH!
CRACK!
BUFF
CRACK!
BUFF

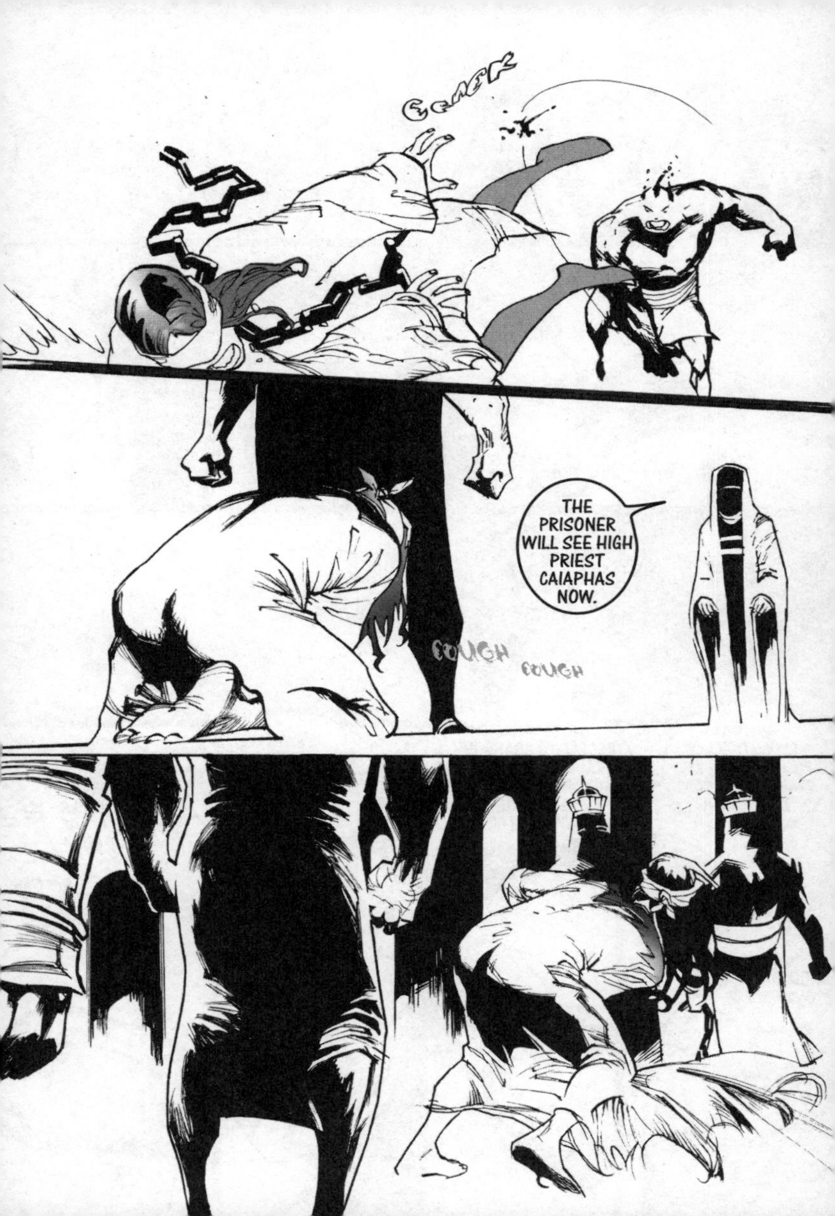
CRACK
THE PRISONER WILL SEE HIGH PRIEST CAIAPHAS NOW.
COUGH
COUGH

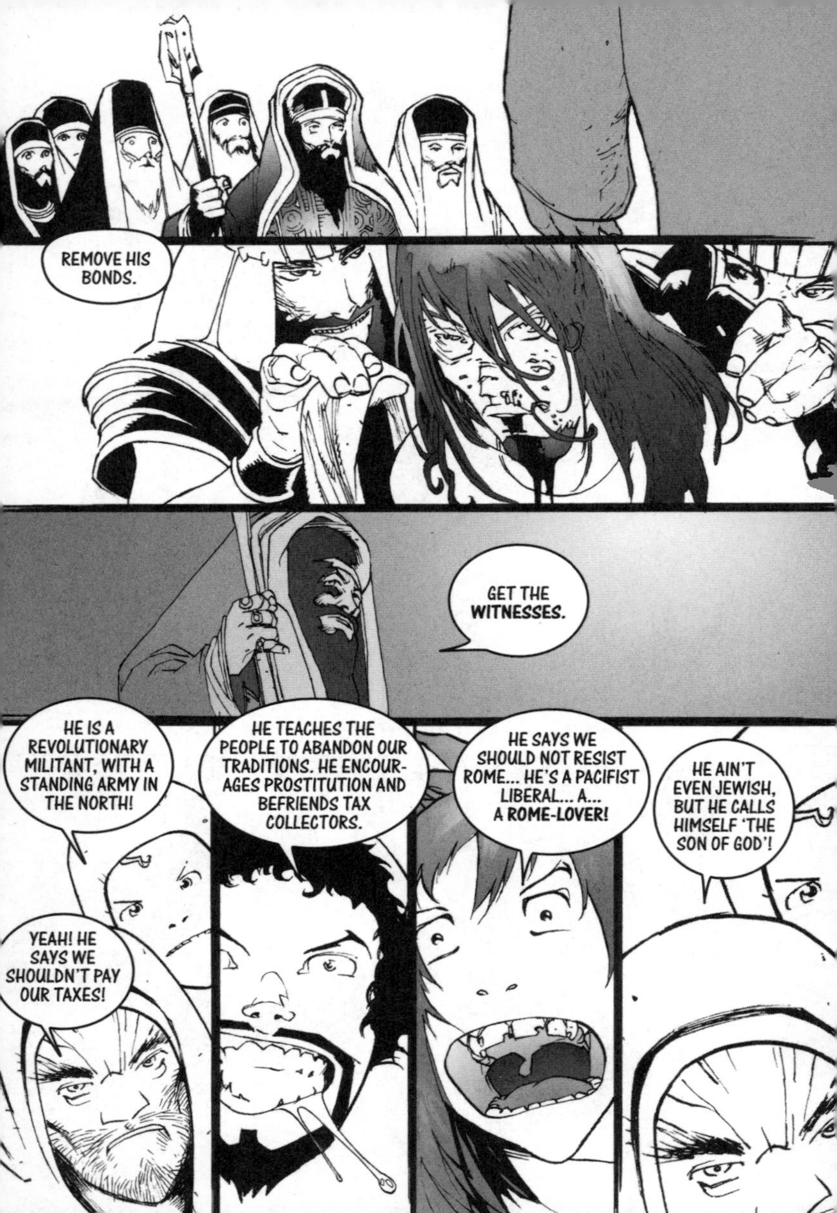
REMOVE HIS BONDS.
GET THE WITNESSES.
HE IS A REVOLUTIONARY MILITANT, WITH A STANDING ARMY IN THE NORTH!
YEAH! HE SAYS WE SHOULDN'T PAY OUR TAXES!
HE TEACHES THE PEOPLE TO ABANDON OUR TRADITIONS. HE ENCOURAGES PROSTITUTION AND BEFRIENDS TAX COLLECTORS.
HE SAYS WE SHOULD NOT RESIST ROME... HE'S A PACIFIST LIBERAL... A... A ROME-LOVER!
HE AIN'T EVEN JEWISH, BUT HE CALLS HIMSELF 'THE SON OF GOD'!

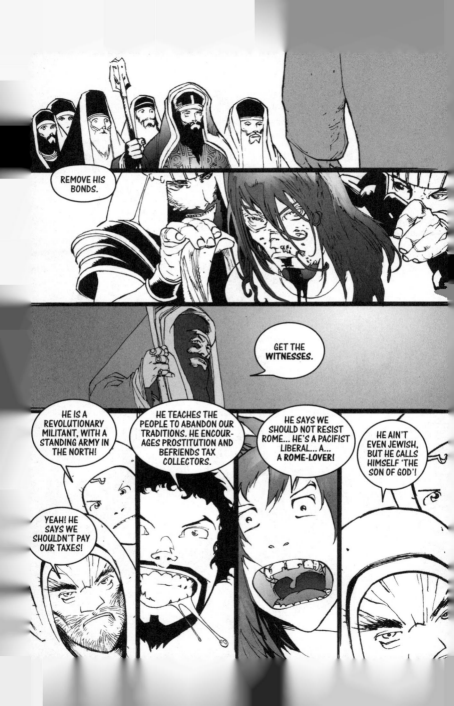

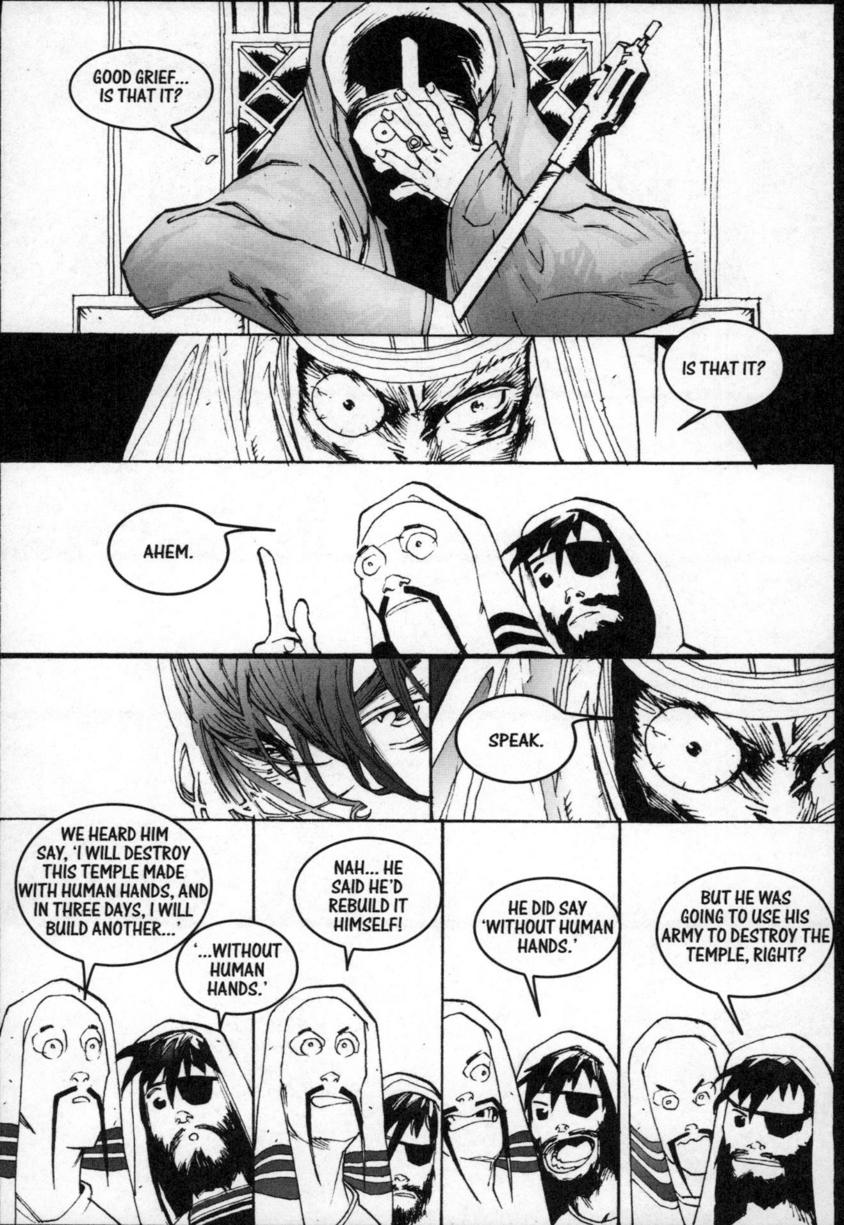
GOOD GRIEF... IS THAT IT?
IS THAT IT?
AHEM.
SPEAK.
WE HEARD HIM SAY, 'I WILL DESTROY THIS TEMPLE MADE WITH HUMAN HANDS, AND IN THREE DAYS, I WILL BUILD ANOTHER...'
'...WITHOUT HUMAN HANDS.'
NAH... HE SAID HE'D REBUILD IT HIMSELF!
HE DID SAY 'WITHOUT HUMAN HANDS.'
BUT HE WAS GOING TO USE HIS ARMY TO DESTROY THE TEMPLE, RIGHT?

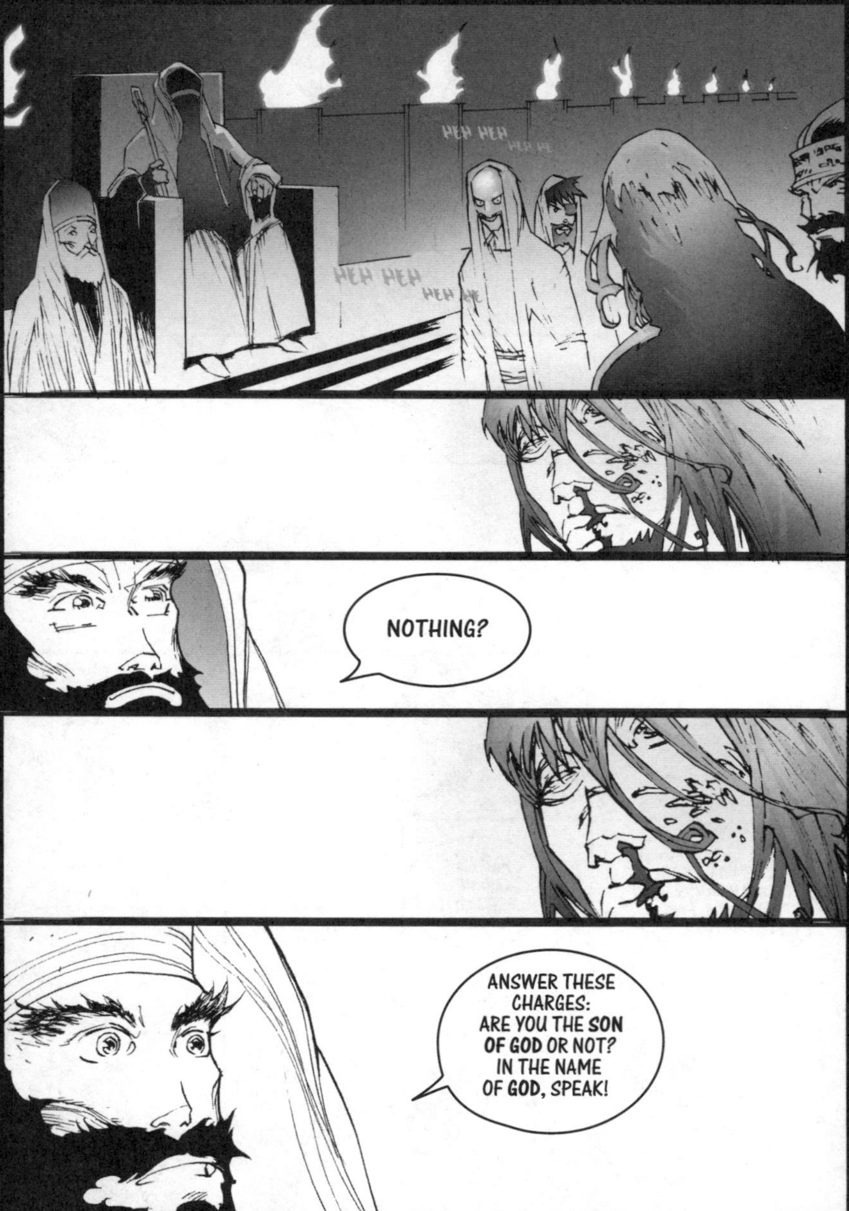
HEH HEH
HEH HE
HEH HEH
HEH HE
NOTHING?
ANSWER THESE CHARGES: ARE YOU THE **SON OF GOD** OR NOT? IN THE NAME OF **GOD**, SPEAK!

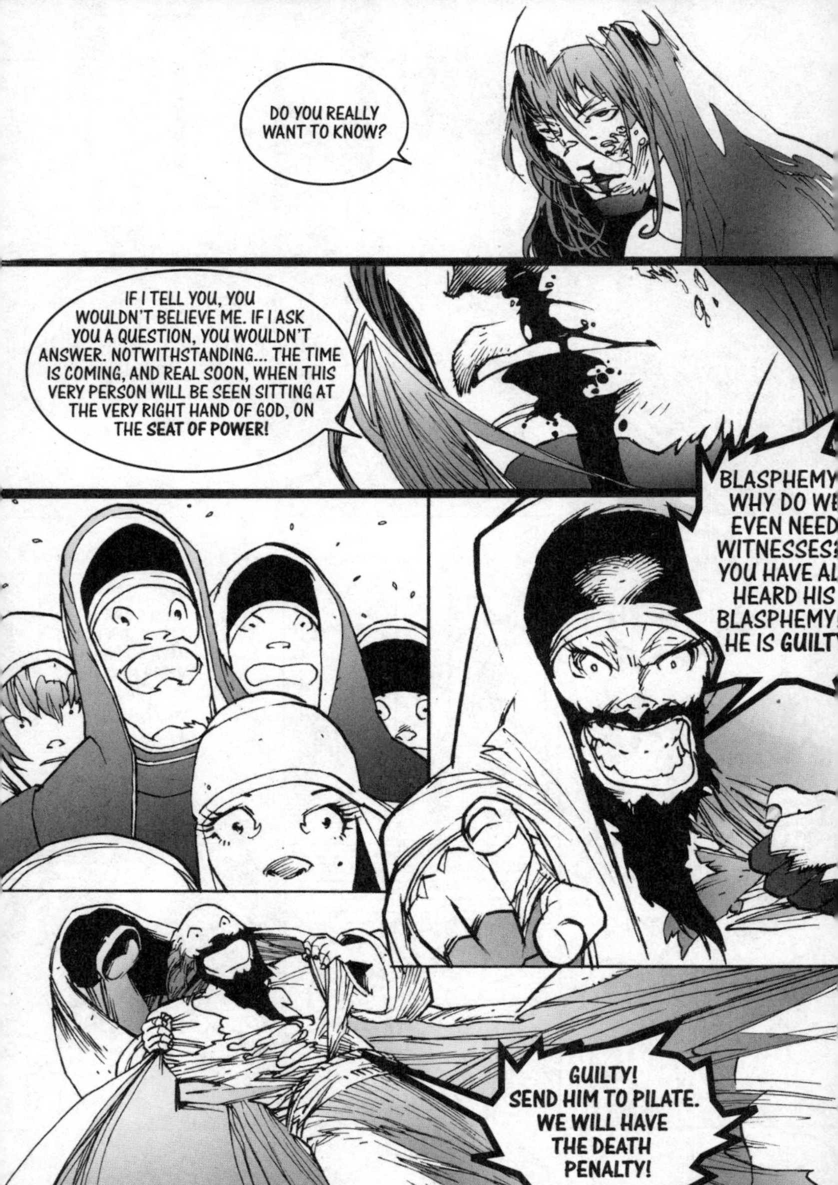
DO YOU REALLY WANT TO KNOW?
IF I TELL YOU, YOU WOULDN'T BELIEVE ME. IF I ASK YOU A QUESTION, YOU WOULDN'T ANSWER. NOTWITHSTANDING... THE TIME IS COMING, AND REAL SOON, WHEN THIS VERY PERSON WILL BE SEEN SITTING AT THE VERY RIGHT HAND OF GOD, ON THE **SEAT OF POWER!**
BLASPHEMY WHY DO WE EVEN NEED WITNESSES YOU HAVE AL HEARD HIS BLASPHEMY HE IS **GUILT**
GUILTY! SEND HIM TO PILATE. WE WILL HAVE THE DEATH PENALTY!

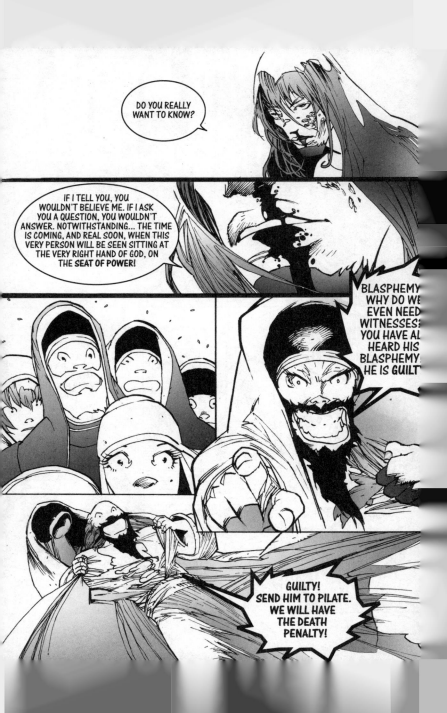

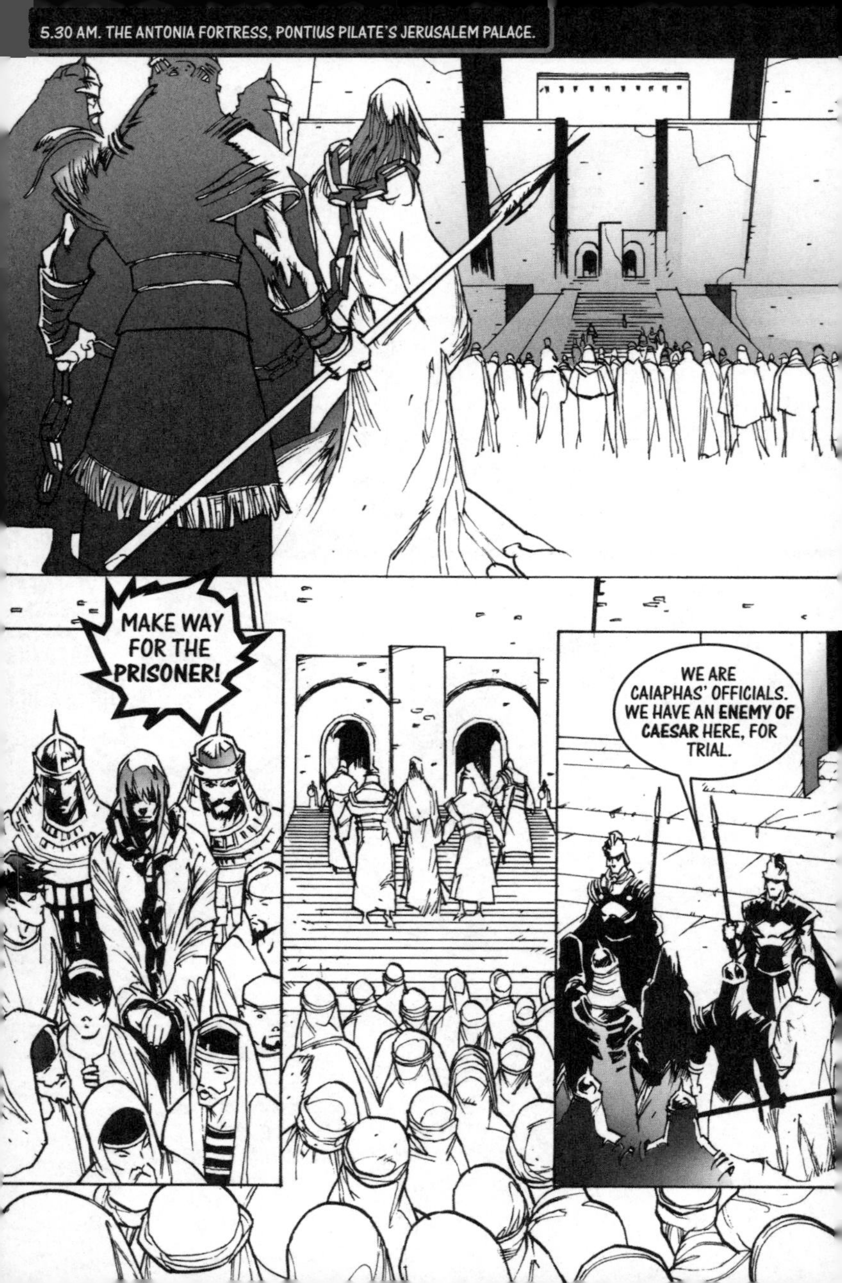
5.30 AM. THE ANTONIA FORTRESS, PONTIUS PILATE'S JERUSALEM PALACE.
MAKE WAY FOR THE PRISONER!
WE ARE CAIAPHAS' OFFICIALS. WE HAVE AN ENEMY OF CAESAR HERE, FOR TRIAL.

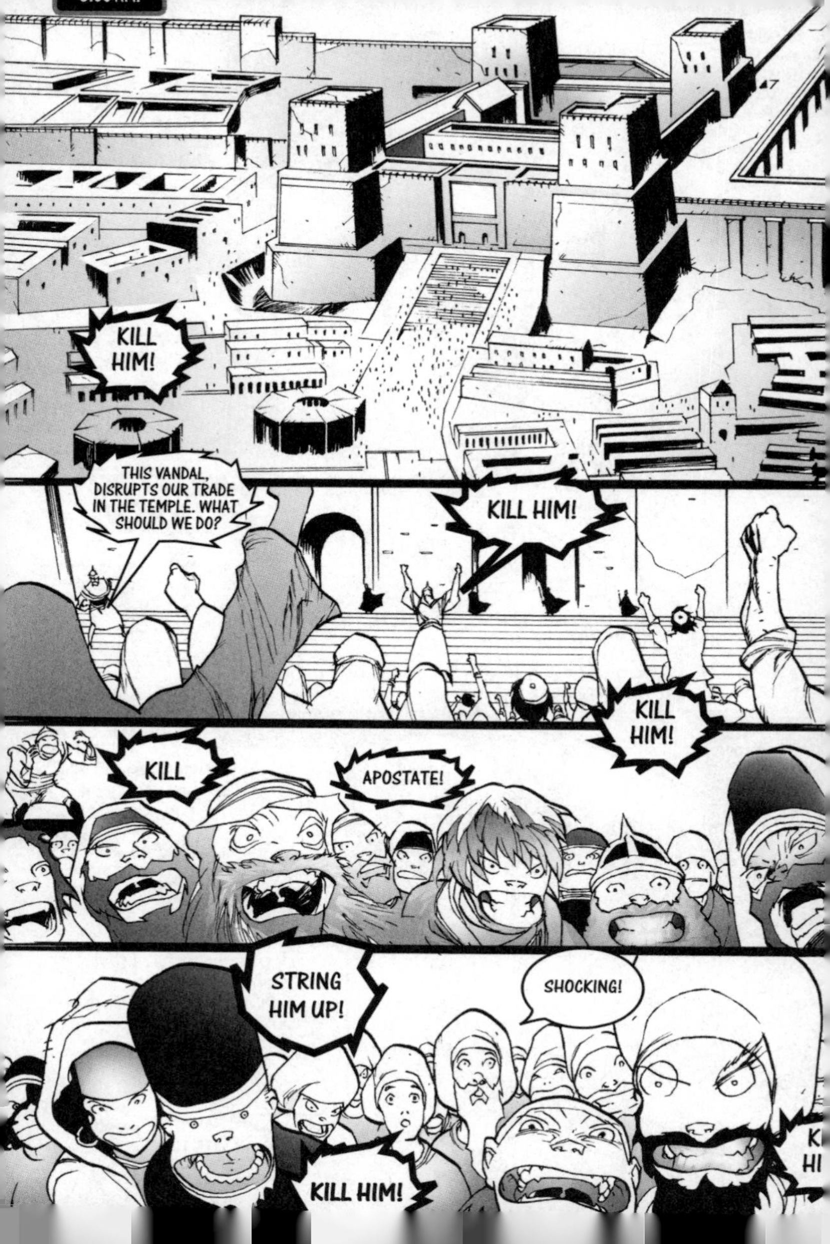
KILL HIM!
THIS VANDAL, DISRUPTS OUR TRADE IN THE TEMPLE. WHAT SHOULD WE DO?
KILL HIM!
KILL HIM!
KILL
APOSTATE!
STRING HIM UP!
SHOCKING!
KILL HIM!

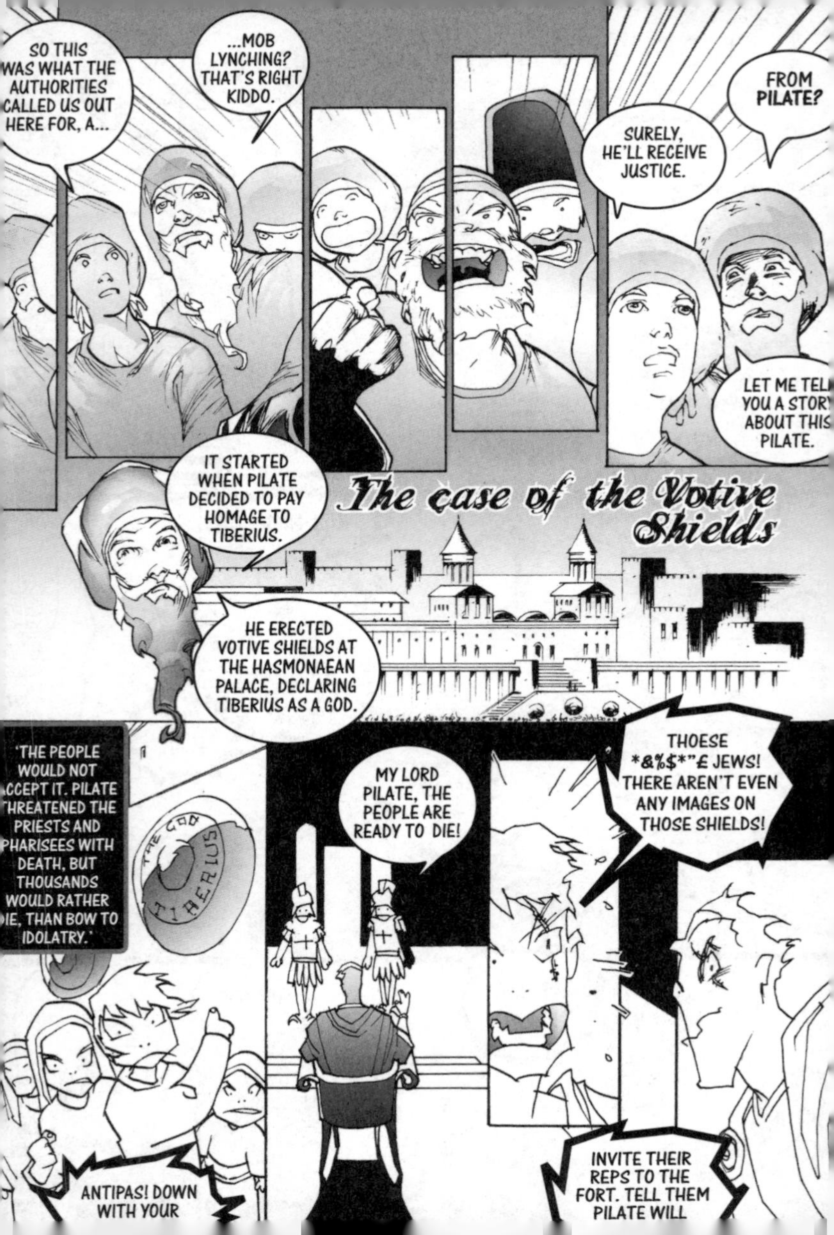
SO THIS WAS WHAT THE AUTHORITIES CALLED US OUT HERE FOR, A...
...MOB LYNCHING? THAT'S RIGHT KIDDO.
SURELY, HE'LL RECEIVE JUSTICE.
FROM PILATE?
LET ME TELL YOU A STORY ABOUT THIS PILATE.
IT STARTED WHEN PILATE DECIDED TO PAY HOMAGE TO TIBERIUS.
The case of the Votive Shields
HE ERECTED VOTIVE SHIELDS AT THE HASMONAEAN PALACE, DECLARING TIBERIUS AS A GOD.
'THE PEOPLE WOULD NOT ACCEPT IT. PILATE THREATENED THE PRIESTS AND PHARISEES WITH DEATH, BUT THOUSANDS WOULD RATHER DIE, THAN BOW TO IDOLATRY.'
THE GOD TIBERIUS
MY LORD PILATE, THE PEOPLE ARE READY TO DIE!
THOESE *&%$*"£ JEWS! THERE AREN'T EVEN ANY IMAGES ON THOSE SHIELDS!
ANTIPAS! DOWN WITH YOUR
INVITE THEIR REPS TO THE FORT. TELL THEM PILATE WILL

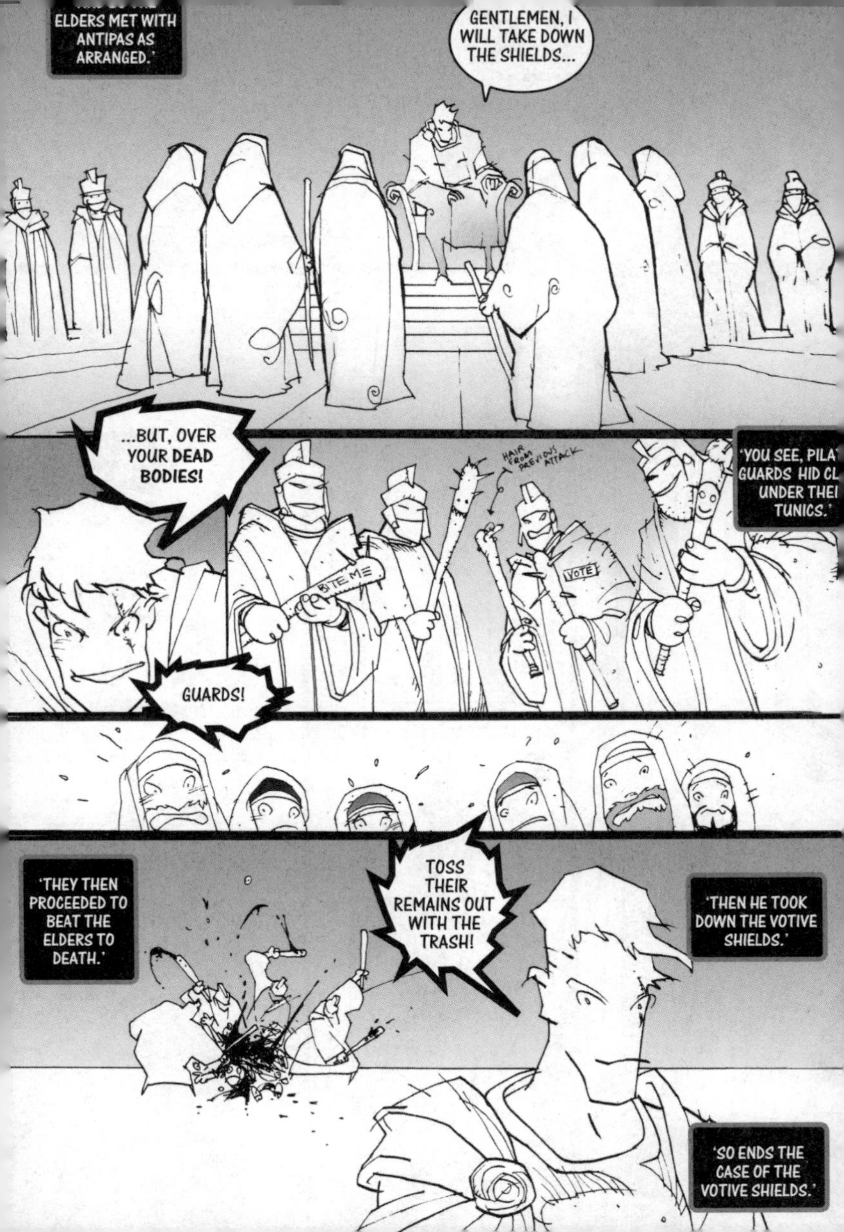
ELDERS MET WITH ANTIPAS AS ARRANGED.'
GENTLEMEN, I WILL TAKE DOWN THE SHIELDS...
...BUT, OVER YOUR DEAD BODIES!
'YOU SEE, PILA
GUARDS HID CL
UNDER THEI
TUNICS.'
BITE ME
HAIR FROM PREVIOUS ATTACK
VOTE
GUARDS!
'THEY THEN PROCEEDED TO BEAT THE ELDERS TO DEATH.'
TOSS THEIR REMAINS OUT WITH THE TRASH!
'THEN HE TOOK DOWN THE VOTIVE SHIELDS.'
'SO ENDS THE CASE OF THE VOTIVE SHIELDS.'

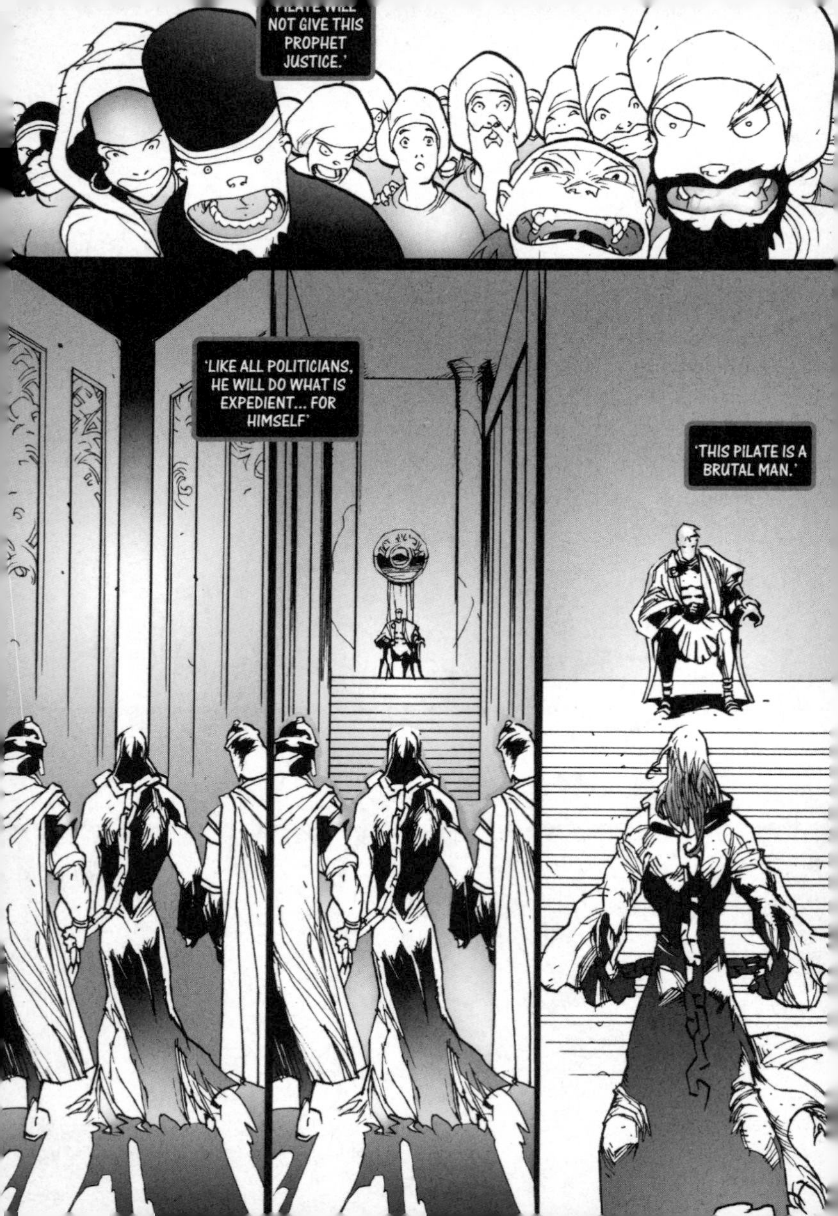
NOT GIVE THIS PROPHET JUSTICE.'
'LIKE ALL POLITICIANS, HE WILL DO WHAT IS EXPEDIENT... FOR HIMSELF'
'THIS PILATE IS A BRUTAL MAN.'

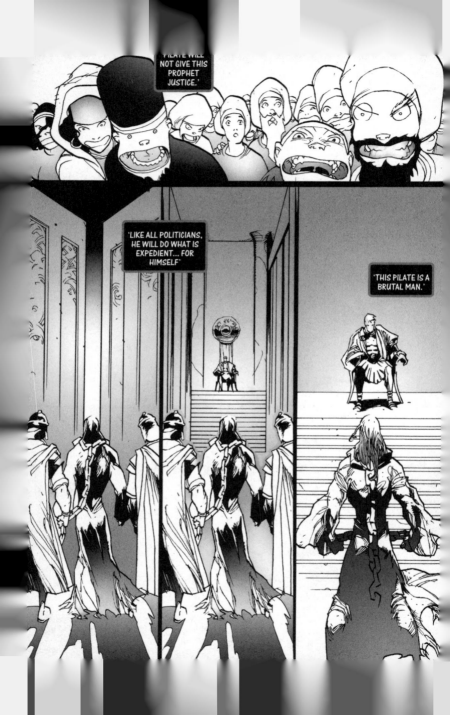

Chapter 2
Trial and error part 2

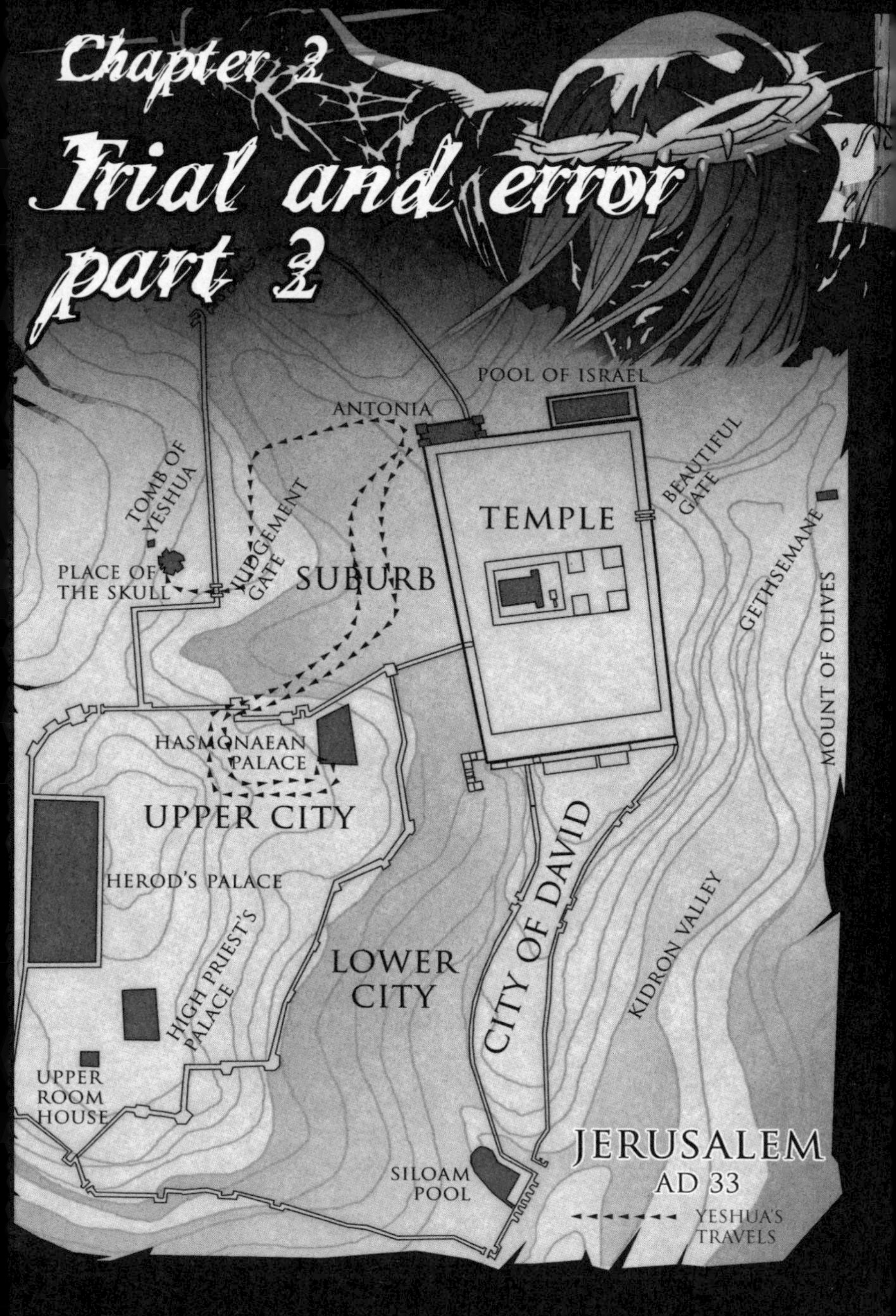
POOL OF ISRAEL
ANTONIA
TOMB OF YESHUA
JUDGEMENT GATE
BEAUTIFUL GATE
TEMPLE
GETHSEMANE
PLACE OF THE SKULL
SUBURB
MOUNT OF OLIVES
HASMONAEAN PALACE
UPPER CITY
HEROD'S PALACE
HIGH PRIEST'S PALACE
LOWER CITY
CITY OF DAVID
KIDRON VALLEY
UPPER ROOM HOUSE
SILOAM POOL
JERUSALEM
AD 33
YESHUA'S TRAVELS

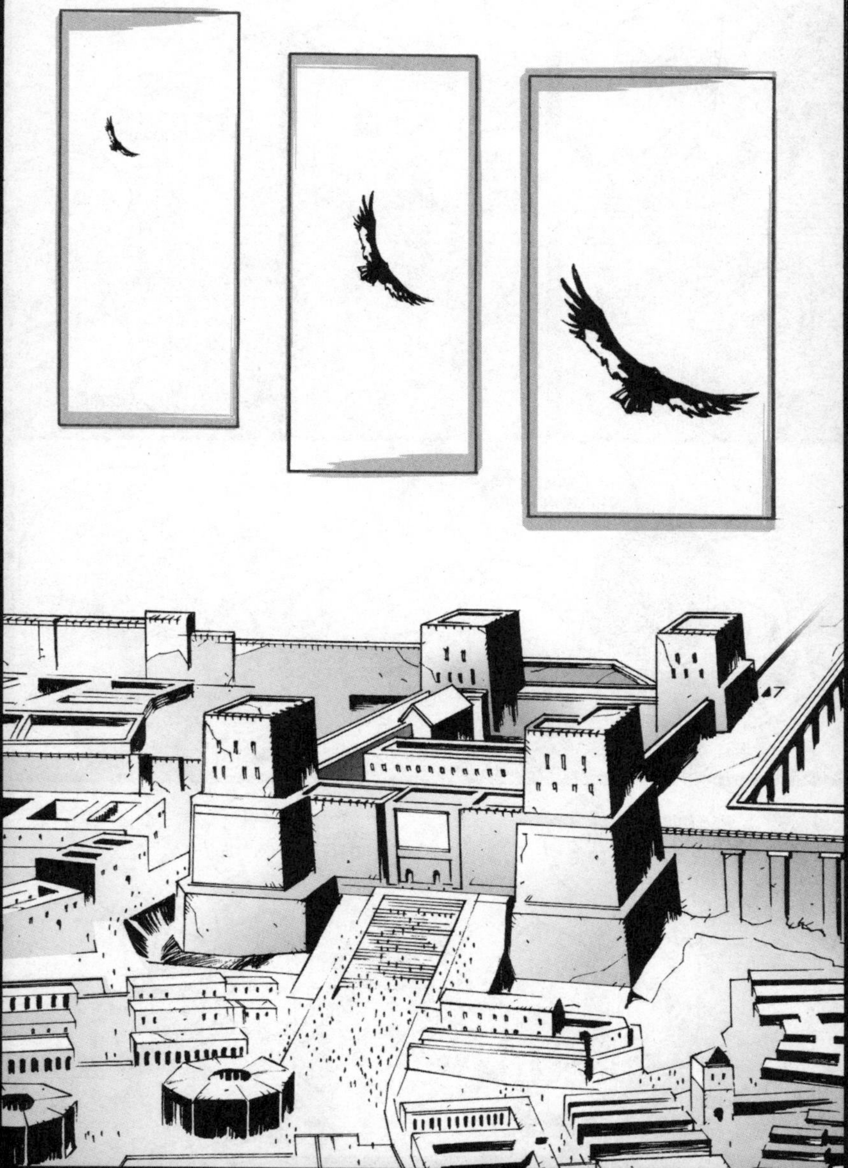

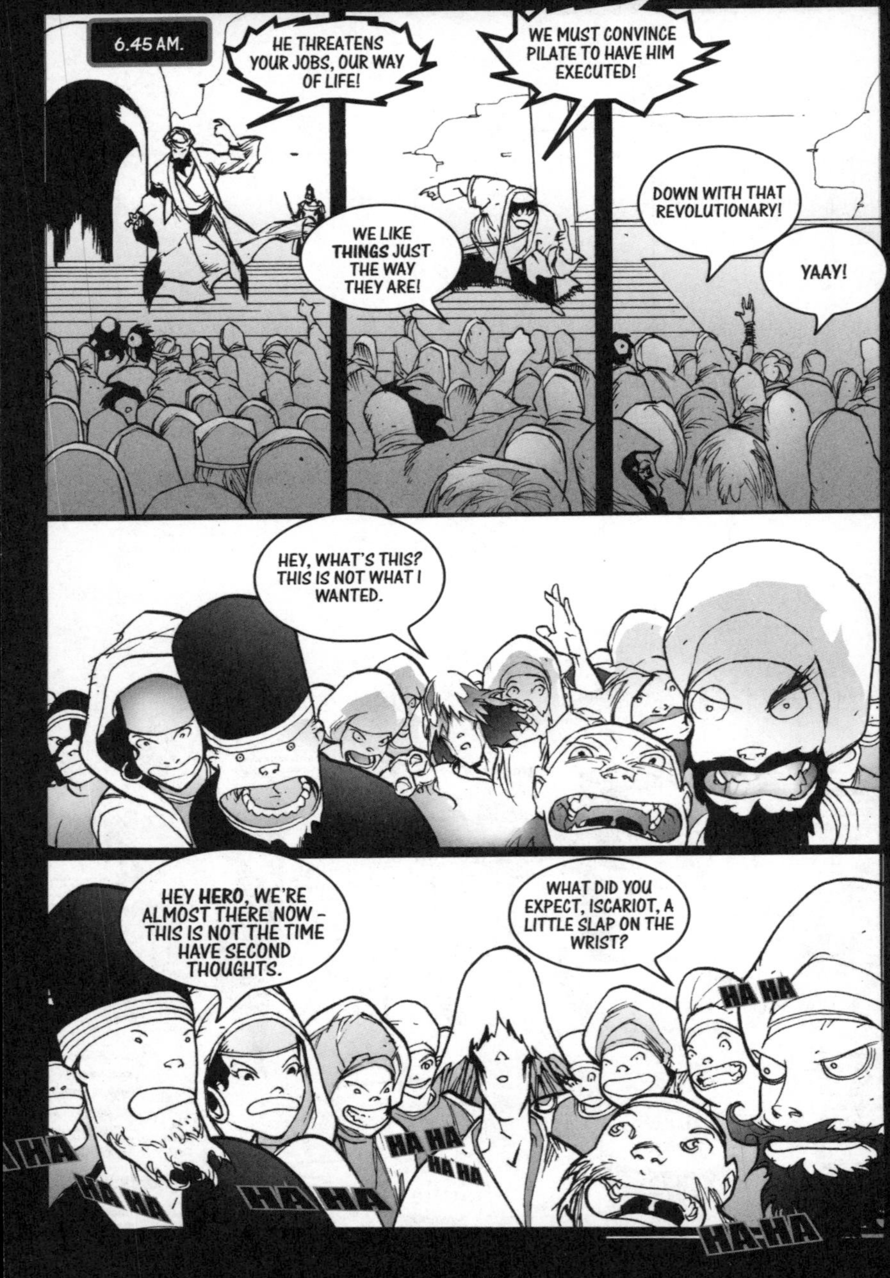
6.45 AM.
HE THREATENS YOUR JOBS, OUR WAY OF LIFE!
WE MUST CONVINCE PILATE TO HAVE HIM EXECUTED!
WE LIKE THINGS JUST THE WAY THEY ARE!
DOWN WITH THAT REVOLUTIONARY!
YAAY!
HEY, WHAT'S THIS? THIS IS NOT WHAT I WANTED.
HEY HERO, WE'RE ALMOST THERE NOW - THIS IS NOT THE TIME HAVE SECOND THOUGHTS.
WHAT DID YOU EXPECT, ISCARIOT, A LITTLE SLAP ON THE WRIST?
HA HA
HA HA
HA HA
HA HA
HA HA
HA-HA

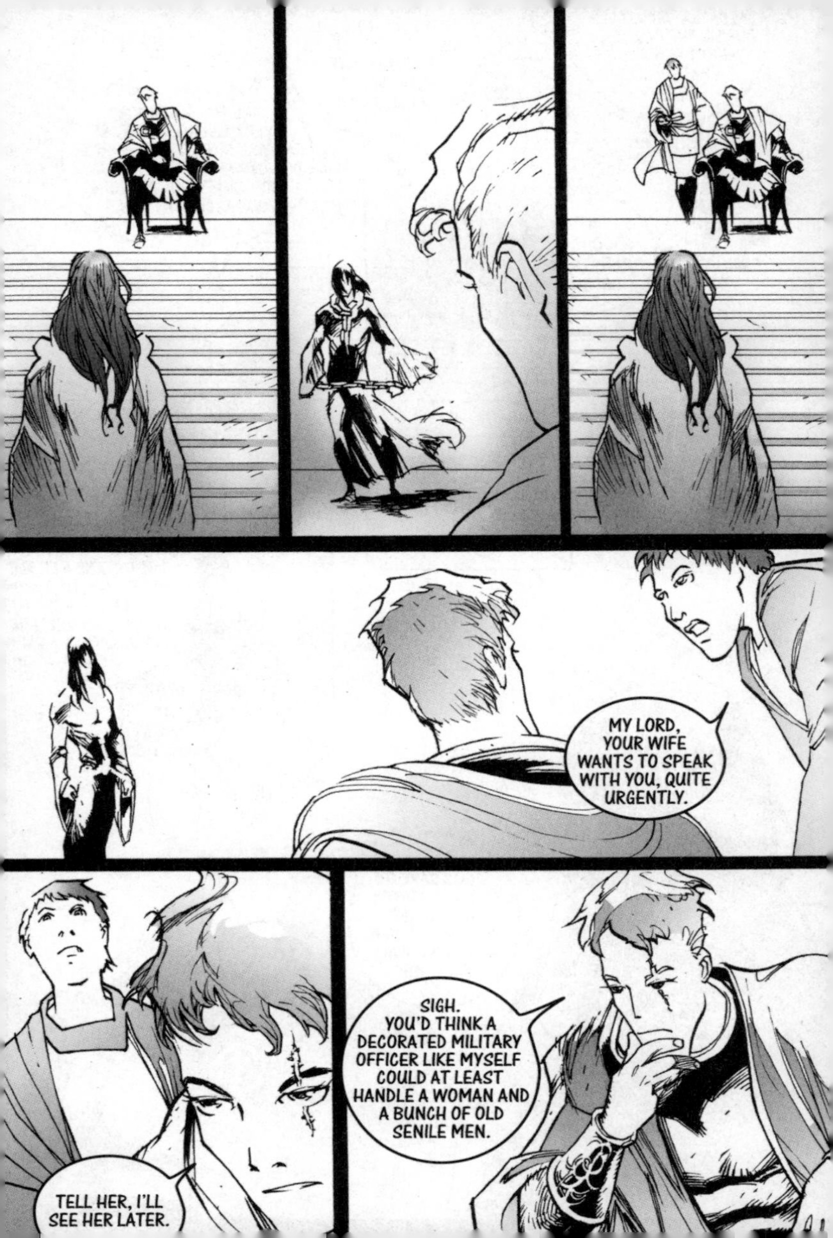
MY LORD, YOUR WIFE WANTS TO SPEAK WITH YOU, QUITE URGENTLY.
TELL HER, I'LL SEE HER LATER.
SIGH. YOU'D THINK A DECORATED MILITARY OFFICER LIKE MYSELF COULD AT LEAST HANDLE A WOMAN AND A BUNCH OF OLD SENILE MEN.

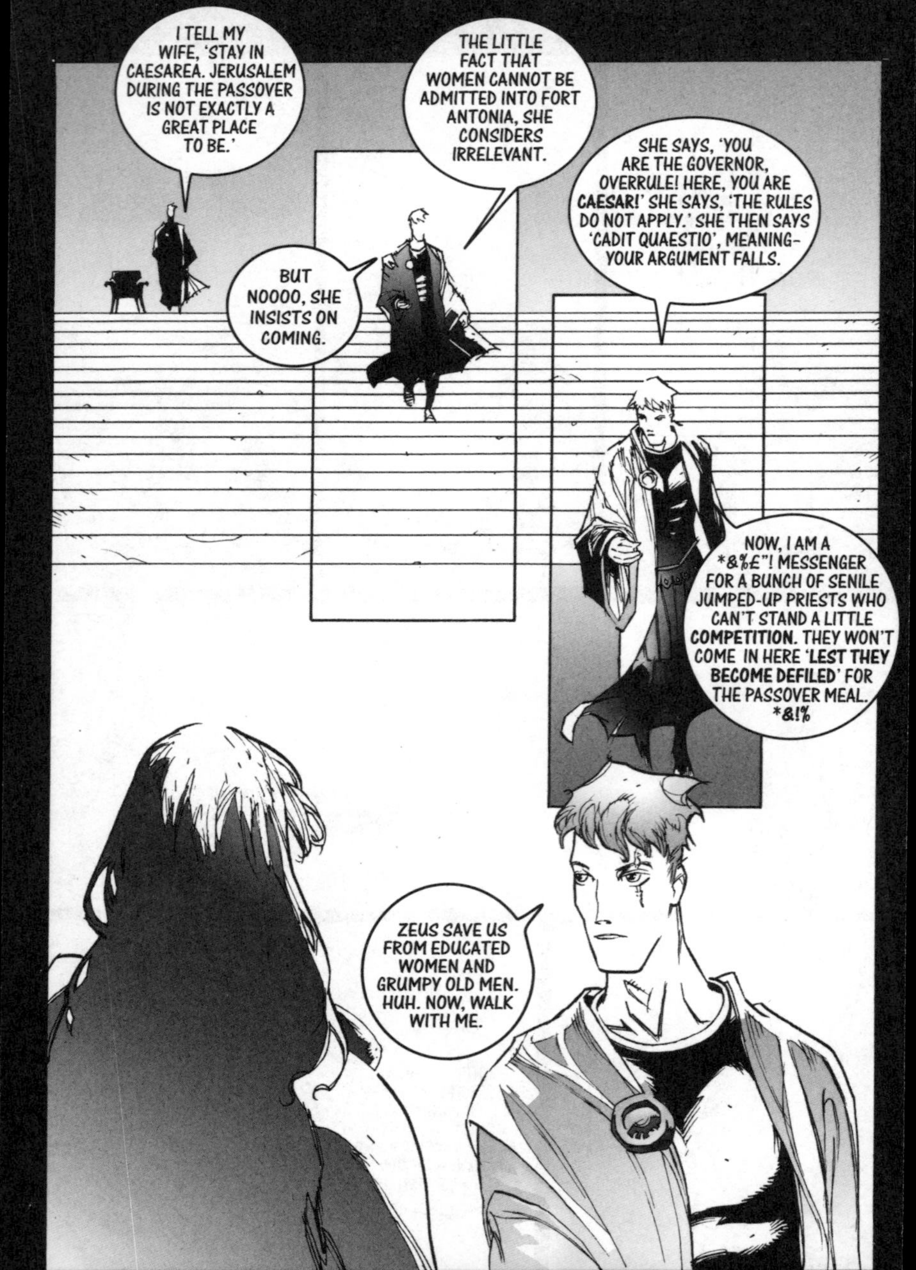
I TELL MY WIFE, 'STAY IN CAESAREA. JERUSALEM DURING THE PASSOVER IS NOT EXACTLY A GREAT PLACE TO BE.'
THE LITTLE FACT THAT WOMEN CANNOT BE ADMITTED INTO FORT ANTONIA, SHE CONSIDERS IRRELEVANT.
BUT NOOOO, SHE INSISTS ON COMING.
SHE SAYS, 'YOU ARE THE GOVERNOR, OVERRULE! HERE, YOU ARE CAESAR!' SHE SAYS, 'THE RULES DO NOT APPLY.' SHE THEN SAYS 'CADIT QUAESTIO', MEANING- YOUR ARGUMENT FALLS.
NOW, I AM A *&%£"! MESSENGER FOR A BUNCH OF SENILE JUMPED-UP PRIESTS WHO CAN'T STAND A LITTLE COMPETITION. THEY WON'T COME IN HERE 'LEST THEY BECOME DEFILED' FOR THE PASSOVER MEAL. *&!%
ZEUS SAVE US FROM EDUCATED WOMEN AND GRUMPY OLD MEN. HUH. NOW, WALK WITH ME.

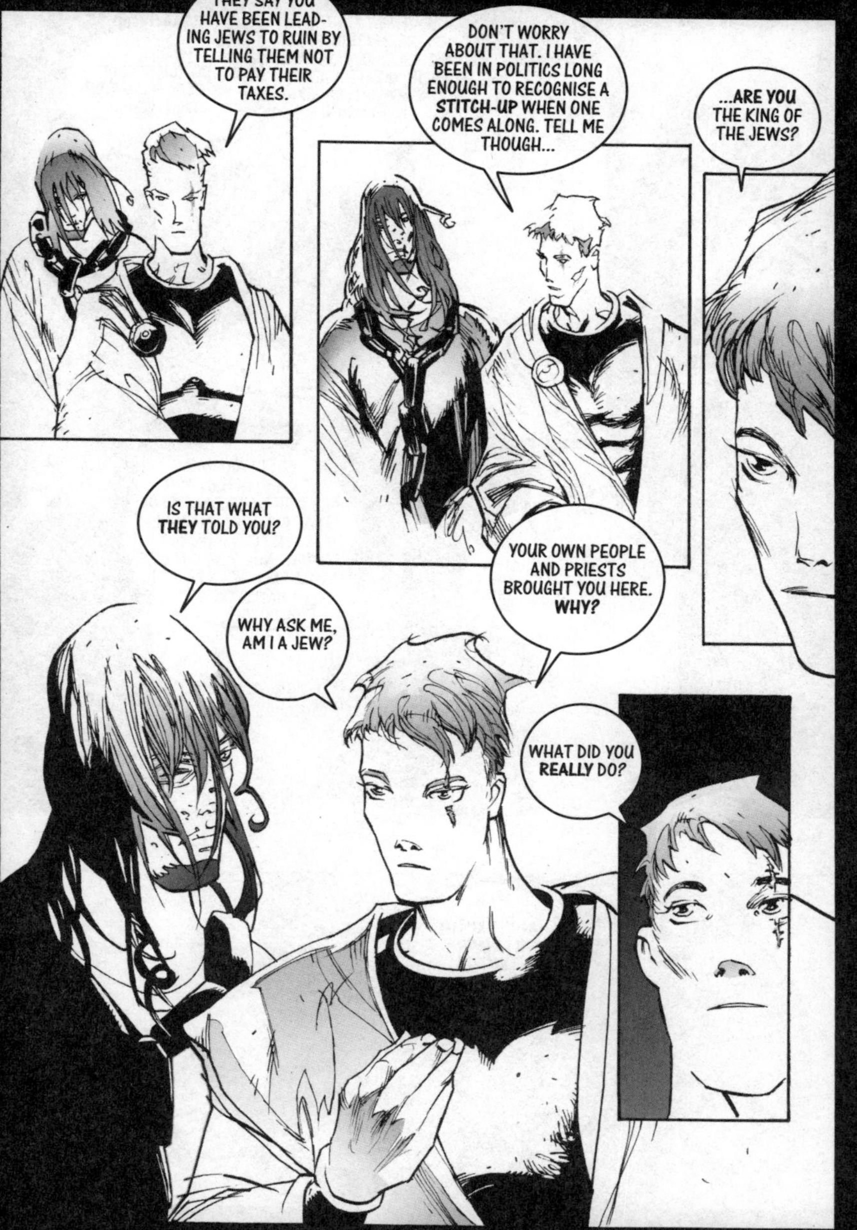
THEY SAY YOU HAVE BEEN LEAD-ING JEWS TO RUIN BY TELLING THEM NOT TO PAY THEIR TAXES.
DON'T WORRY ABOUT THAT. I HAVE BEEN IN POLITICS LONG ENOUGH TO RECOGNISE A STITCH-UP WHEN ONE COMES ALONG. TELL ME THOUGH...
...ARE YOU THE KING OF THE JEWS?
IS THAT WHAT THEY TOLD YOU?
WHY ASK ME, AM I A JEW?
YOUR OWN PEOPLE AND PRIESTS BROUGHT YOU HERE. WHY?
WHAT DID YOU REALLY DO?

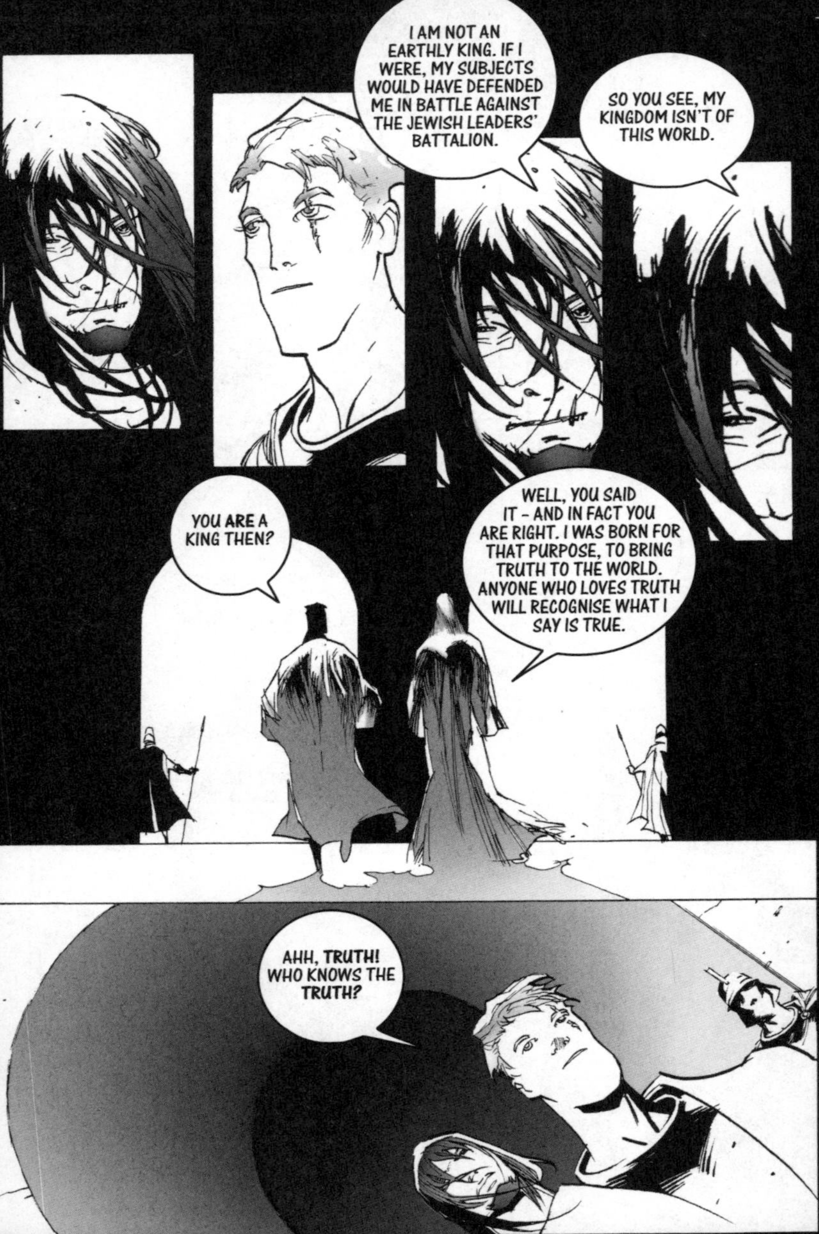
I AM NOT AN EARTHLY KING. IF I WERE, MY SUBJECTS WOULD HAVE DEFENDED ME IN BATTLE AGAINST THE JEWISH LEADERS' BATTALION.
SO YOU SEE, MY KINGDOM ISN'T OF THIS WORLD.
YOU ARE A KING THEN?
WELL, YOU SAID IT - AND IN FACT YOU ARE RIGHT. I WAS BORN FOR THAT PURPOSE, TO BRING TRUTH TO THE WORLD. ANYONE WHO LOVES TRUTH WILL RECOGNISE WHAT I SAY IS TRUE.
AHH, TRUTH! WHO KNOWS THE TRUTH?

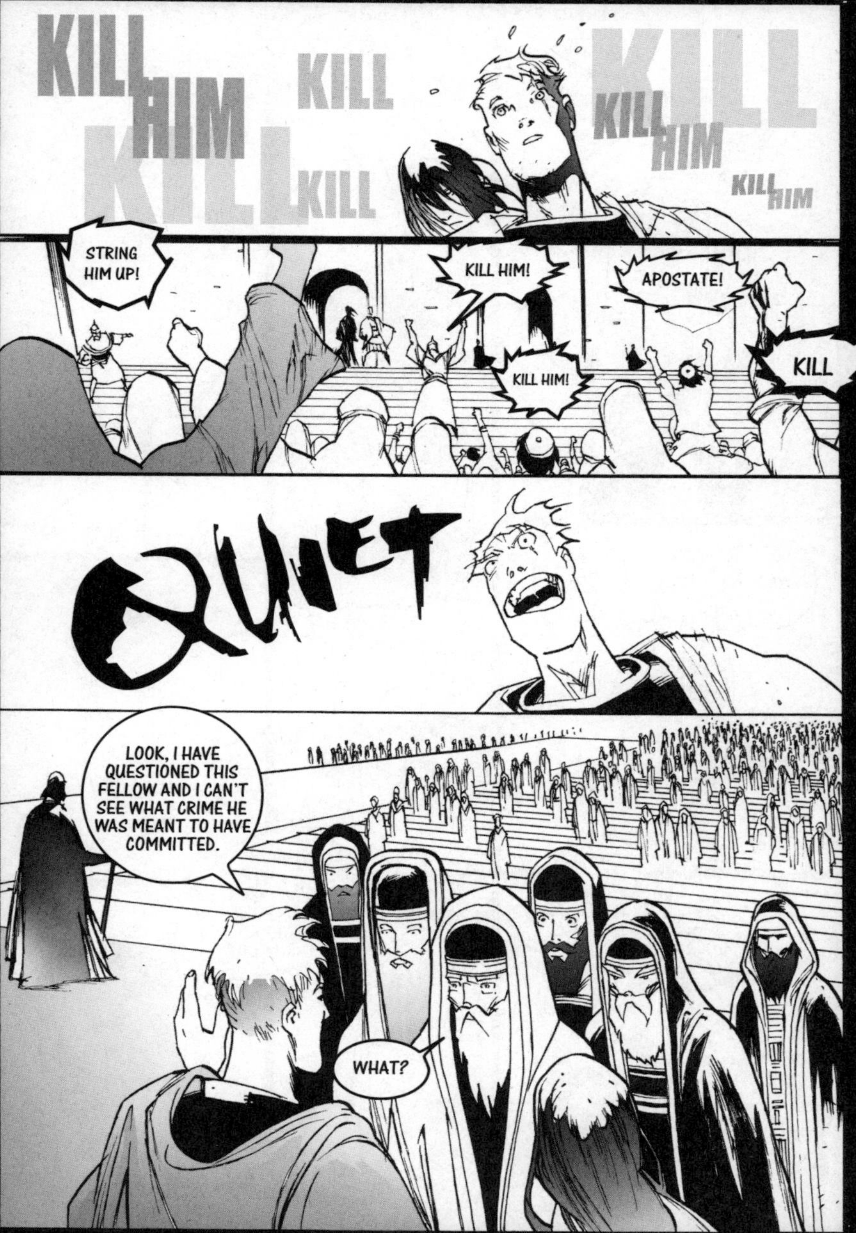
KILL HIM KILL KILL KILL
KILL KILL HIM KILL HIM
STRING HIM UP!
KILL HIM!
APOSTATE!
KILL HIM!
KILL
QUIET
LOOK, I HAVE QUESTIONED THIS FELLOW AND I CAN'T SEE WHAT CRIME HE WAS MEANT TO HAVE COMMITTED.
WHAT?

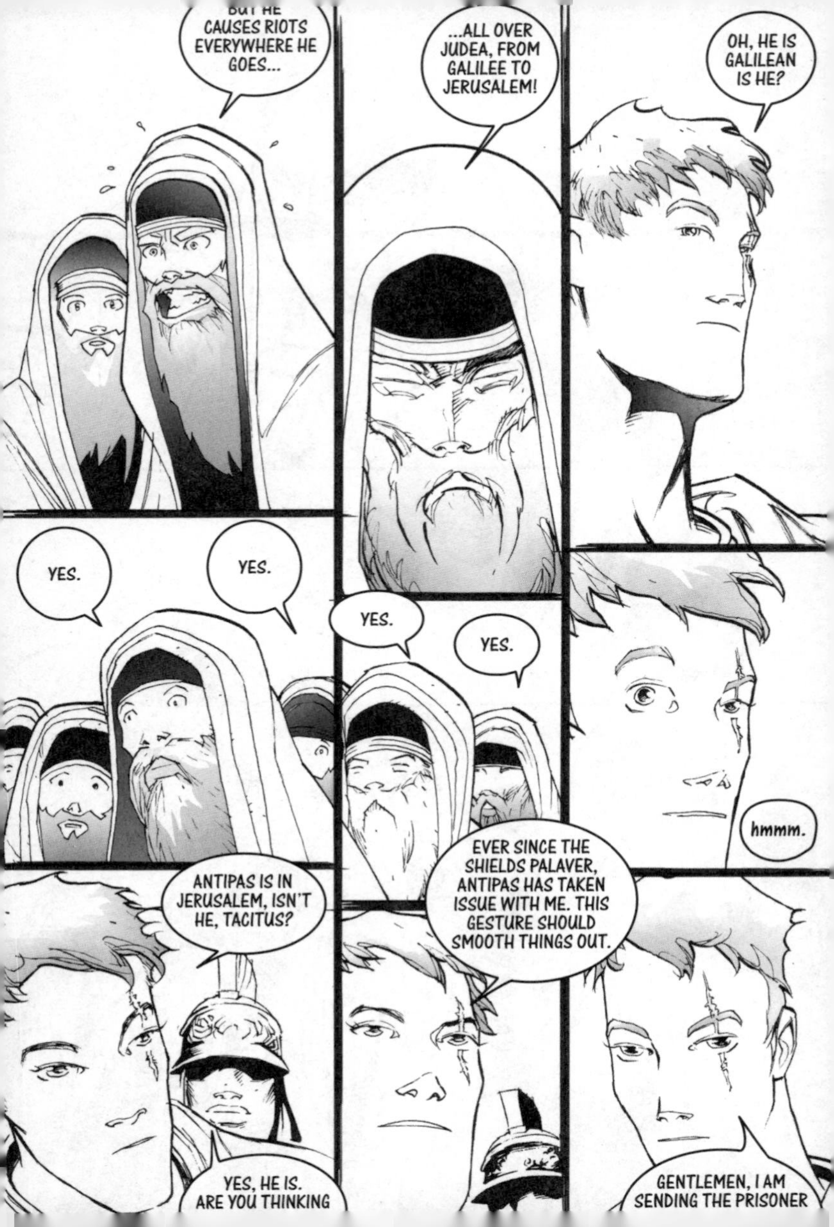
BUT HE CAUSES RIOTS EVERYWHERE HE GOES...
...ALL OVER JUDEA, FROM GALILEE TO JERUSALEM!
OH, HE IS GALILEAN IS HE?
YES.
YES.
YES.
YES.
hmmm.
ANTIPAS IS IN JERUSALEM, ISN'T HE, TACITUS?
YES, HE IS. ARE YOU THINKING
EVER SINCE THE SHIELDS PALAVER, ANTIPAS HAS TAKEN ISSUE WITH ME. THIS GESTURE SHOULD SMOOTH THINGS OUT.
GENTLEMEN, I AM SENDING THE PRISONER

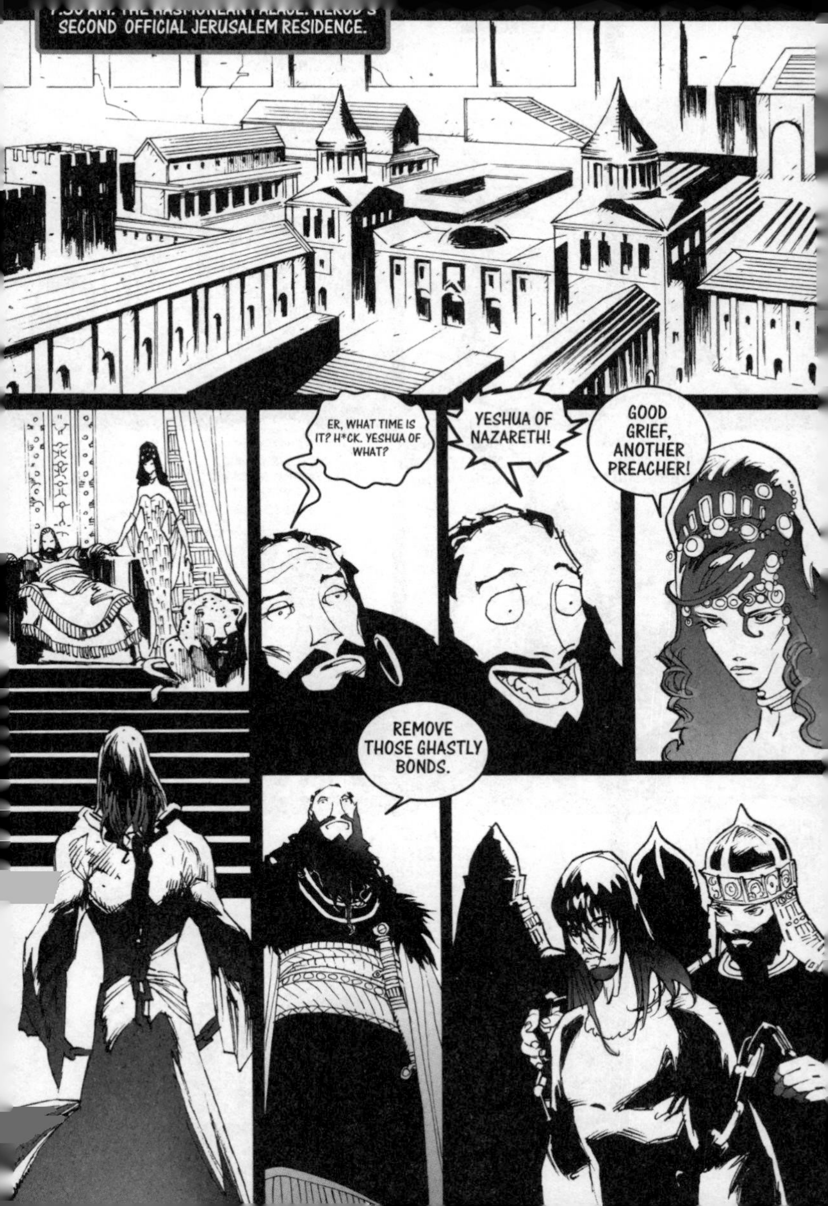

SECOND OFFICIAL JERUSALEM RESIDENCE.
ER, WHAT TIME IS IT? H*CK. YESHUA OF WHAT?
YESHUA OF NAZARETH!
GOOD GRIEF, ANOTHER PREACHER!
REMOVE THOSE GHASTLY BONDS.

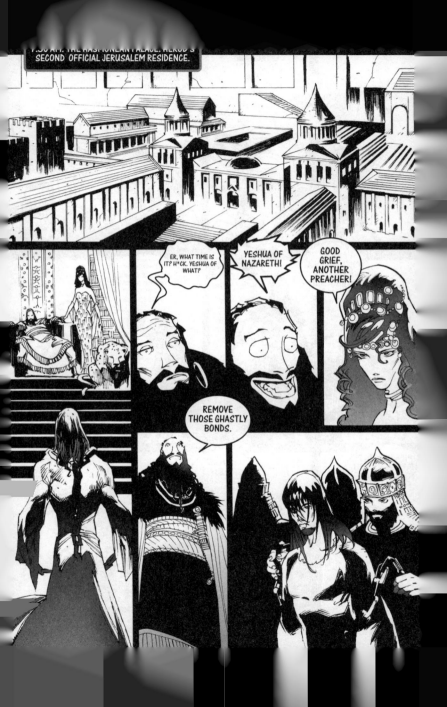

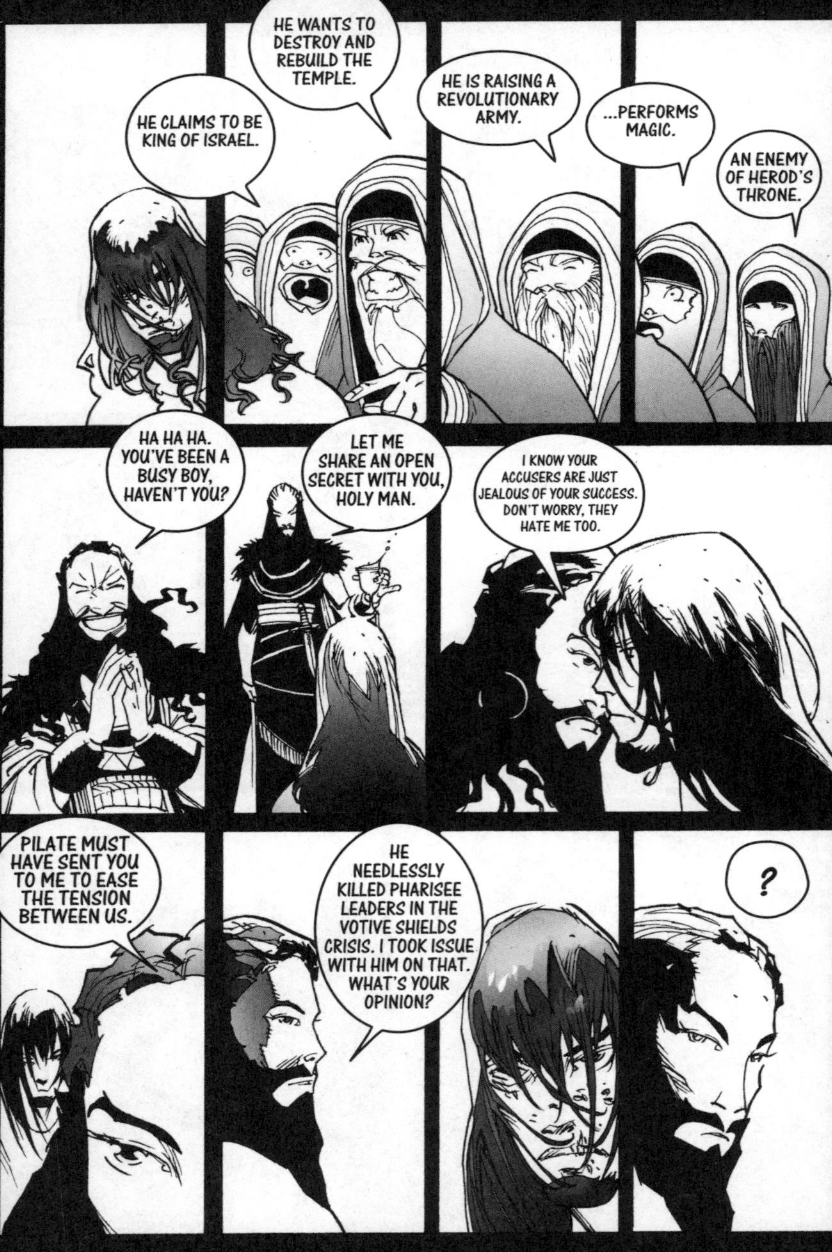
HE CLAIMS TO BE KING OF ISRAEL.
HE WANTS TO DESTROY AND REBUILD THE TEMPLE.
HE IS RAISING A REVOLUTIONARY ARMY.
...PERFORMS MAGIC.
AN ENEMY OF HEROD'S THRONE.
HA HA HA. YOU'VE BEEN A BUSY BOY, HAVEN'T YOU?
LET ME SHARE AN OPEN SECRET WITH YOU, HOLY MAN.
I KNOW YOUR ACCUSERS ARE JUST JEALOUS OF YOUR SUCCESS. DON'T WORRY, THEY HATE ME TOO.
PILATE MUST HAVE SENT YOU TO ME TO EASE THE TENSION BETWEEN US.
HE NEEDLESSLY KILLED PHARISEE LEADERS IN THE VOTIVE SHIELDS CRISIS. I TOOK ISSUE WITH HIM ON THAT. WHAT'S YOUR OPINION?
?

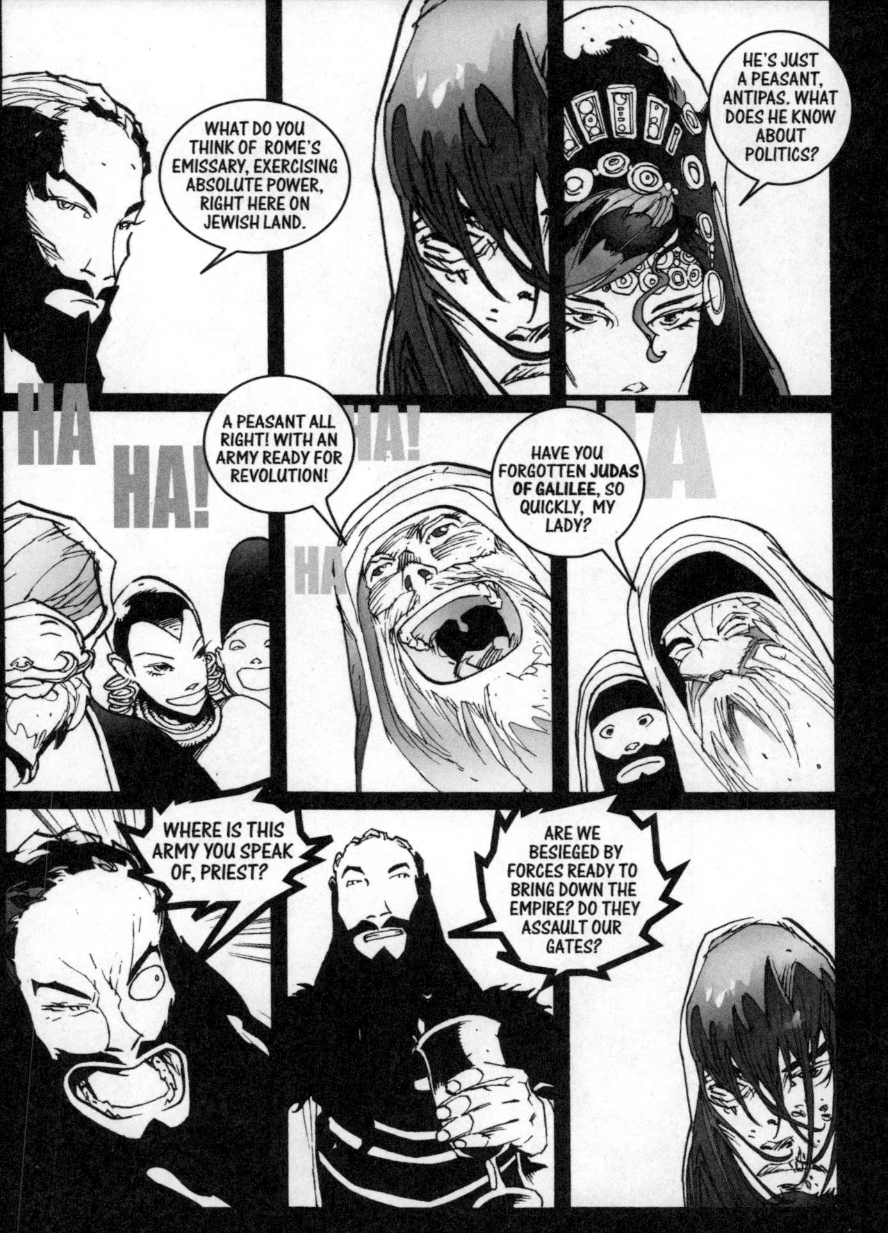
WHAT DO YOU THINK OF ROME'S EMISSARY, EXERCISING ABSOLUTE POWER, RIGHT HERE ON JEWISH LAND.
HE'S JUST A PEASANT, ANTIPAS. WHAT DOES HE KNOW ABOUT POLITICS?
HA HA! HA!
A PEASANT ALL RIGHT! WITH AN ARMY READY FOR REVOLUTION!
HA
HAVE YOU FORGOTTEN JUDAS OF GALILEE, SO QUICKLY, MY LADY?
WHERE IS THIS ARMY YOU SPEAK OF, PRIEST?
ARE WE BESIEGED BY FORCES READY TO BRING DOWN THE EMPIRE? DO THEY ASSAULT OUR GATES?

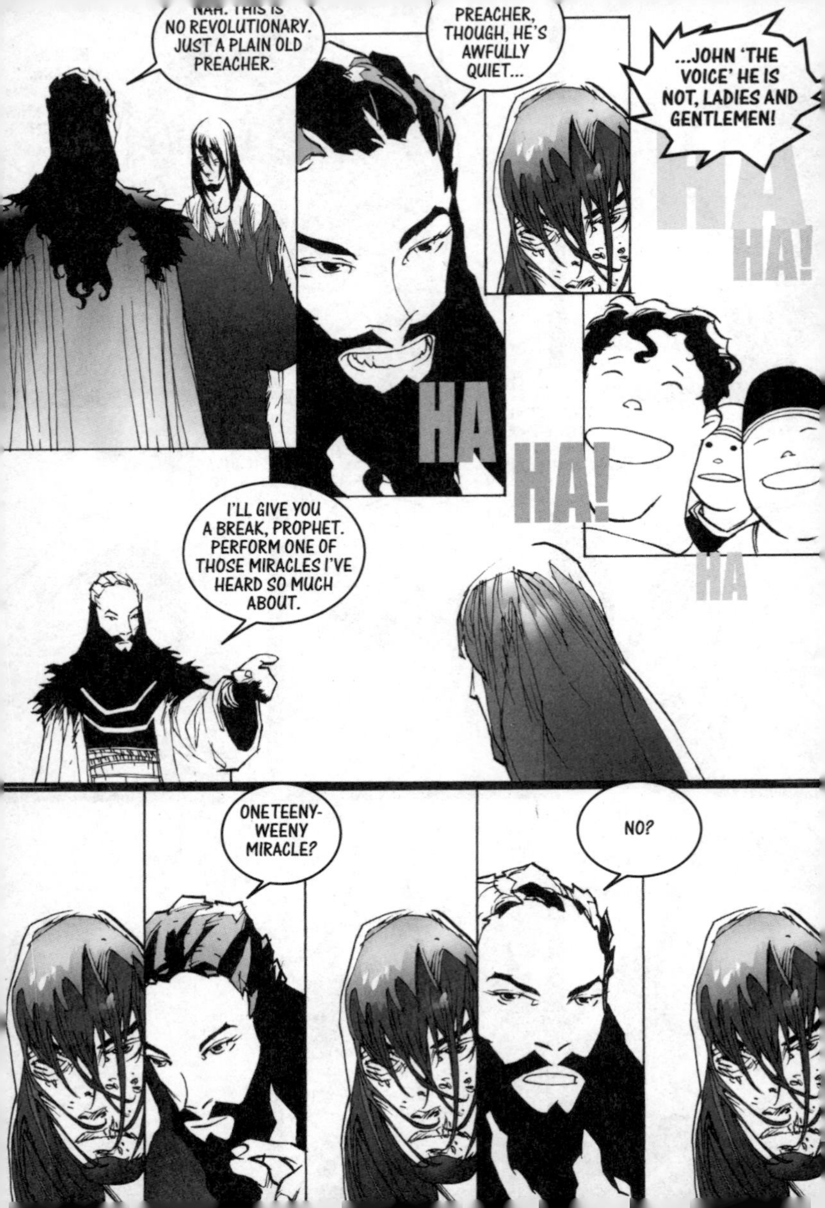
NAH. THIS IS NO REVOLUTIONARY. JUST A PLAIN OLD PREACHER.
PREACHER, THOUGH, HE'S AWFULLY QUIET...
...JOHN 'THE VOICE' HE IS NOT, LADIES AND GENTLEMEN!
HA HA!
HA HA!
HA
I'LL GIVE YOU A BREAK, PROPHET. PERFORM ONE OF THOSE MIRACLES I'VE HEARD SO MUCH ABOUT.
ONE TEENY-WEENY MIRACLE?
NO?

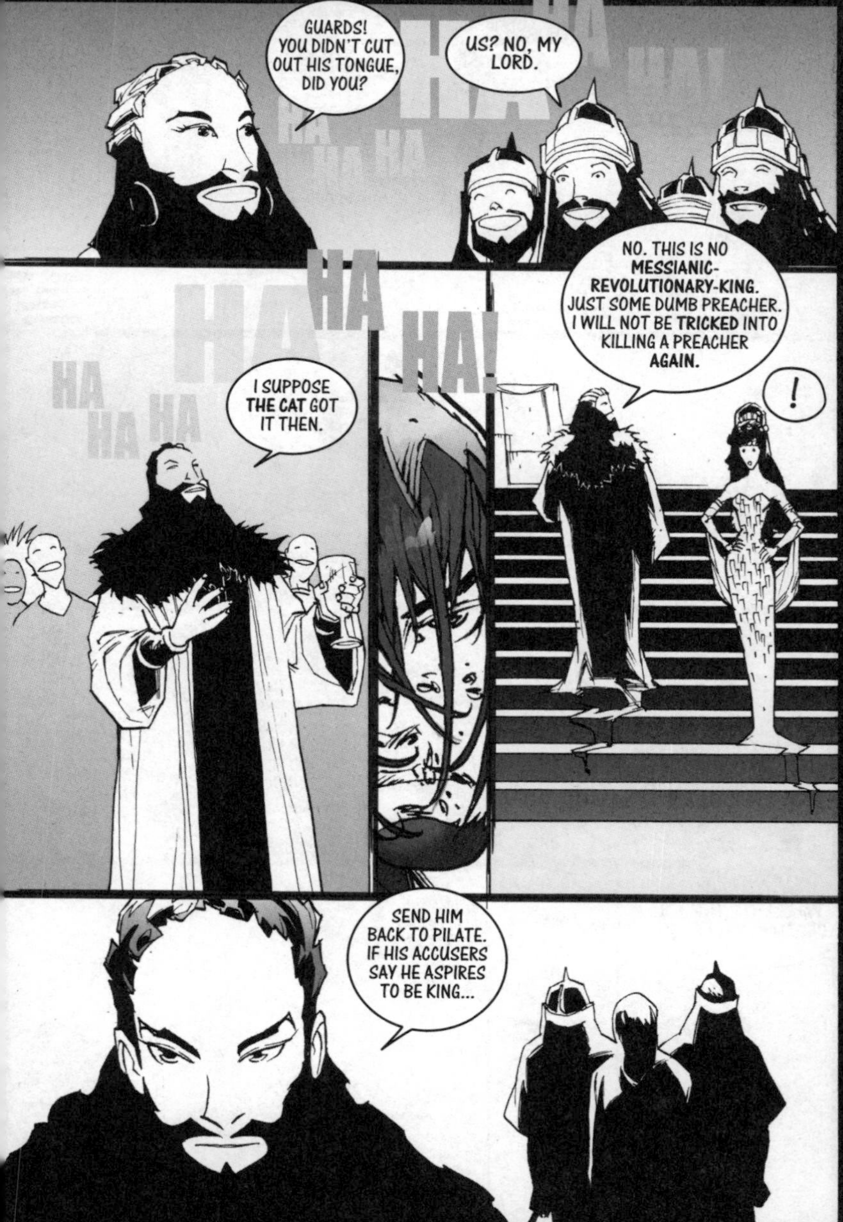
GUARDS! YOU DIDN'T CUT OUT HIS TONGUE, DID YOU?
US? NO, MY LORD.
HA HA HA HA HA HA HA!
HA HA HA HA HA HA!
I SUPPOSE THE CAT GOT IT THEN.
NO. THIS IS NO MESSIANIC-REVOLUTIONARY-KING. JUST SOME DUMB PREACHER. I WILL NOT BE TRICKED INTO KILLING A PREACHER AGAIN.
!
SEND HIM BACK TO PILATE. IF HIS ACCUSERS SAY HE ASPIRES TO BE KING...

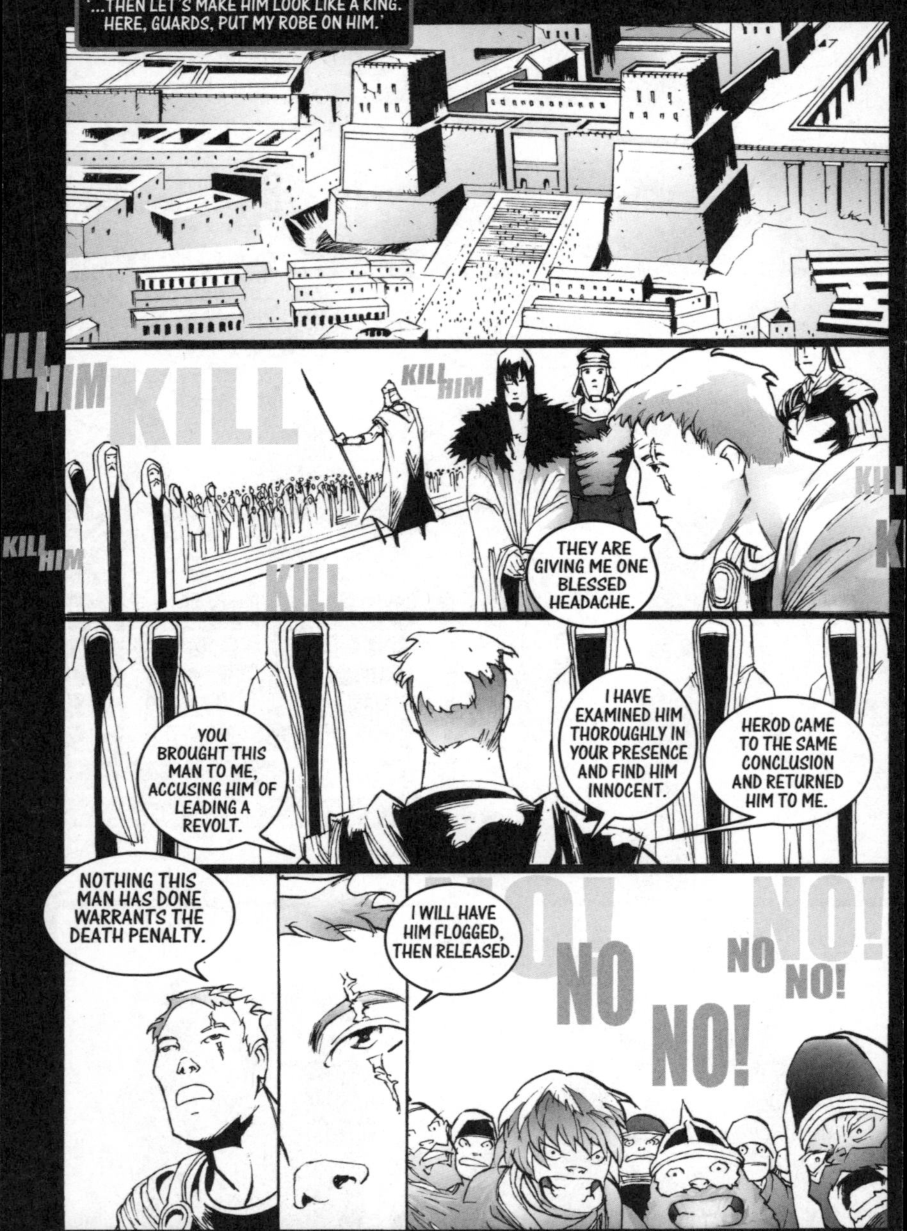
'...THEN LET'S MAKE HIM LOOK LIKE A KING. HERE, GUARDS, PUT MY ROBE ON HIM.'
KILL HIM KILL KILL HIM KILL HIM KILL KILL K
THEY ARE GIVING ME ONE BLESSED HEADACHE.
YOU BROUGHT THIS MAN TO ME, ACCUSING HIM OF LEADING A REVOLT.
I HAVE EXAMINED HIM THOROUGHLY IN YOUR PRESENCE AND FIND HIM INNOCENT.
HEROD CAME TO THE SAME CONCLUSION AND RETURNED HIM TO ME.
NOTHING THIS MAN HAS DONE WARRANTS THE DEATH PENALTY.
I WILL HAVE HIM FLOGGED, THEN RELEASED.
NO! NO! NO NO! NO NO! NO!

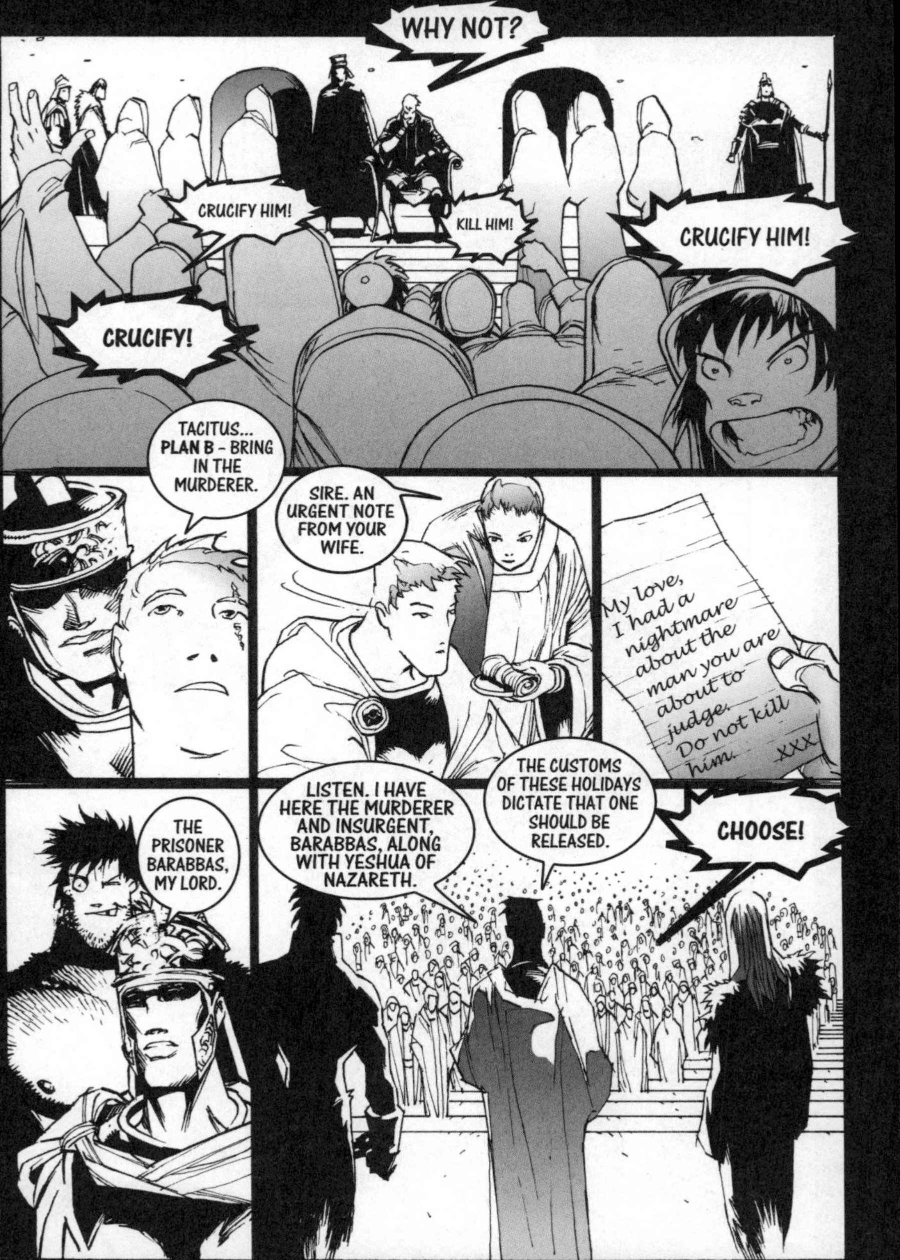
WHY NOT?
CRUCIFY HIM!
KILL HIM!
CRUCIFY HIM!
CRUCIFY!
TACITUS... PLAN B - BRING IN THE MURDERER.
SIRE. AN URGENT NOTE FROM YOUR WIFE.
My love, I had a nightmare about the man you are about to judge. Do not kill him. XXX
THE PRISONER BARABBAS, MY LORD.
LISTEN. I HAVE HERE THE MURDERER AND INSURGENT, BARABBAS, ALONG WITH YESHUA OF NAZARETH.
THE CUSTOMS OF THESE HOLIDAYS DICTATE THAT ONE SHOULD BE RELEASED.
CHOOSE!

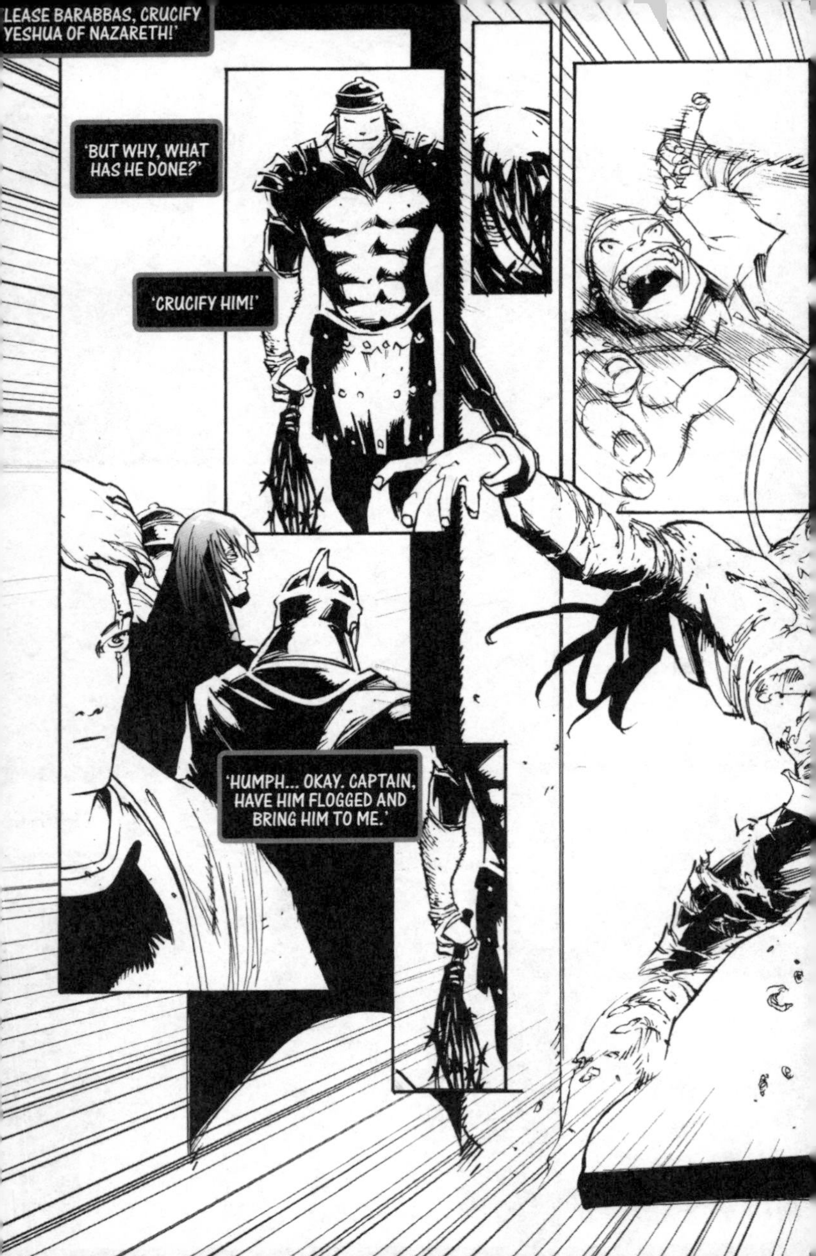
'LEASE BARABBAS, CRUCIFY YESHUA OF NAZARETH!'
'BUT WHY, WHAT HAS HE DONE?'
'CRUCIFY HIM!'
'HUMPH... OKAY. CAPTAIN, HAVE HIM FLOGGED AND BRING HIM TO ME.'

CRACK!

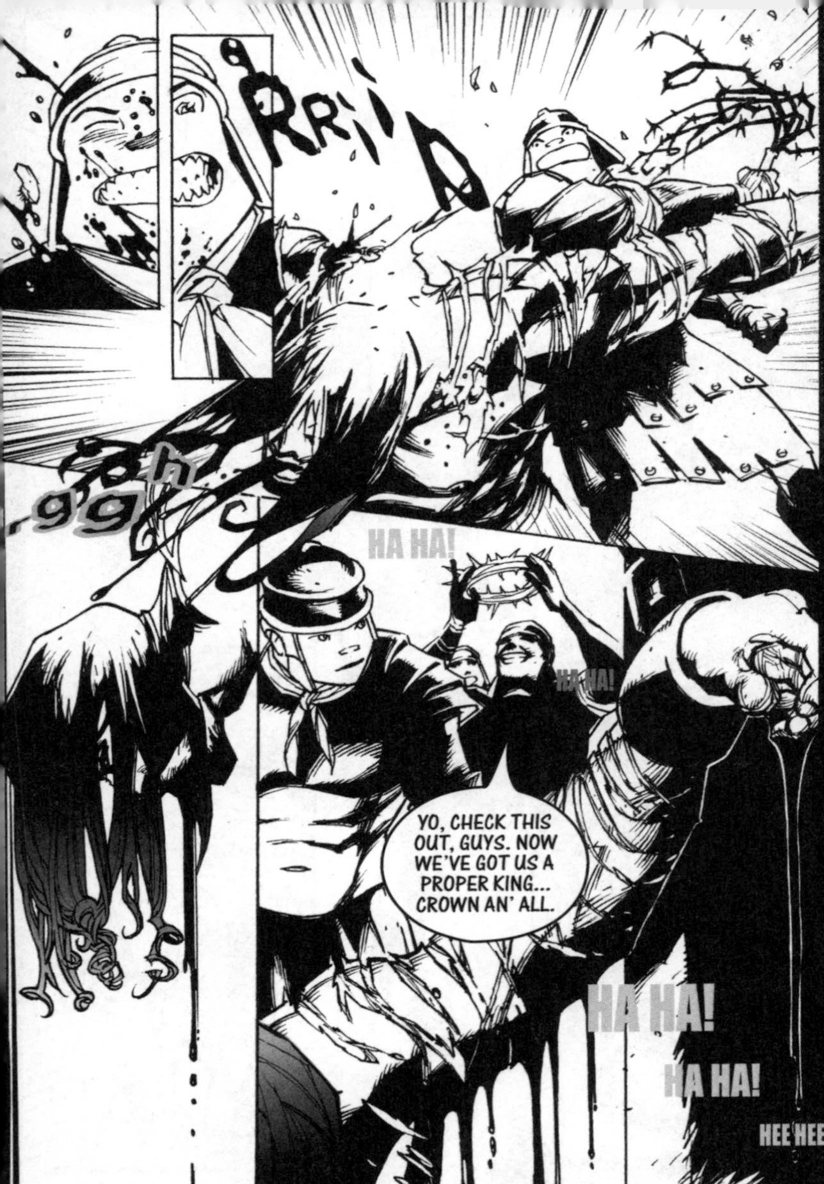
RRIIP
gghh
HA HA!
HA HA!
YO, CHECK THIS OUT, GUYS. NOW WE'VE GOT US A PROPER KING... CROWN AN' ALL.
HA HA!
HA HA!
HEE HEE

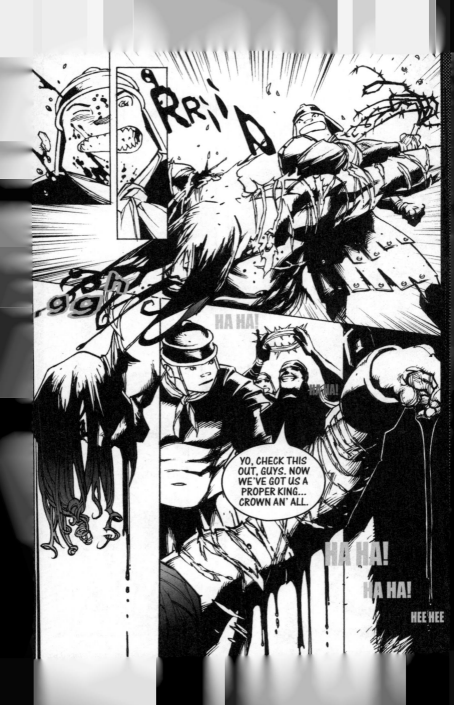

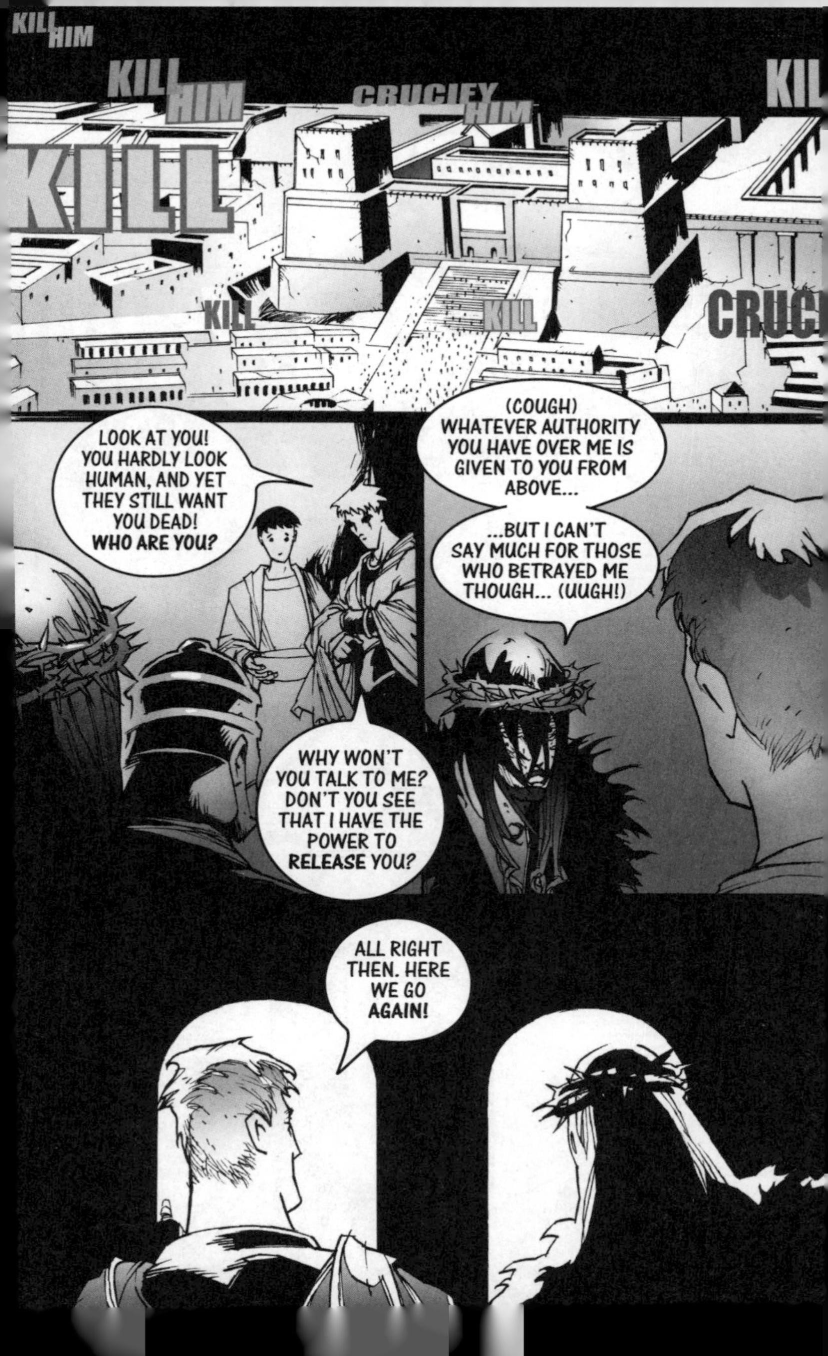

KILL HIM
KILL HIM
CRUCIFY HIM
KILL
KILL
KILL
KILL
CRUC
LOOK AT YOU! YOU HARDLY LOOK HUMAN, AND YET THEY STILL WANT YOU DEAD! WHO ARE YOU?
WHY WON'T YOU TALK TO ME? DON'T YOU SEE THAT I HAVE THE POWER TO RELEASE YOU?
(COUGH) WHATEVER AUTHORITY YOU HAVE OVER ME IS GIVEN TO YOU FROM ABOVE...
...BUT I CAN'T SAY MUCH FOR THOSE WHO BETRAYED ME THOUGH... (UUGH!)
ALL RIGHT THEN. HERE WE GO AGAIN!

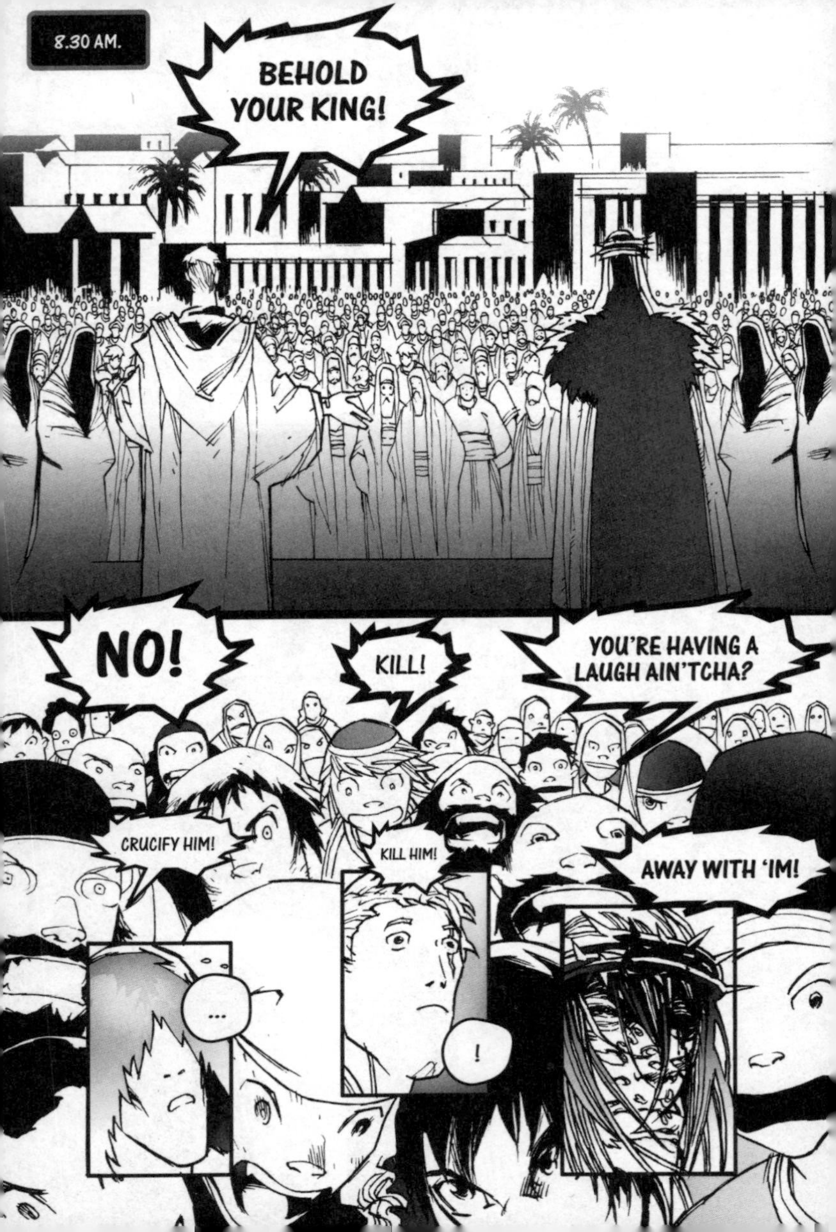
8.30 AM.
BEHOLD YOUR KING!
NO!
KILL!
YOU'RE HAVING A LAUGH AIN'TCHA?
CRUCIFY HIM!
KILL HIM!
AWAY WITH 'IM!
...
!

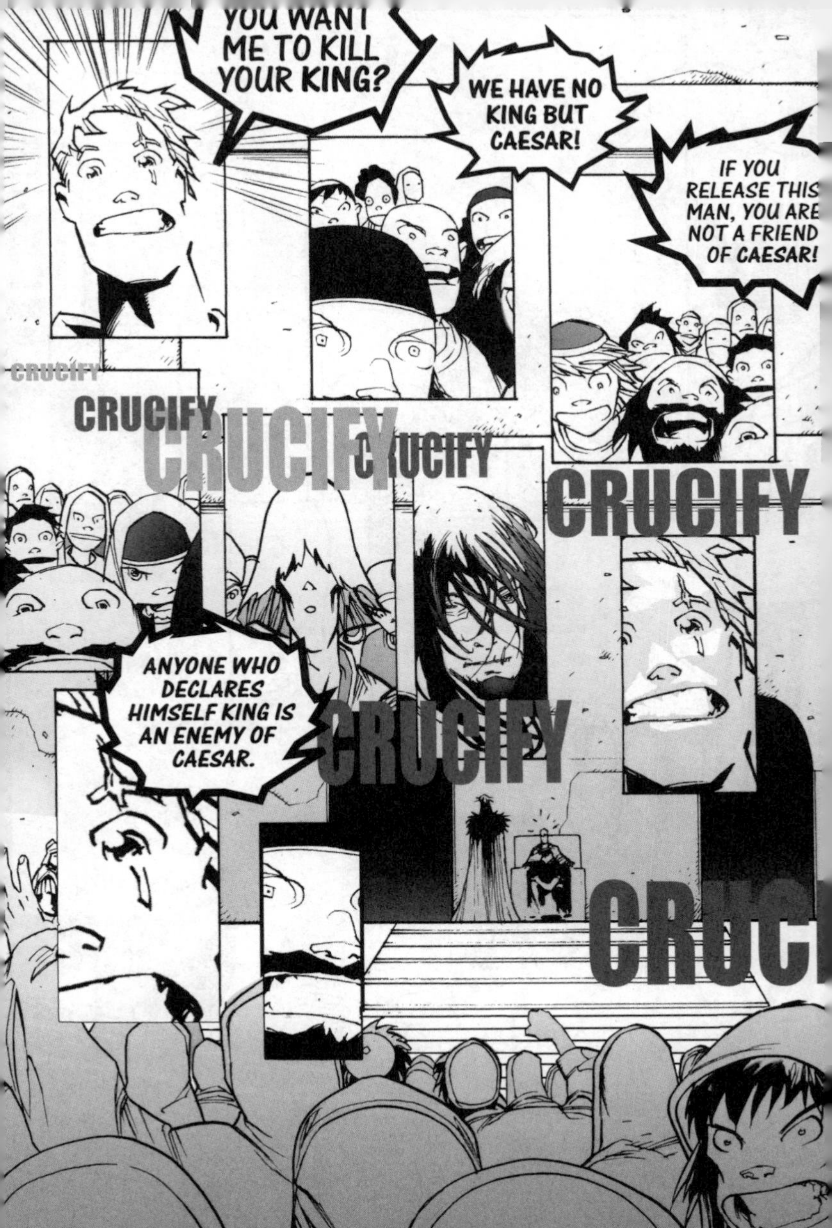
YOU WANT ME TO KILL YOUR KING?
WE HAVE NO KING BUT CAESAR!
IF YOU RELEASE THIS MAN, YOU ARE NOT A FRIEND OF CAESAR!
CRUCIFY
CRUCIFY
CRUCIFY
CRUCIFY
CRUCIFY
ANYONE WHO DECLARES HIMSELF KING IS AN ENEMY OF CAESAR.
CRUCIFY

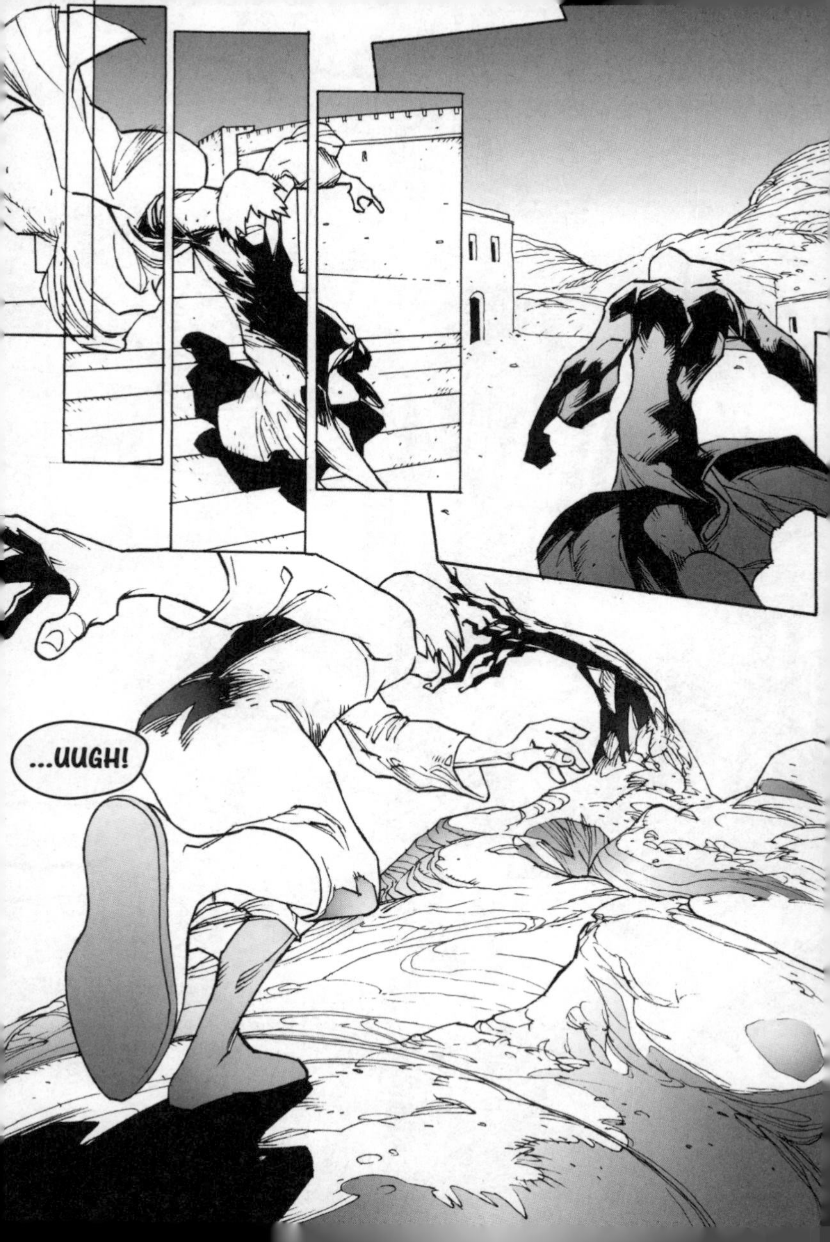
...UUGH!

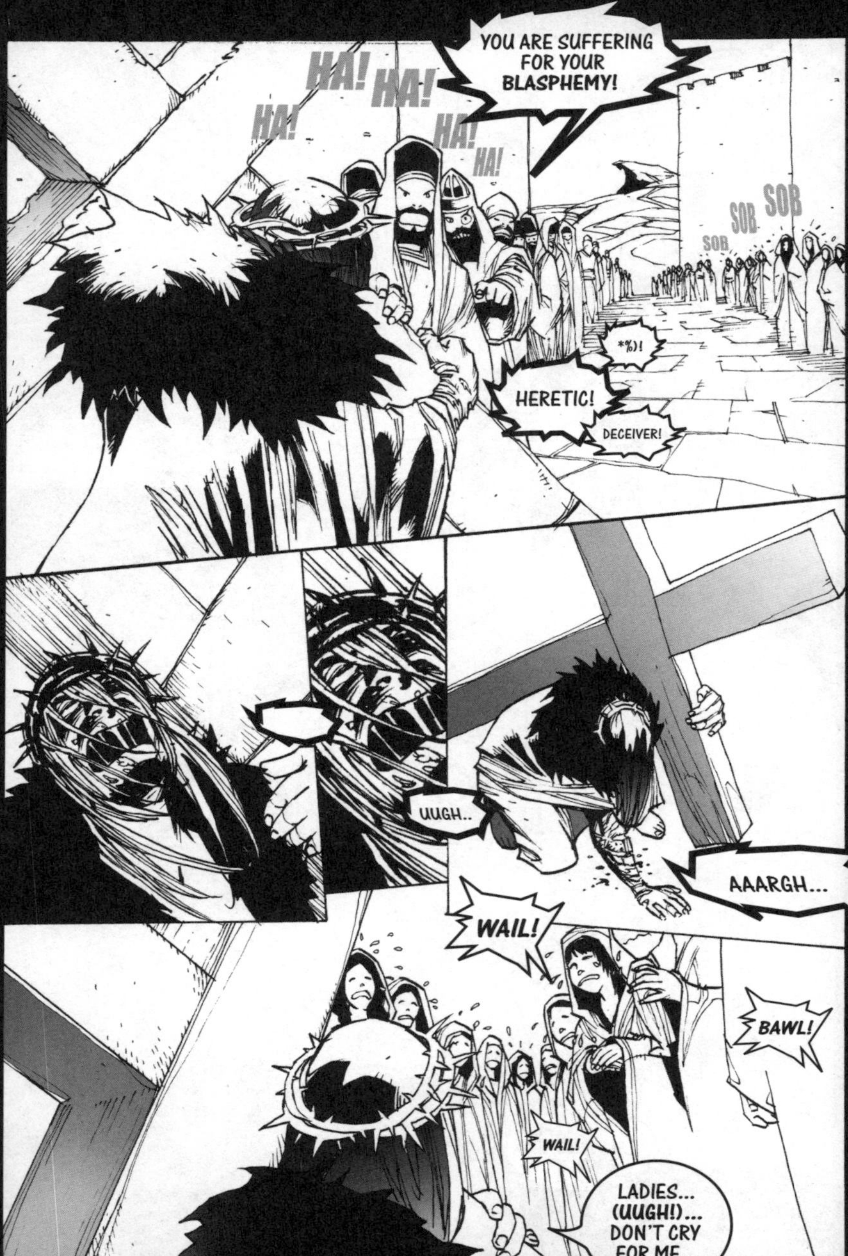
HA!
HA!
HA!
HA!
HA!
YOU ARE SUFFERING FOR YOUR BLASPHEMY!
SOB
SOB
SOB
*%)!
HERETIC!
DECEIVER!
UUGH..
AAARGH...
WAIL!
BAWL!
WAIL!
LADIES... (UUGH!)... DON'T CRY FOR ME...

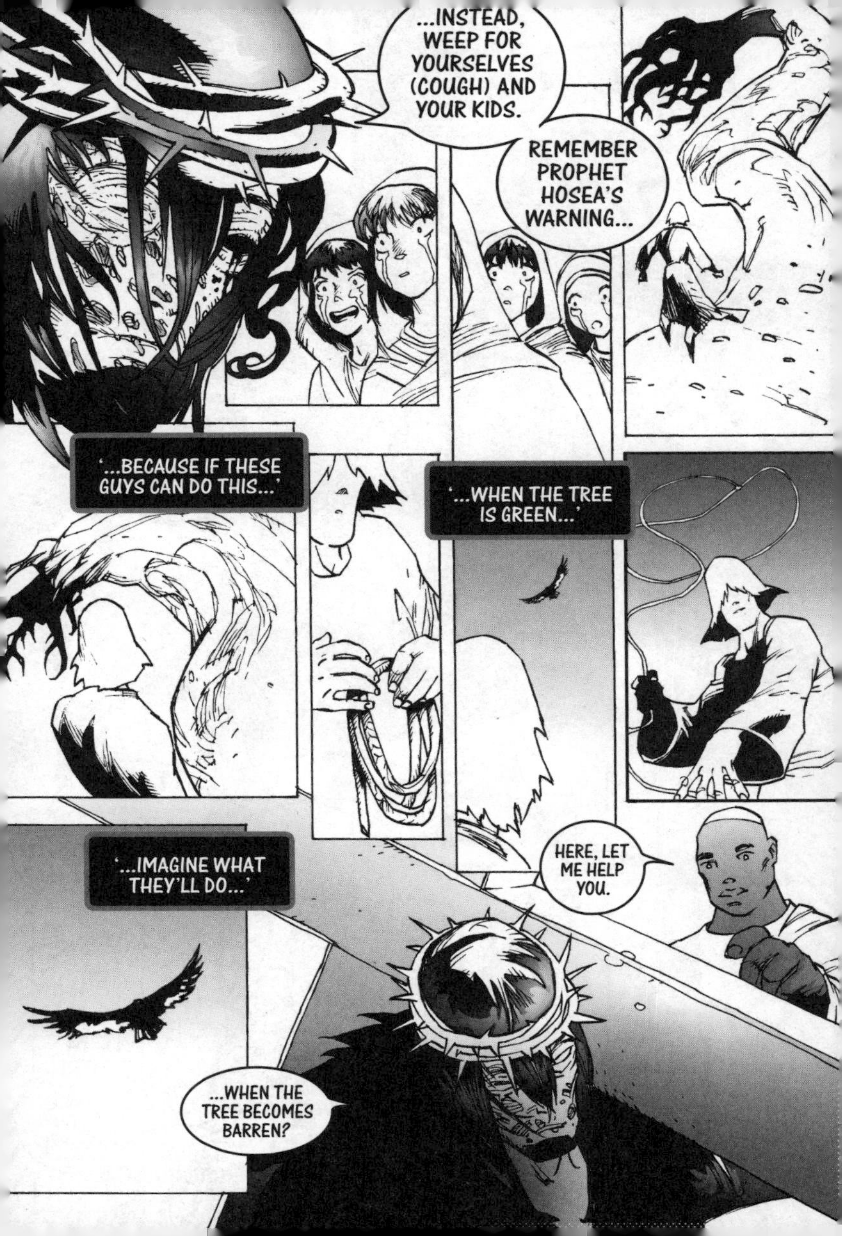
...INSTEAD, WEEP FOR YOURSELVES (COUGH) AND YOUR KIDS.
REMEMBER PROPHET HOSEA'S WARNING...
'...BECAUSE IF THESE GUYS CAN DO THIS...'
'...WHEN THE TREE IS GREEN...'
'...IMAGINE WHAT THEY'LL DO...'
HERE, LET ME HELP YOU.
...WHEN THE TREE BECOMES BARREN?

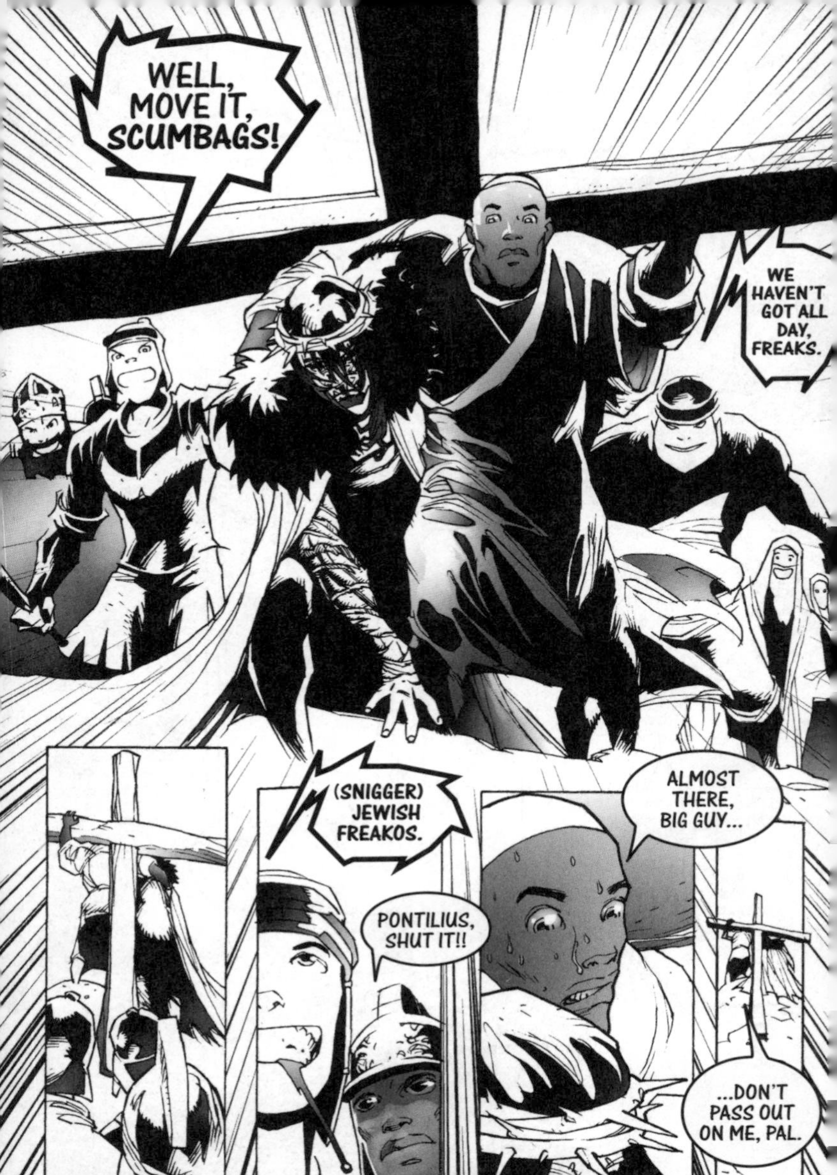
WELL, MOVE IT, SCUMBAGS!
WE HAVEN'T GOT ALL DAY, FREAKS.
(SNIGGER) JEWISH FREAKOS.
PONTILIUS, SHUT IT!!
ALMOST THERE, BIG GUY...
...DON'T PASS OUT ON ME, PAL.

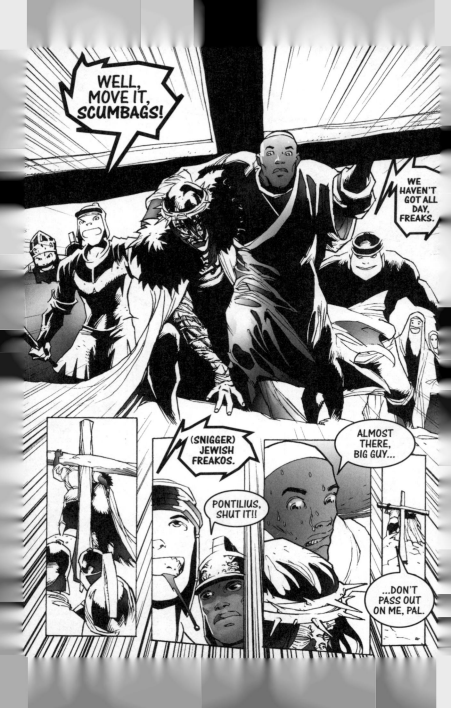

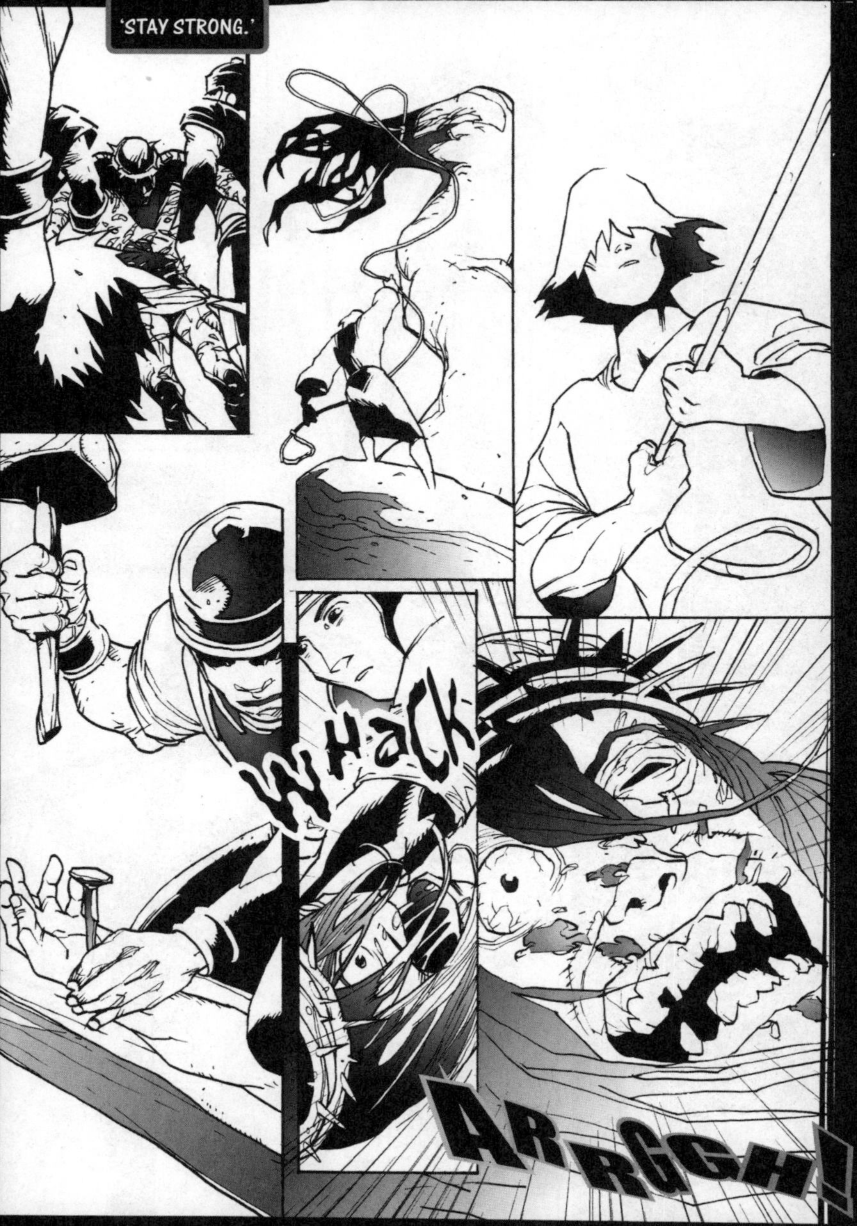
'STAY STRONG.'
WHACK
ARRGGH!

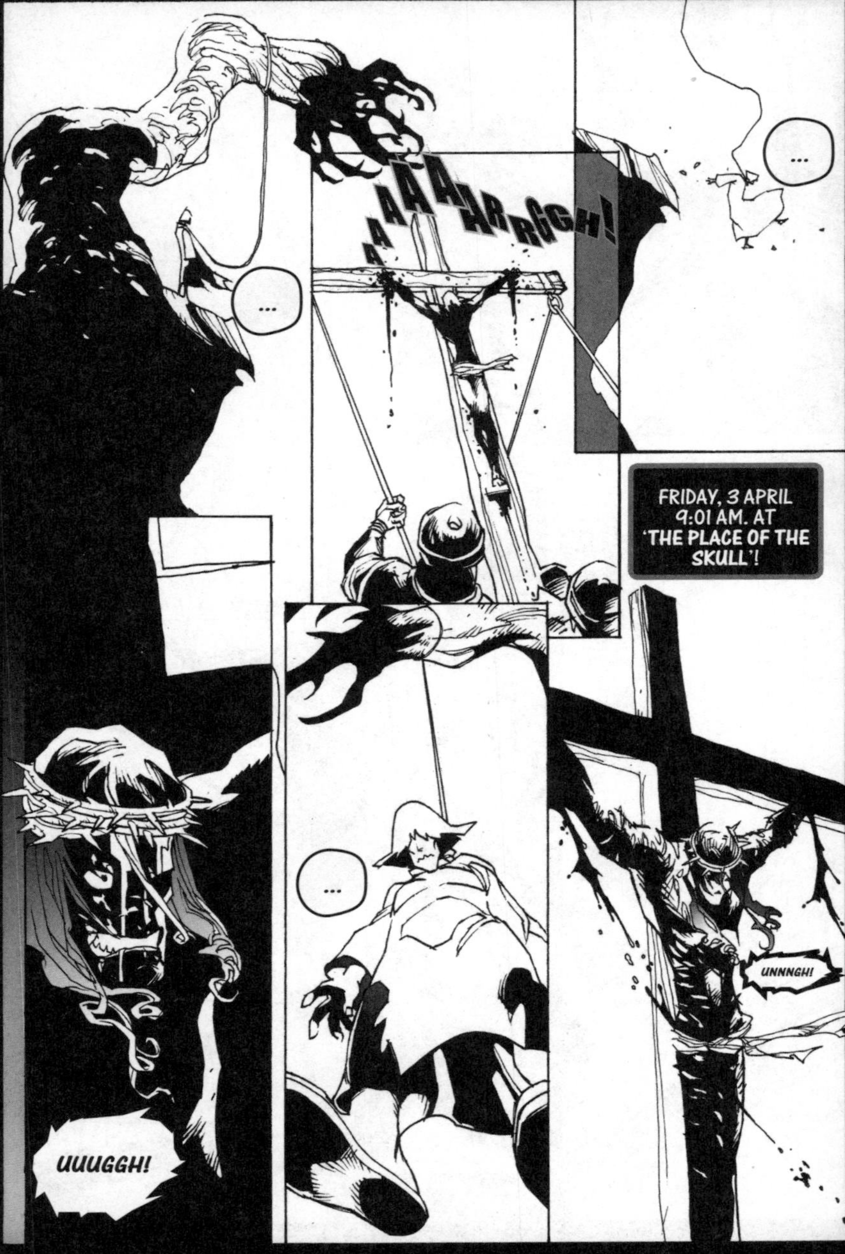
...
AAAAAARRGGH!
...
FRIDAY, 3 APRIL 9:01 AM. AT 'THE PLACE OF THE SKULL'!
...
UNNNGH!
UUUGGH!

Chapter 3
Auf wiedersehen

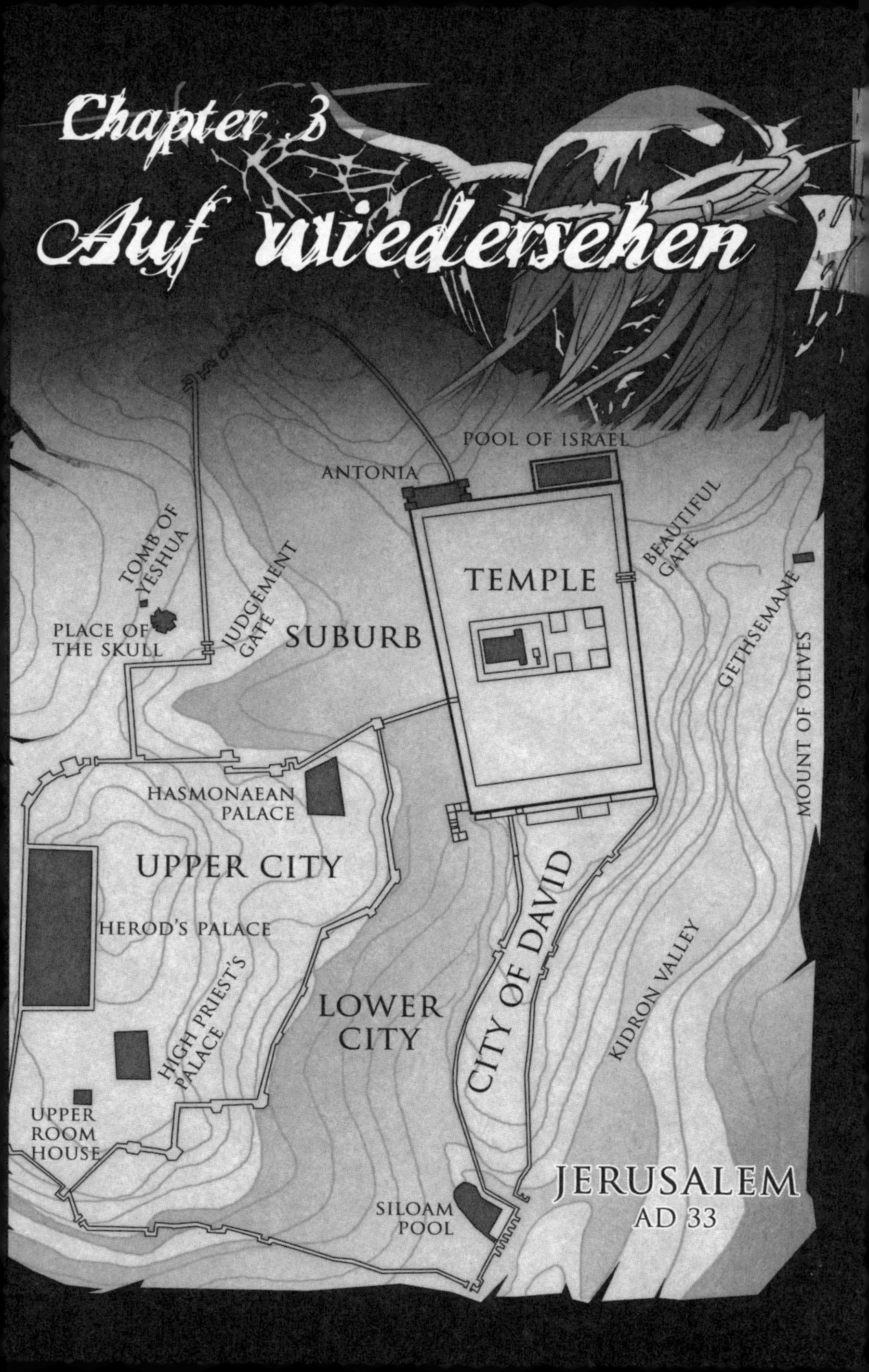
POOL OF ISRAEL
ANTONIA
TOMB OF YESHUA
JUDGEMENT GATE
TEMPLE
BEAUTIFUL GATE
PLACE OF THE SKULL
SUBURB
GETHSEMANE
MOUNT OF OLIVES
HASMONAEAN PALACE
UPPER CITY
CITY OF DAVID
HEROD'S PALACE
KIDRON VALLEY
HIGH PRIEST'S PALACE
LOWER CITY
UPPER ROOM HOUSE
SILOAM POOL
JERUSALEM
AD 33

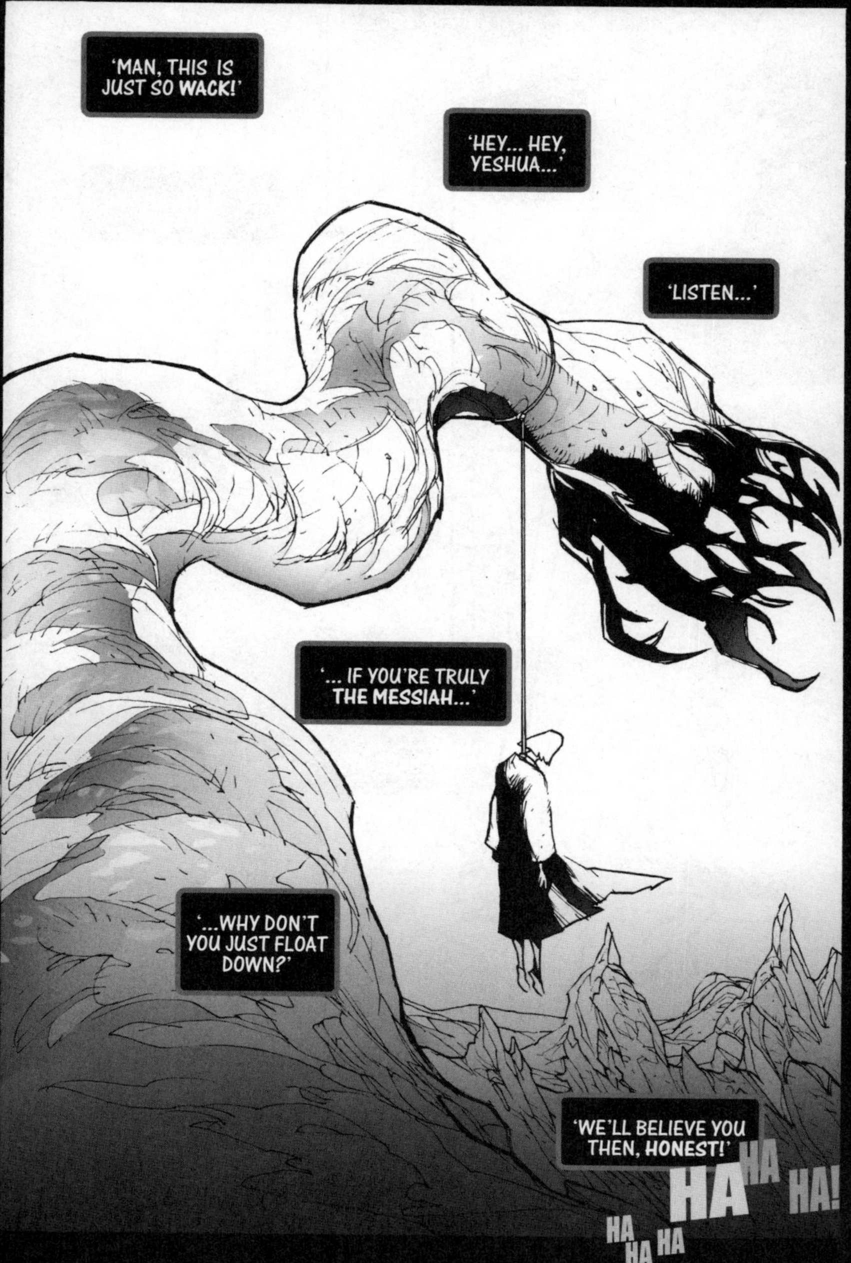
'MAN, THIS IS JUST SO WACK!'
'HEY... HEY, YESHUA...'
'LISTEN...'
'... IF YOU'RE TRULY THE MESSIAH...'
'...WHY DON'T YOU JUST FLOAT DOWN?'
'WE'LL BELIEVE YOU THEN, HONEST!'
HA HA HA HA HA HA HA!

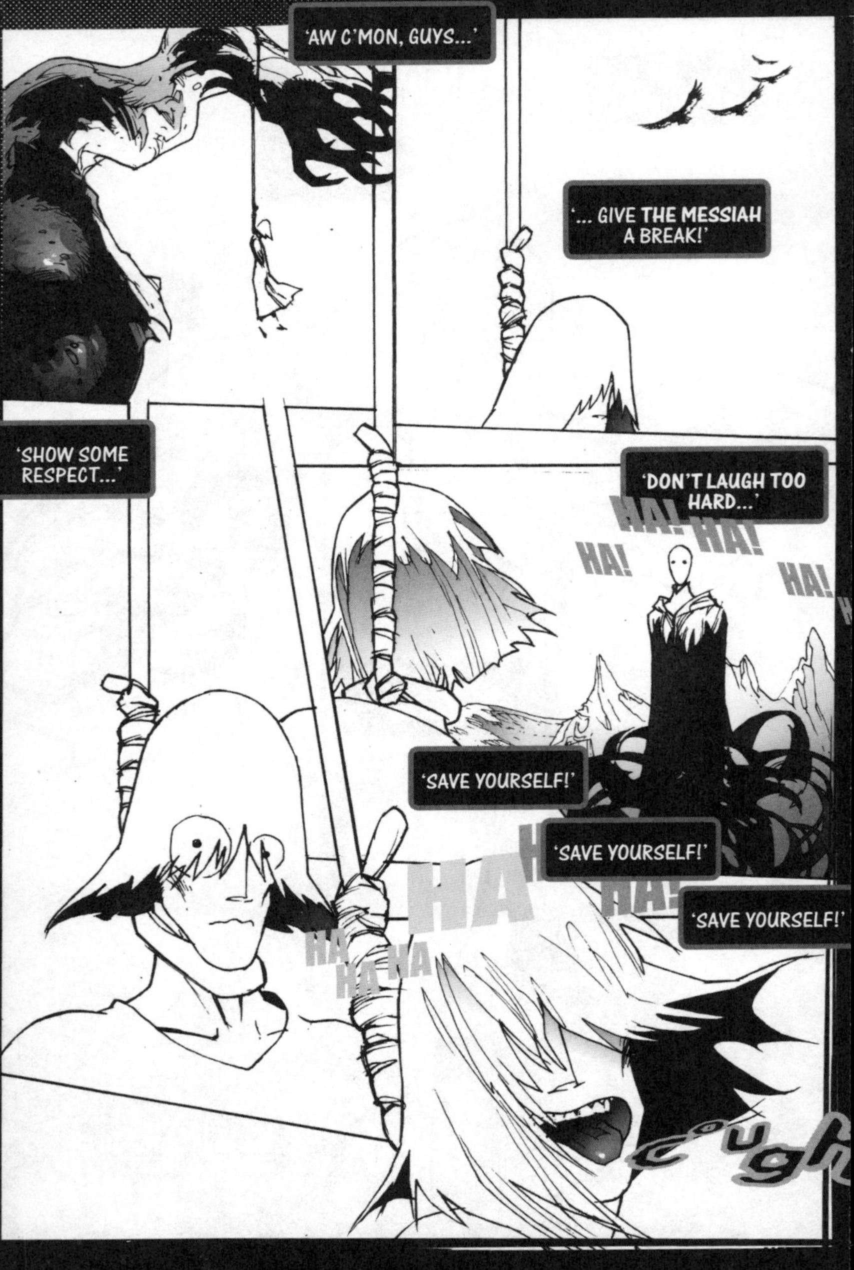
'AW C'MON, GUYS...'
'... GIVE THE MESSIAH A BREAK!'
'SHOW SOME RESPECT...'
'DON'T LAUGH TOO HARD...'
HA! HA! HA! HA!
'SAVE YOURSELF!'
'SAVE YOURSELF!'
'SAVE YOURSELF!'
HA HA HA HA HA
cough

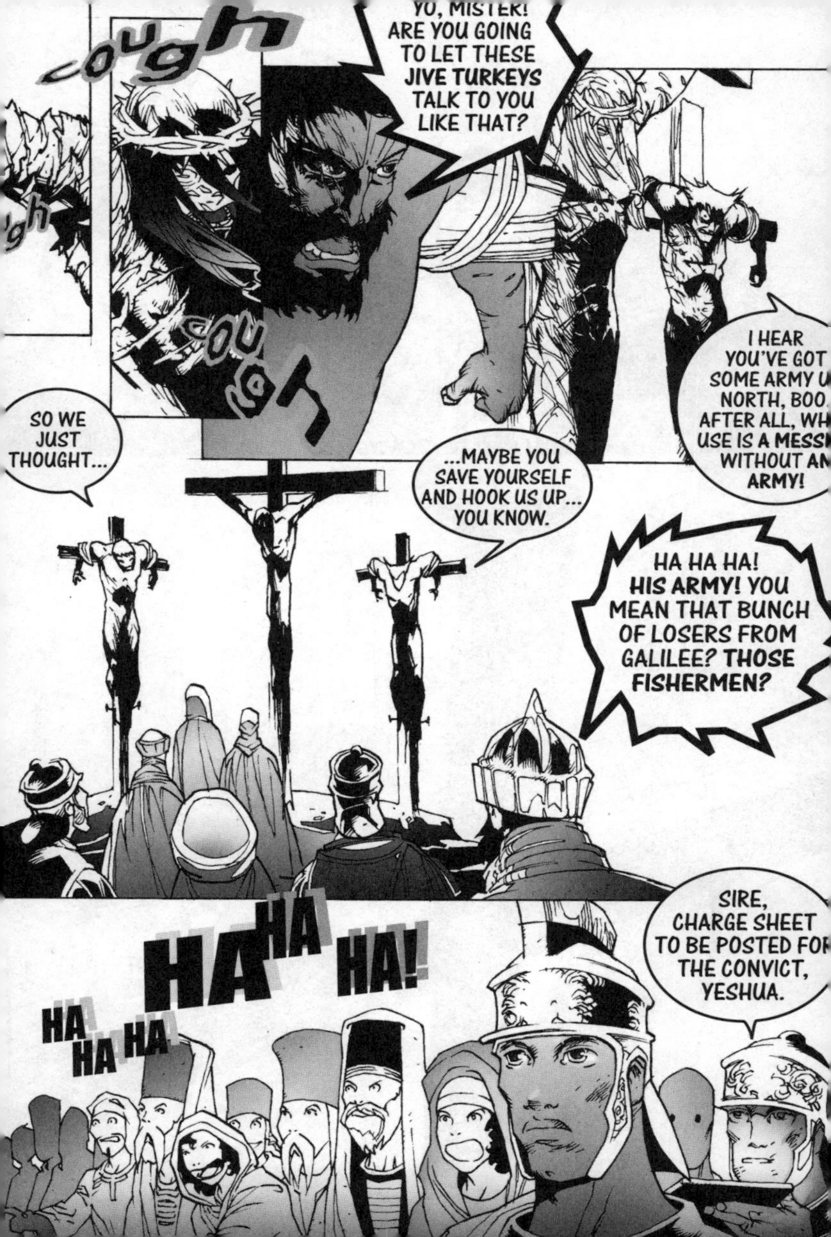
cough
YO, MISTER! ARE YOU GOING TO LET THESE JIVE TURKEYS TALK TO YOU LIKE THAT?
cough
SO WE JUST THOUGHT...
...MAYBE YOU SAVE YOURSELF AND HOOK US UP... YOU KNOW.
I HEAR YOU'VE GOT SOME ARMY U NORTH, BOO AFTER ALL, WH USE IS A MESS WITHOUT AN ARMY!
HA HA HA! HIS ARMY! YOU MEAN THAT BUNCH OF LOSERS FROM GALILEE? THOSE FISHERMEN?
HA HA HA!
HA HA HA
SIRE, CHARGE SHEET TO BE POSTED FO THE CONVICT, YESHUA.

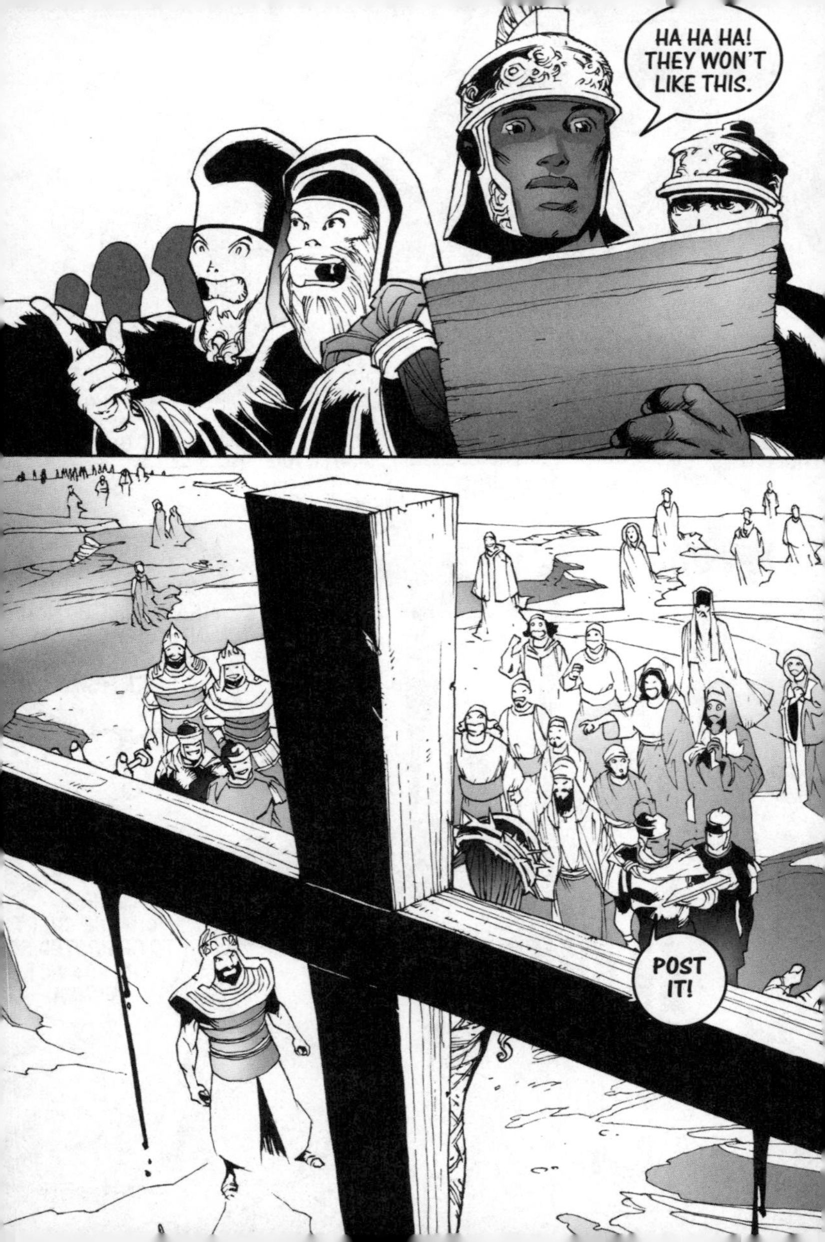
HA HA HA! THEY WON'T LIKE THIS.
POST IT!

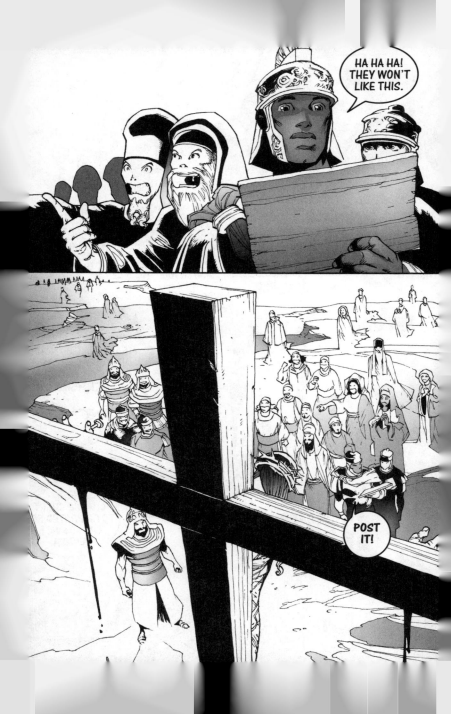

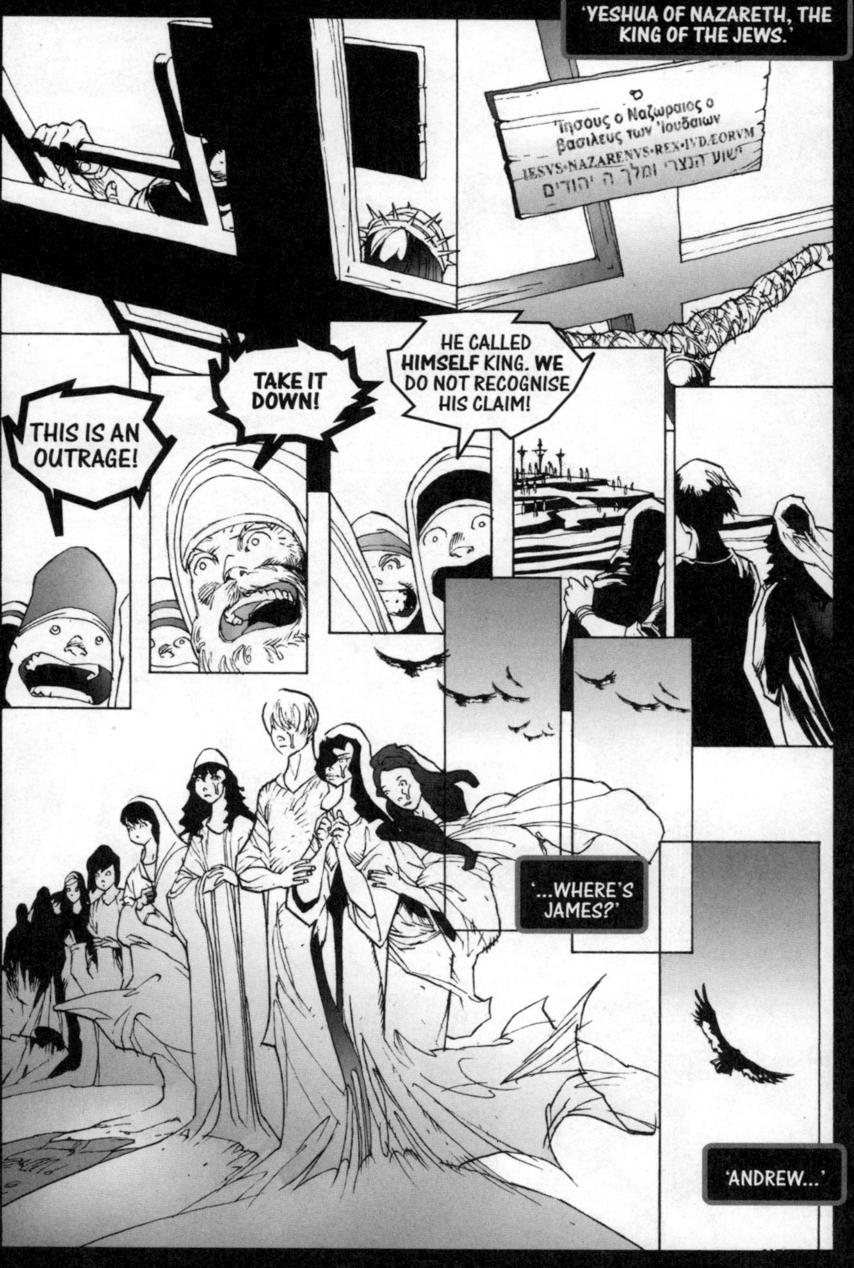
'YESHUA OF NAZARETH, THE KING OF THE JEWS.'
'Ιησους ο Ναζωραιος ο βασιλευς των 'Ιουδαιων
IESVS·NAZARENVS·REX·IVDÆORVM
ישוע הנצרי ומלך ה יהודים
THIS IS AN OUTRAGE!
TAKE IT DOWN!
HE CALLED HIMSELF KING. WE DO NOT RECOGNISE HIS CLAIM!
'...WHERE'S JAMES?'
'ANDREW...'

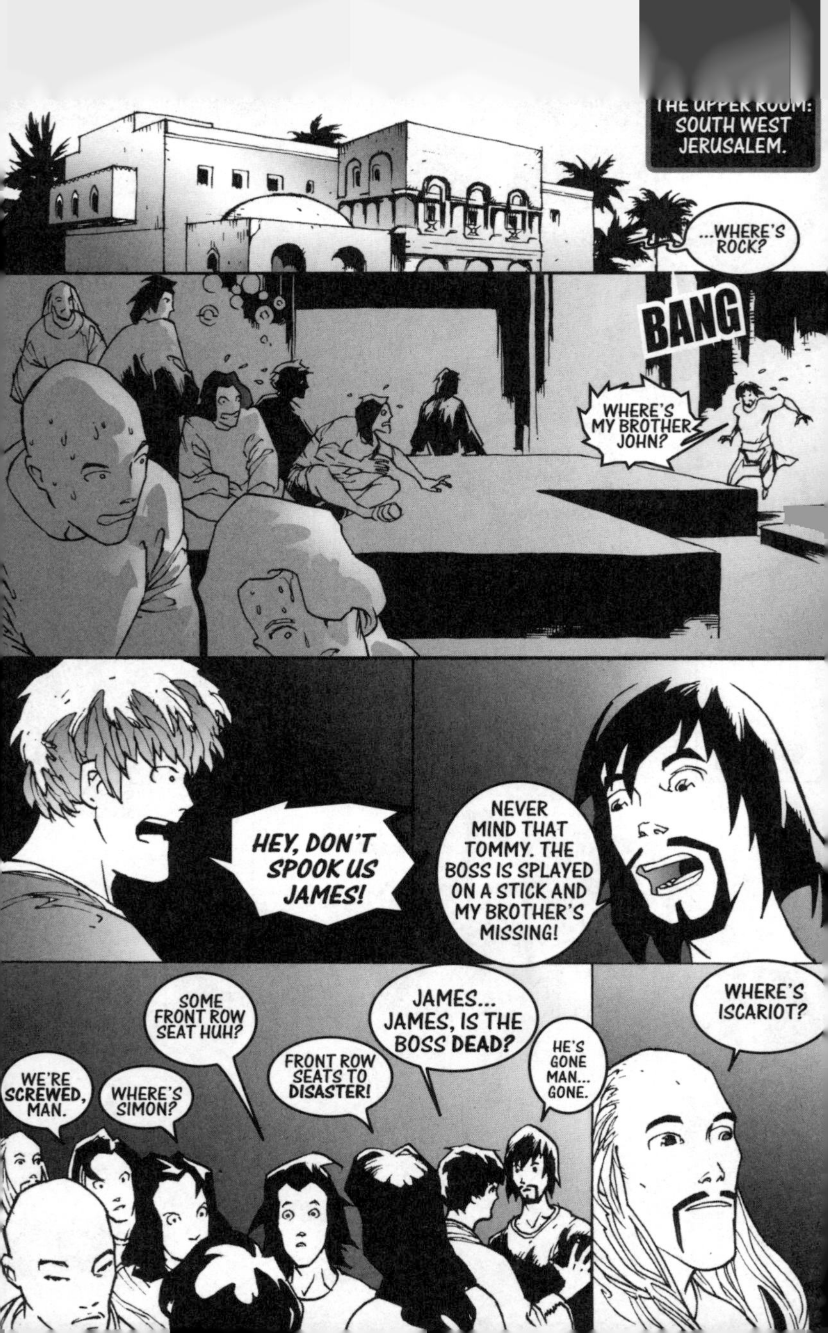
THE UPPER ROOM: SOUTH WEST JERUSALEM.
...WHERE'S ROCK?
BANG
WHERE'S MY BROTHER JOHN?
HEY, DON'T SPOOK US JAMES!
NEVER MIND THAT TOMMY. THE BOSS IS SPLAYED ON A STICK AND MY BROTHER'S MISSING!
WE'RE SCREWED, MAN.
WHERE'S SIMON?
SOME FRONT ROW SEAT HUH?
FRONT ROW SEATS TO DISASTER!
JAMES... JAMES, IS THE BOSS DEAD?
HE'S GONE MAN... GONE.
WHERE'S ISCARIOT?

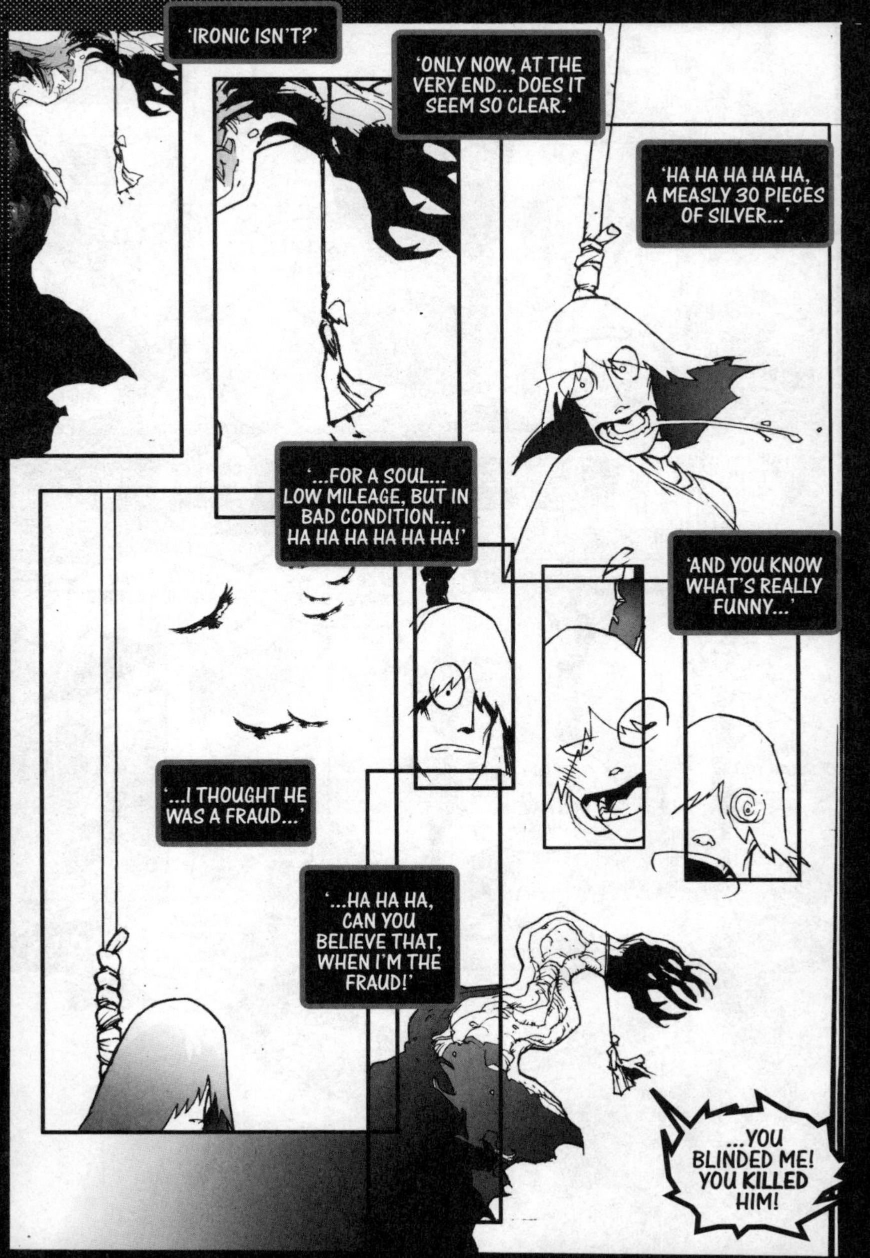
'IRONIC ISN'T?'
'ONLY NOW, AT THE VERY END... DOES IT SEEM SO CLEAR.'
'HA HA HA HA HA, A MEASLY 30 PIECES OF SILVER...'
'...FOR A SOUL... LOW MILEAGE, BUT IN BAD CONDITION... HA HA HA HA HA HA!'
'AND YOU KNOW WHAT'S REALLY FUNNY...'
'...I THOUGHT HE WAS A FRAUD...'
'...HA HA HA, CAN YOU BELIEVE THAT, WHEN I'M THE FRAUD!'
...YOU BLINDED ME! YOU KILLED HIM!

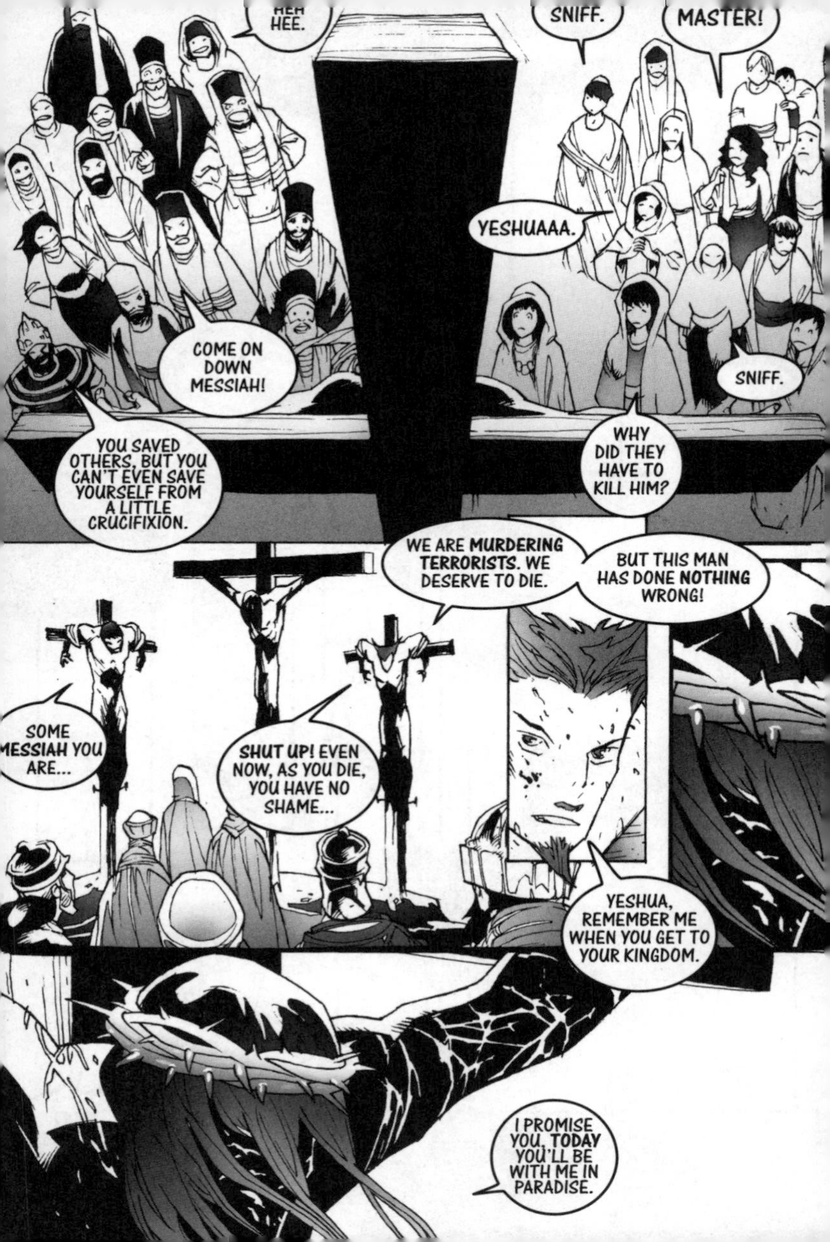
HEH HEE.
SNIFF.
MASTER!
YESHUAAA.
COME ON DOWN MESSIAH!
SNIFF.
YOU SAVED OTHERS, BUT YOU CAN'T EVEN SAVE YOURSELF FROM A LITTLE CRUCIFIXION.
WHY DID THEY HAVE TO KILL HIM?
WE ARE MURDERING TERRORISTS. WE DESERVE TO DIE.
BUT THIS MAN HAS DONE NOTHING WRONG!
SOME MESSIAH YOU ARE...
SHUT UP! EVEN NOW, AS YOU DIE, YOU HAVE NO SHAME...
YESHUA, REMEMBER ME WHEN YOU GET TO YOUR KINGDOM.
I PROMISE YOU, TODAY YOU'LL BE WITH ME IN PARADISE.

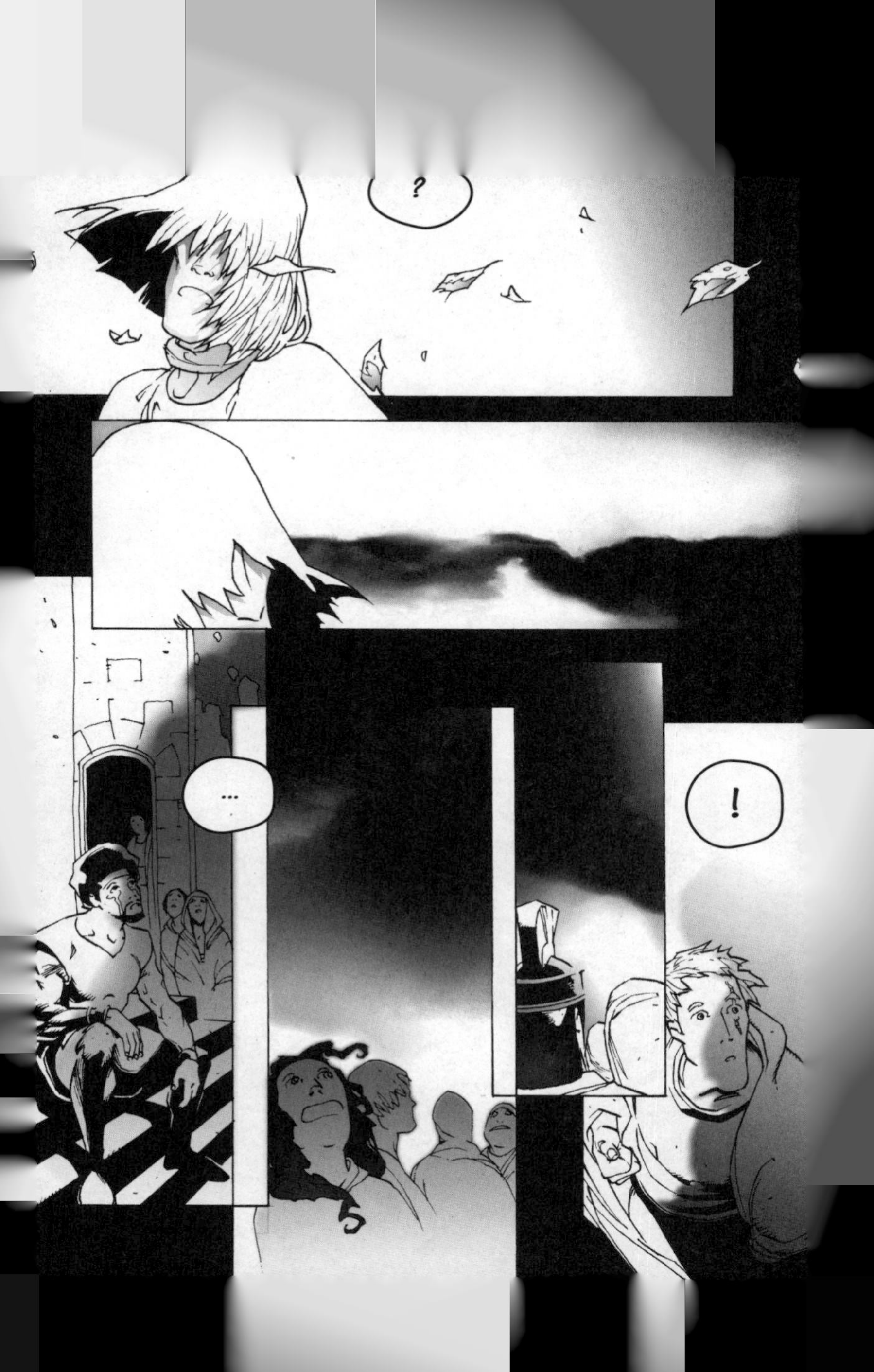
?
...
!

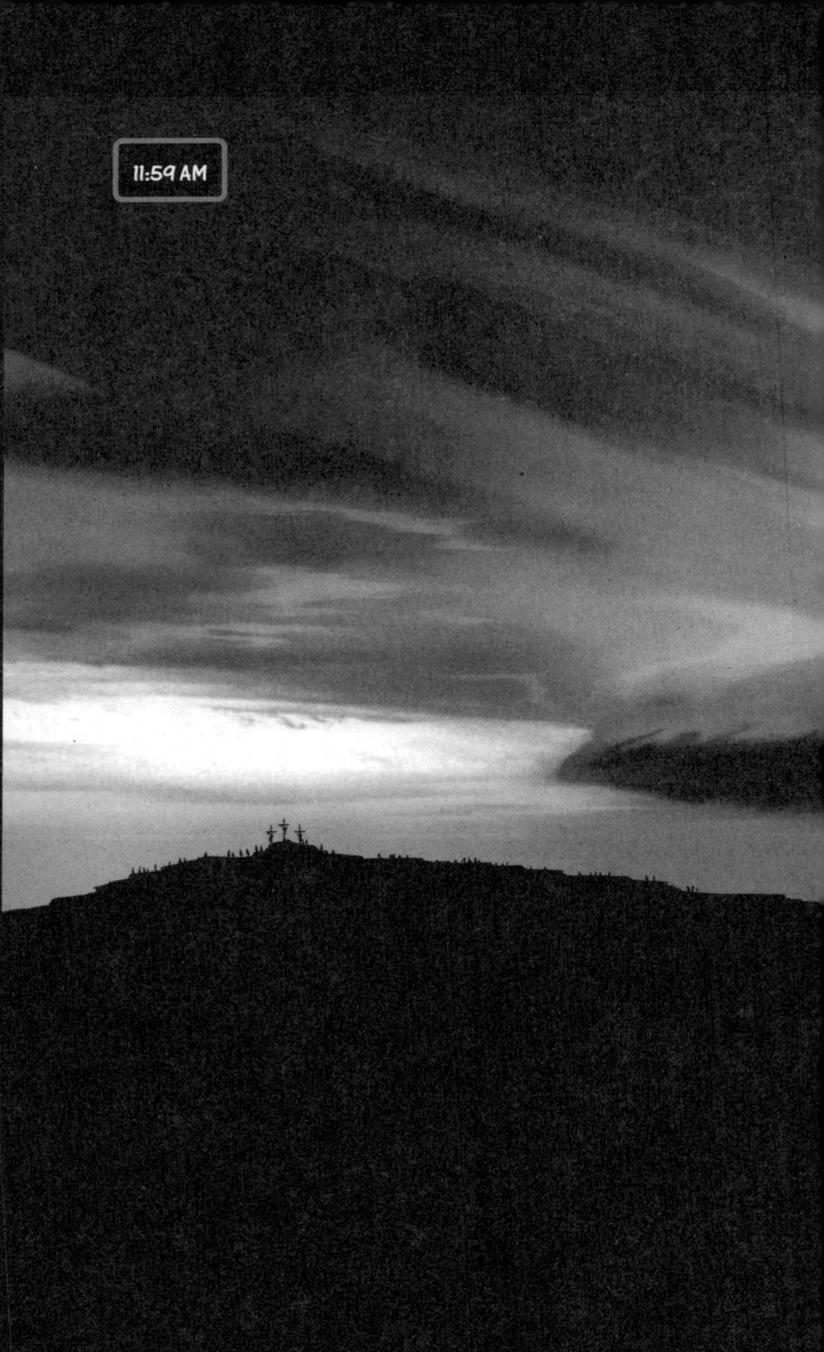

11:59 AM

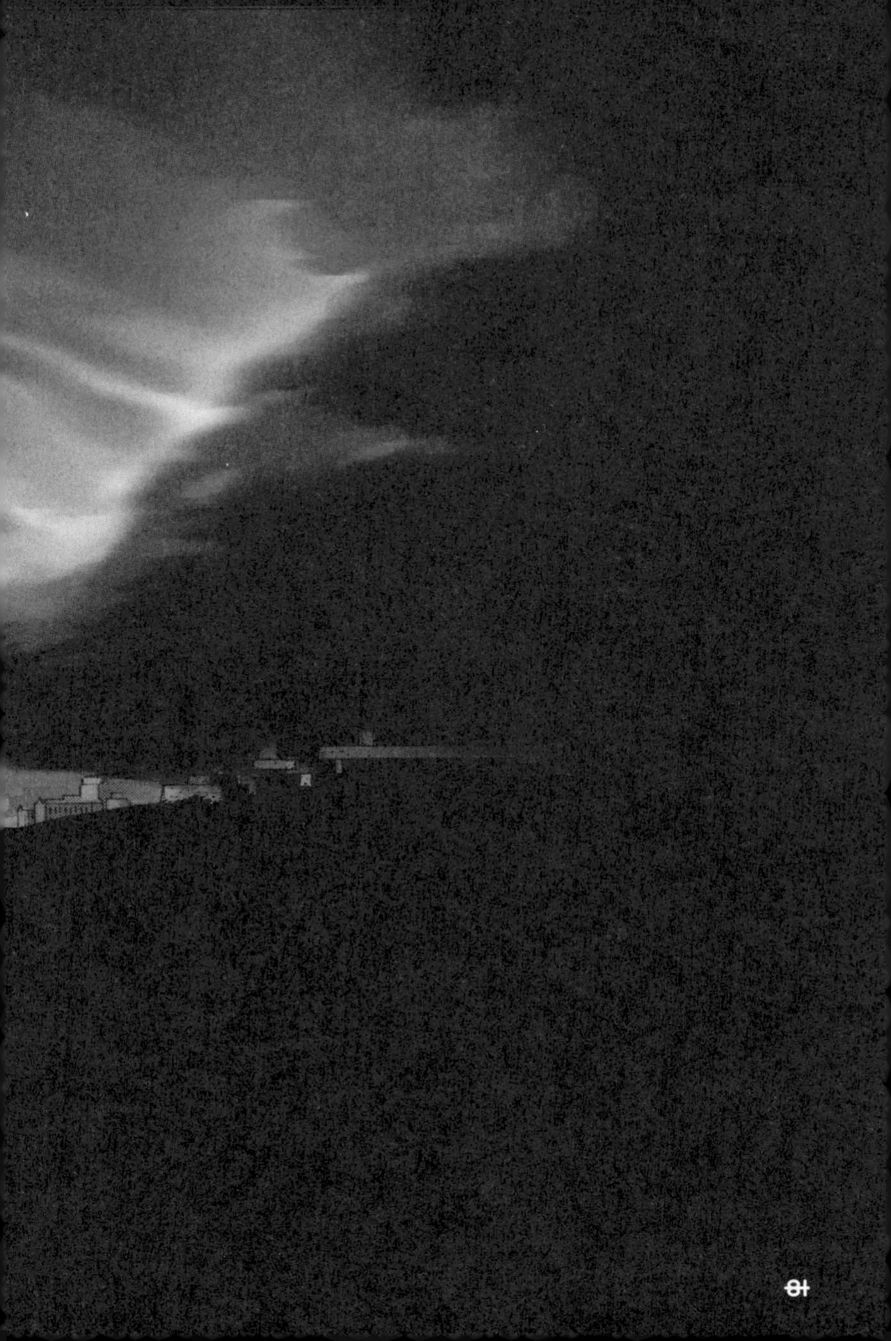

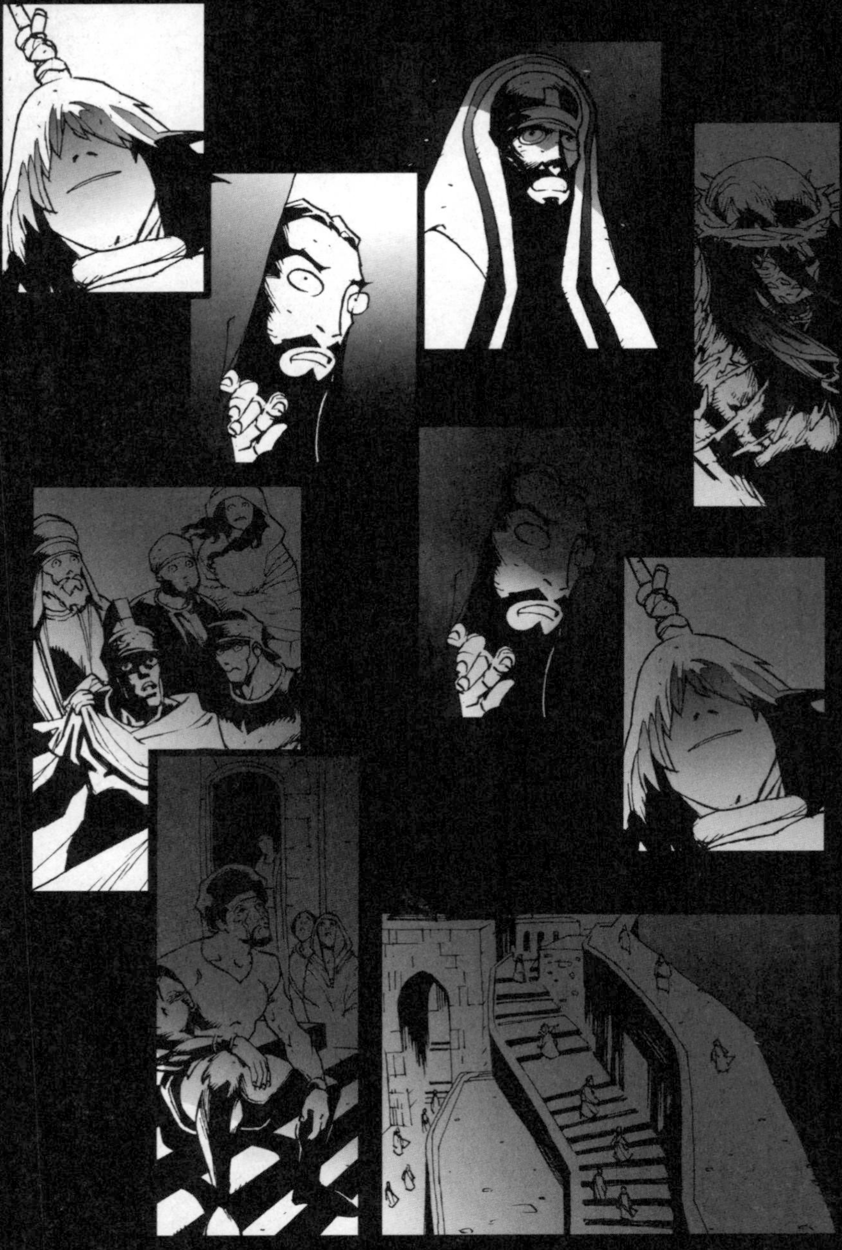

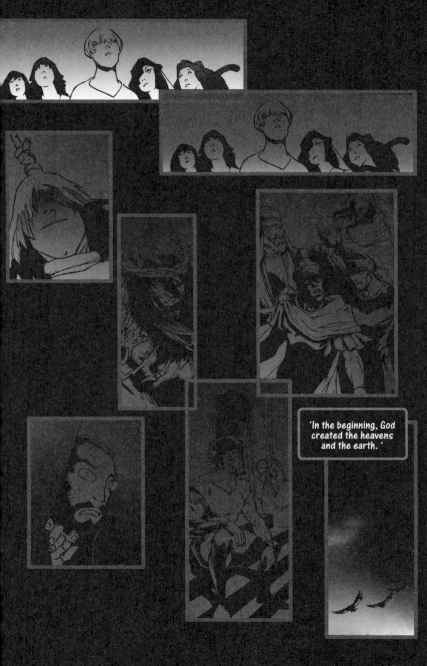

'In the beginning, God created the heavens and the earth.'

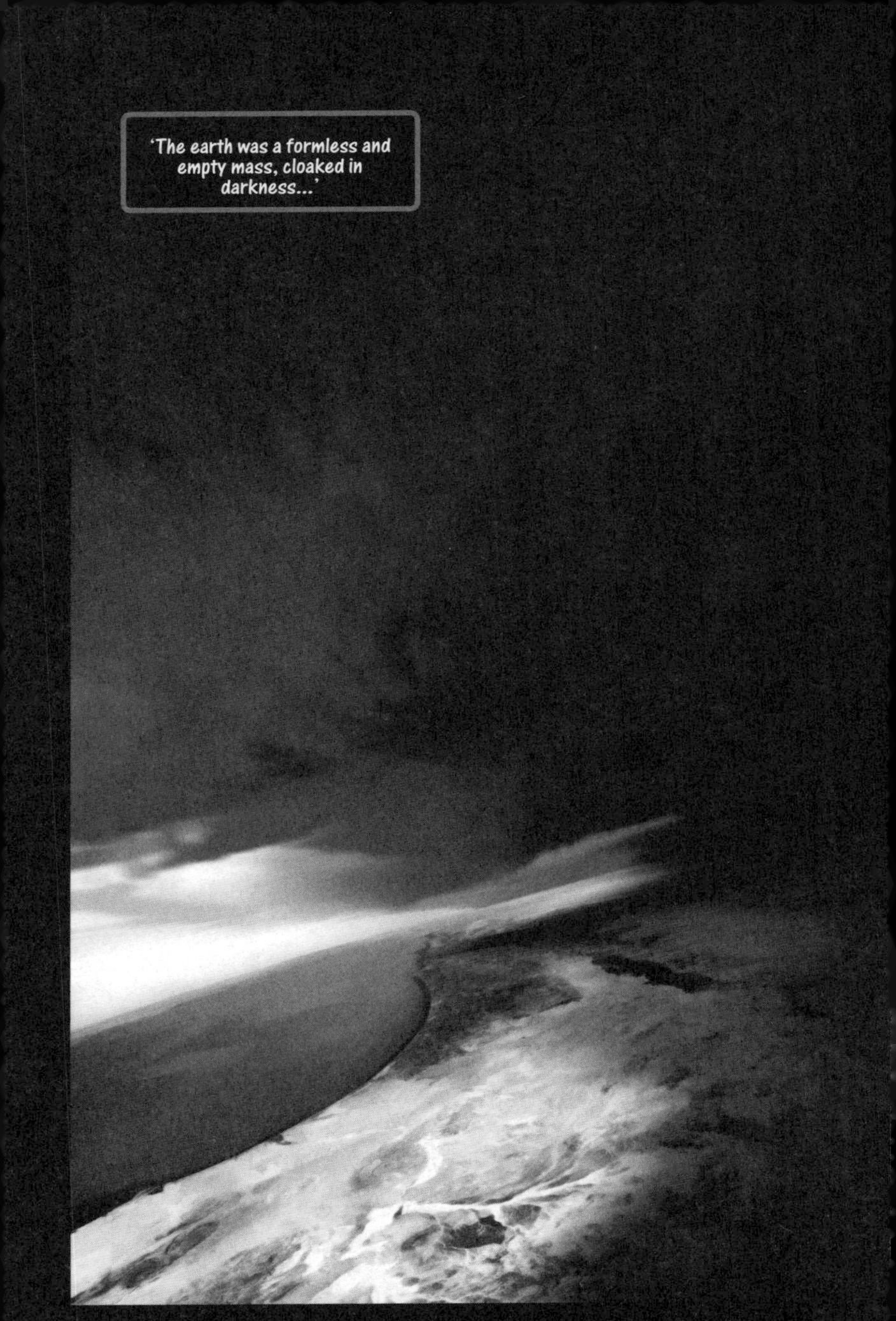
'The earth was a formless and empty mass, cloaked in darkness...'

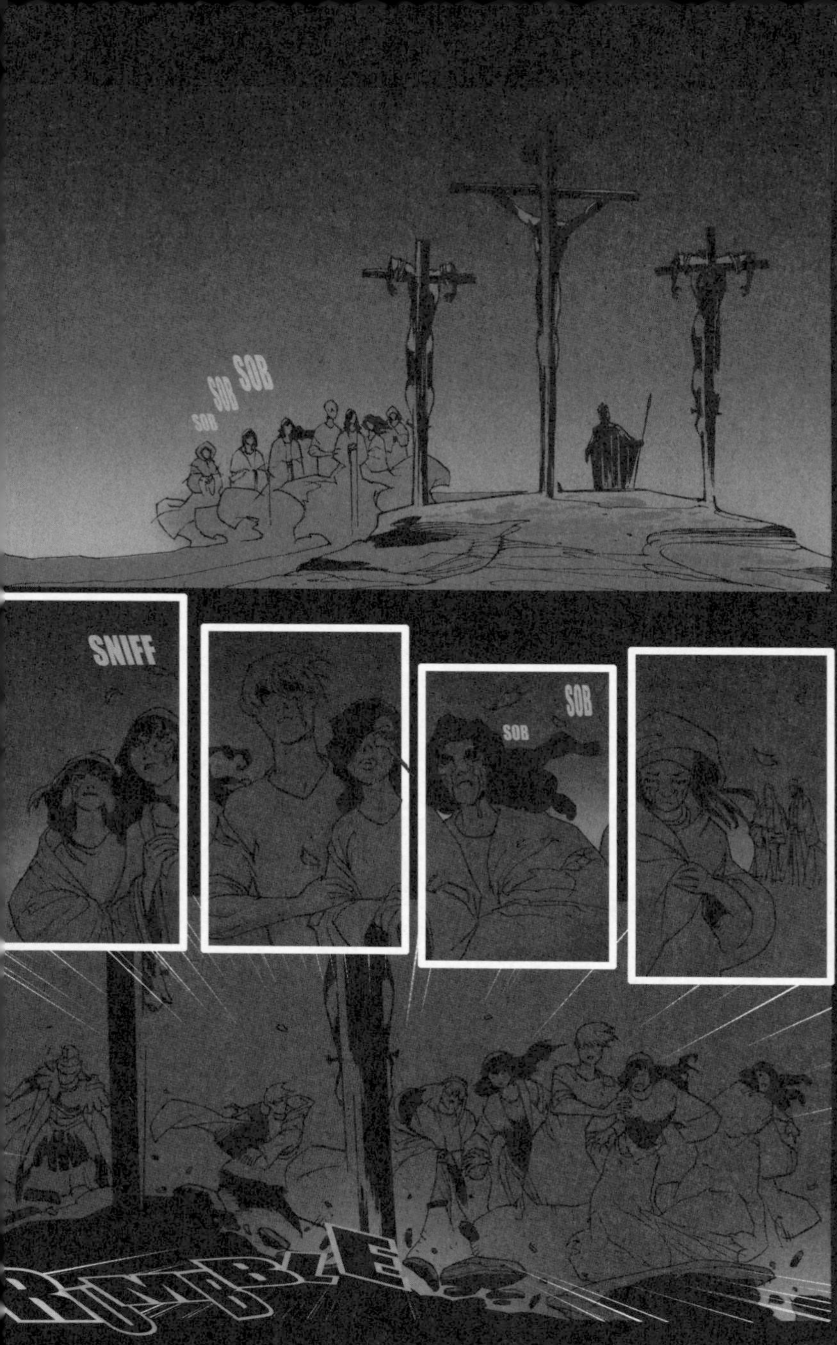
SOB
SOB
SOB
SNIFF
SOB
SOB
RUMBLE

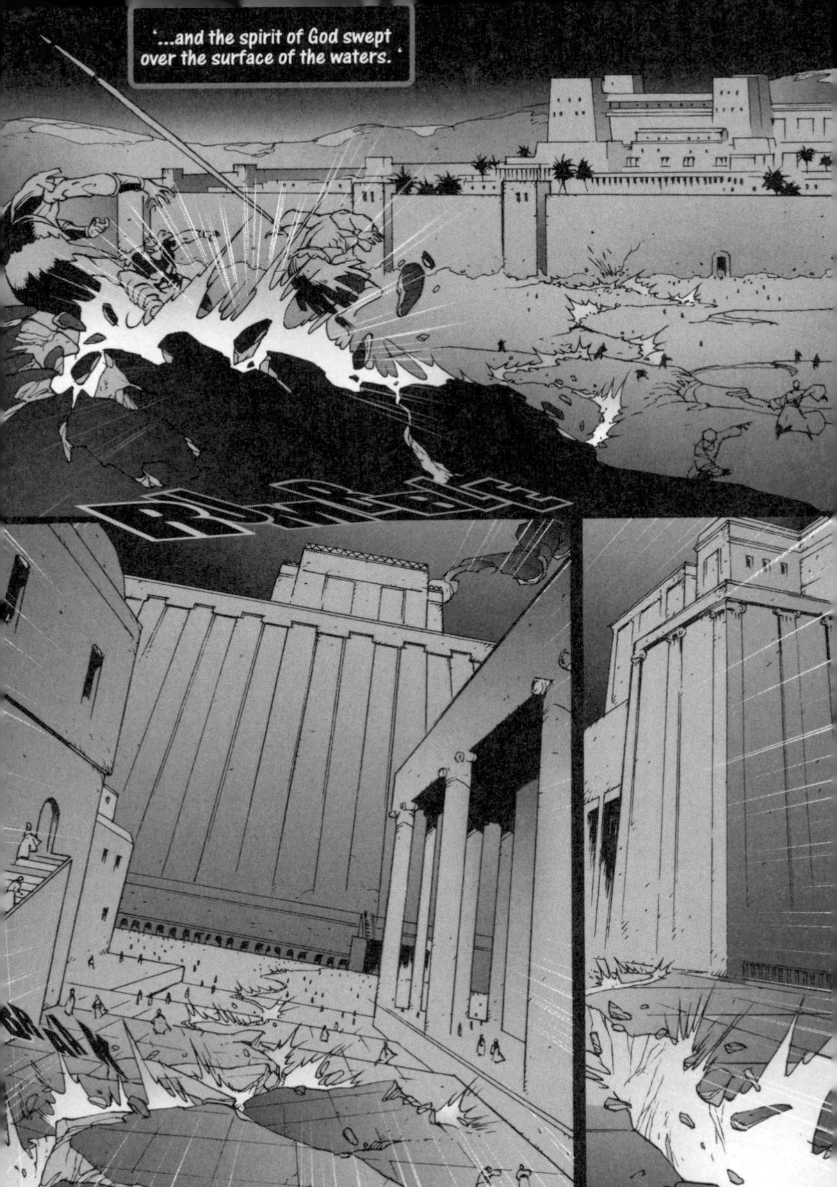
'...and the spirit of God swept over the surface of the waters. '

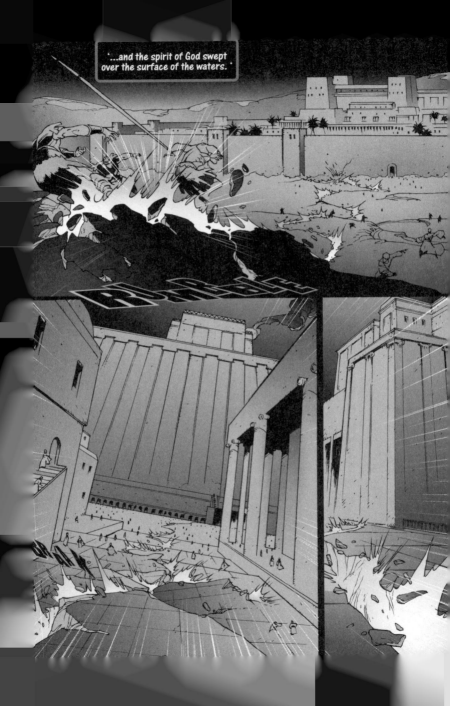

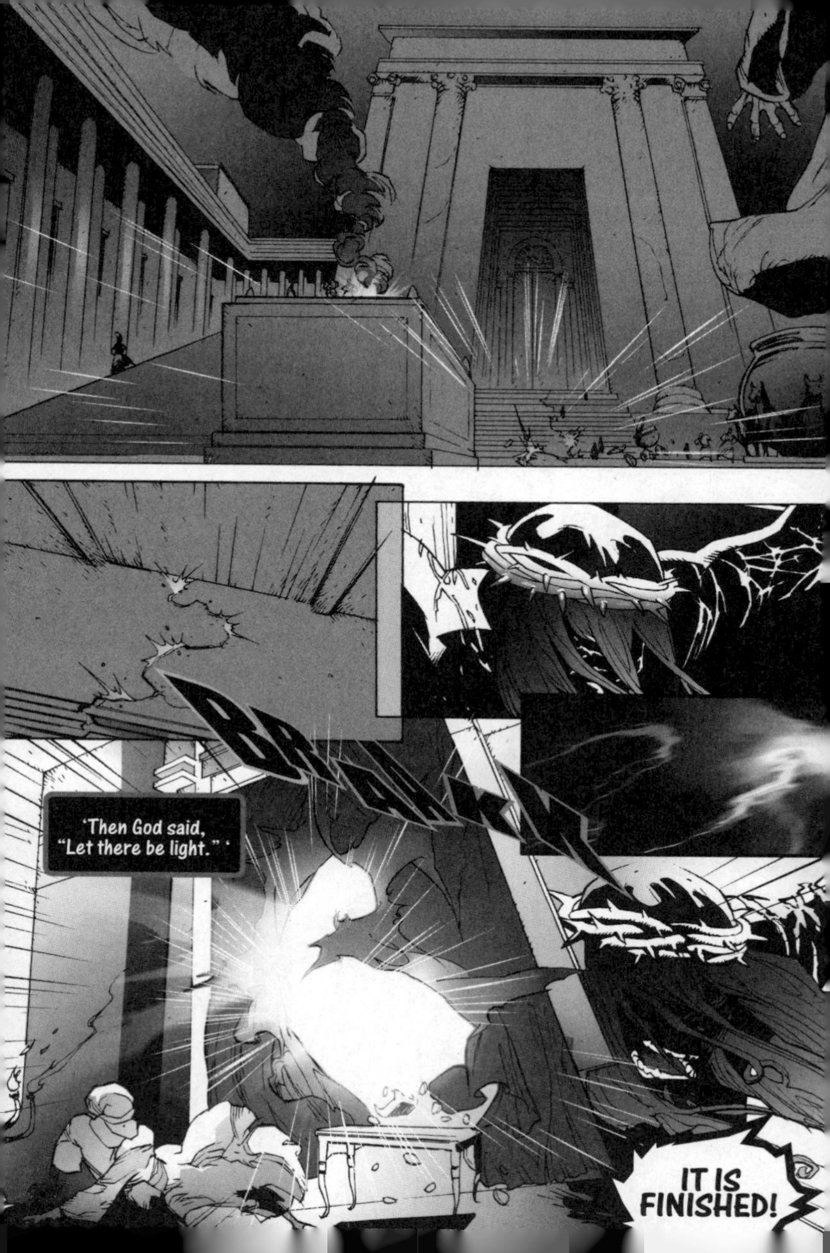
'Then God said,
"Let there be light." '
IT IS
FINISHED!

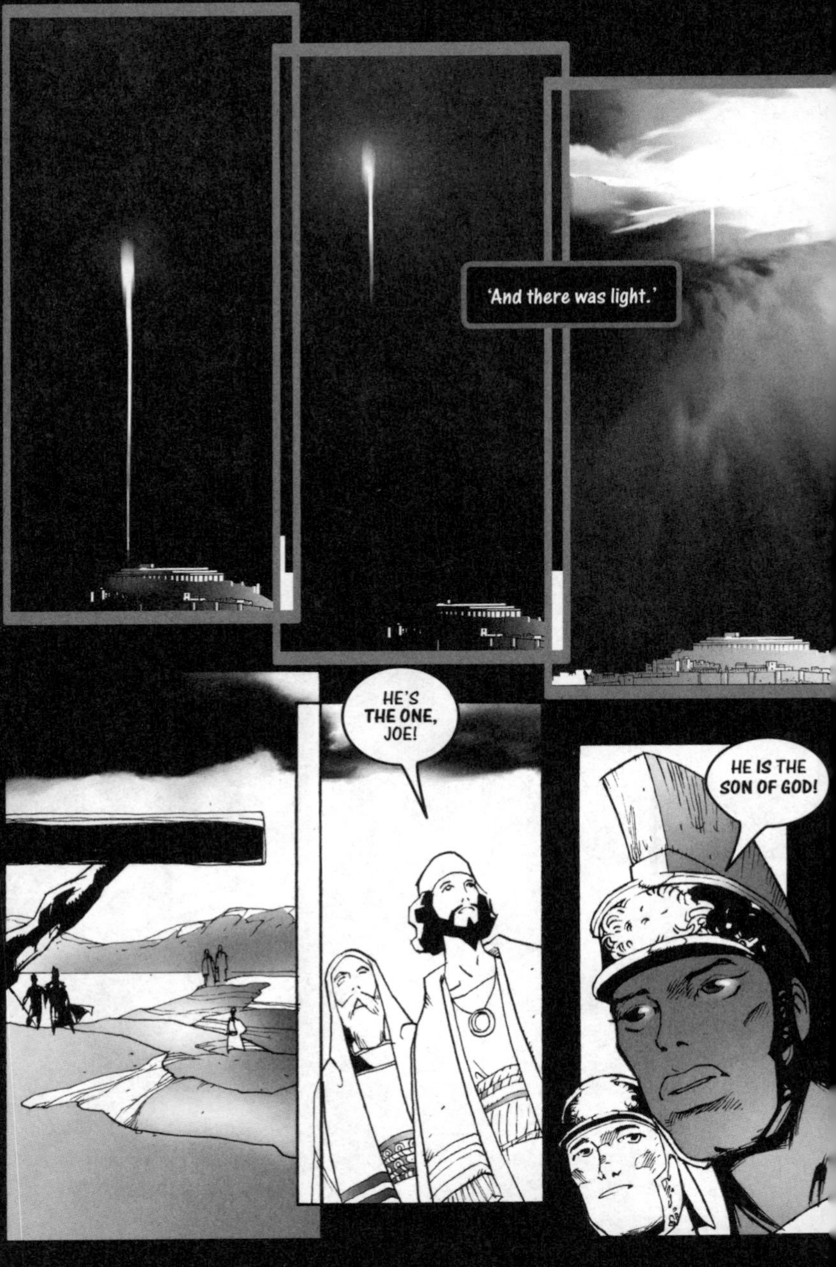
'And there was light.'
HE'S THE ONE, JOE!
HE IS THE SON OF GOD!

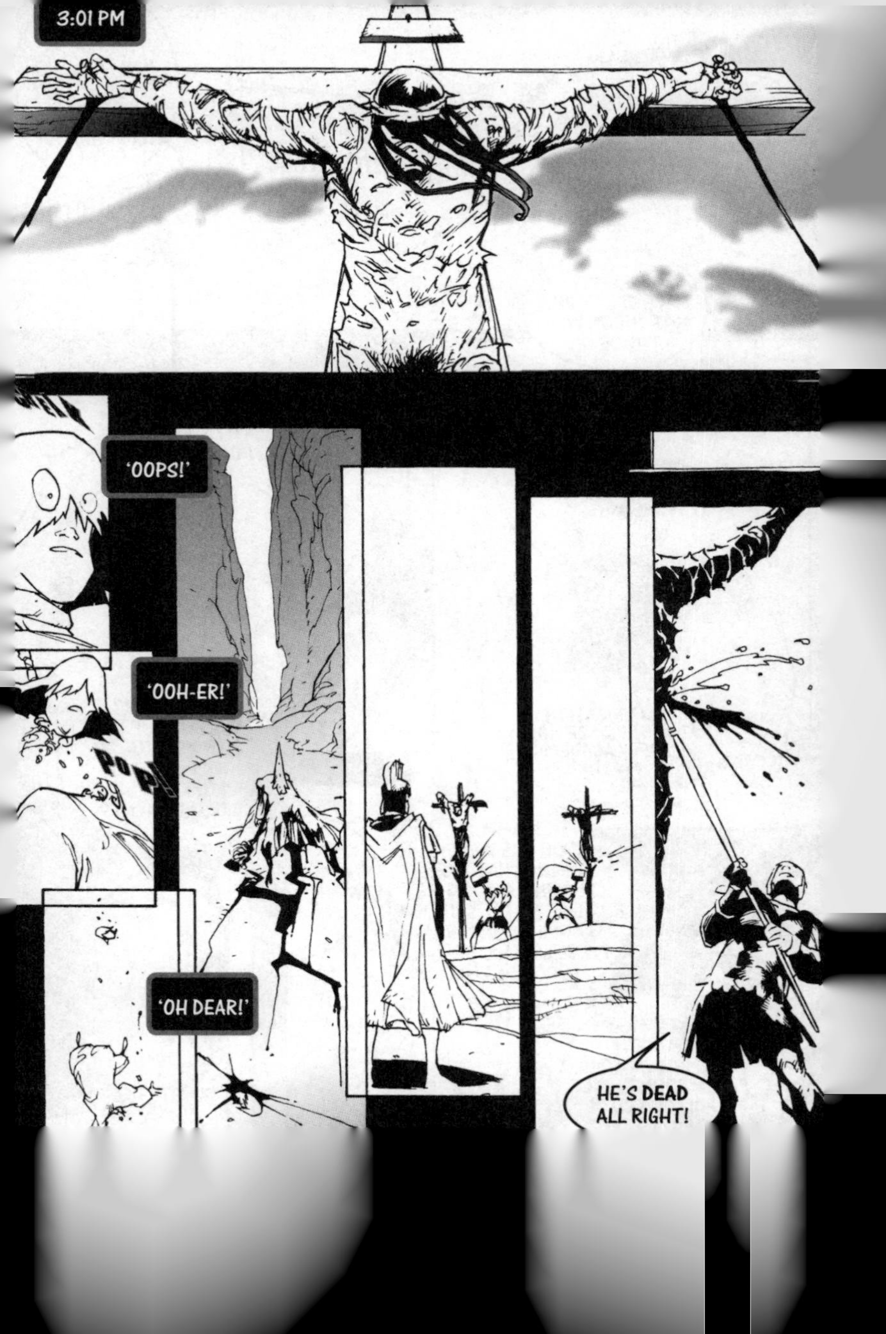

3:01 PM
'OOPS!'
'OOH-ER!'
POP!
'OH DEAR!'
HE'S DEAD ALL RIGHT!

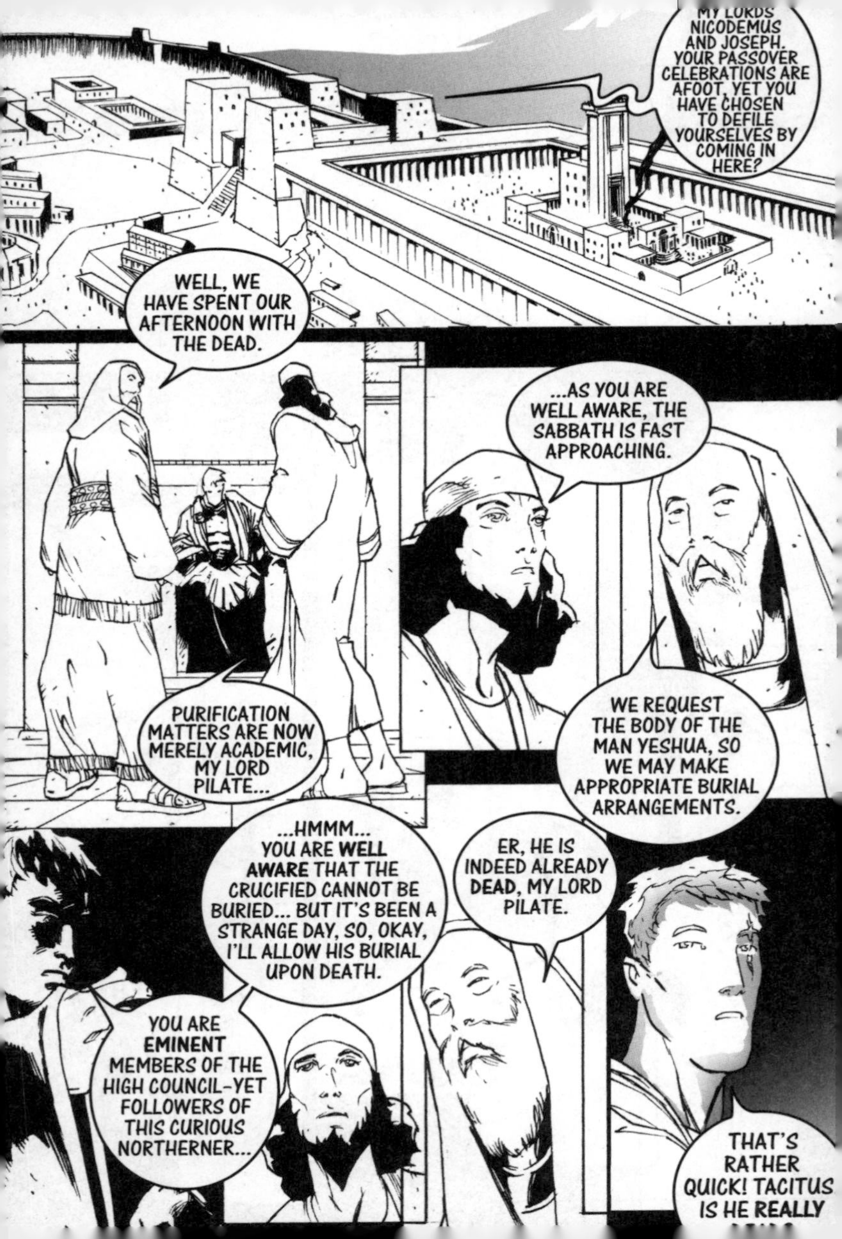
MY LORDS NICODEMUS AND JOSEPH. YOUR PASSOVER CELEBRATIONS ARE AFOOT, YET YOU HAVE CHOSEN TO DEFILE YOURSELVES BY COMING IN HERE?
WELL, WE HAVE SPENT OUR AFTERNOON WITH THE DEAD.
PURIFICATION MATTERS ARE NOW MERELY ACADEMIC, MY LORD PILATE...
...AS YOU ARE WELL AWARE, THE SABBATH IS FAST APPROACHING.
WE REQUEST THE BODY OF THE MAN YESHUA, SO WE MAY MAKE APPROPRIATE BURIAL ARRANGEMENTS.
YOU ARE EMINENT MEMBERS OF THE HIGH COUNCIL-YET FOLLOWERS OF THIS CURIOUS NORTHERNER...
...HMMM... YOU ARE WELL AWARE THAT THE CRUCIFIED CANNOT BE BURIED... BUT IT'S BEEN A STRANGE DAY, SO, OKAY, I'LL ALLOW HIS BURIAL UPON DEATH.
ER, HE IS INDEED ALREADY DEAD, MY LORD PILATE.
THAT'S RATHER QUICK! TACITUS IS HE REALLY

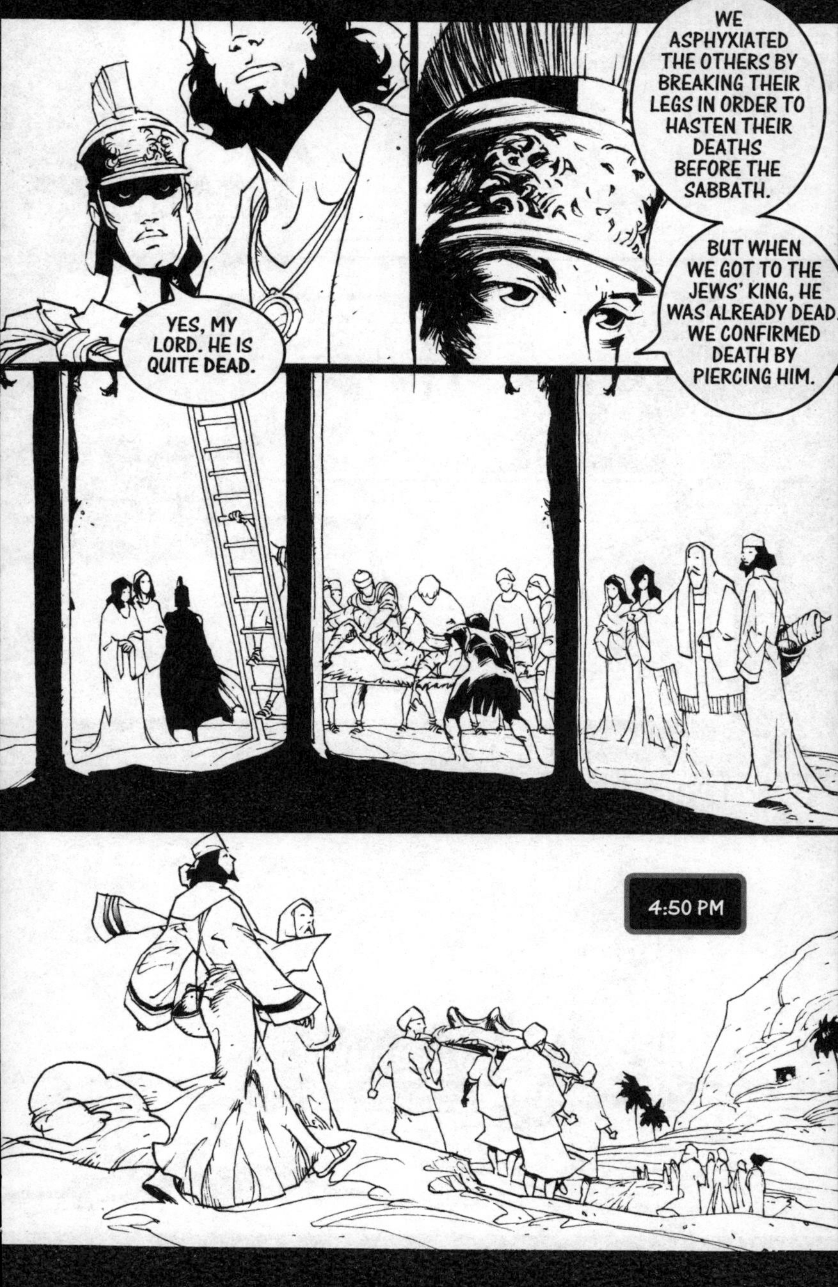
YES, MY LORD. HE IS QUITE DEAD.
WE ASPHYXIATED THE OTHERS BY BREAKING THEIR LEGS IN ORDER TO HASTEN THEIR DEATHS BEFORE THE SABBATH.
BUT WHEN WE GOT TO THE JEWS' KING, HE WAS ALREADY DEAD. WE CONFIRMED DEATH BY PIERCING HIM.
4:50 PM

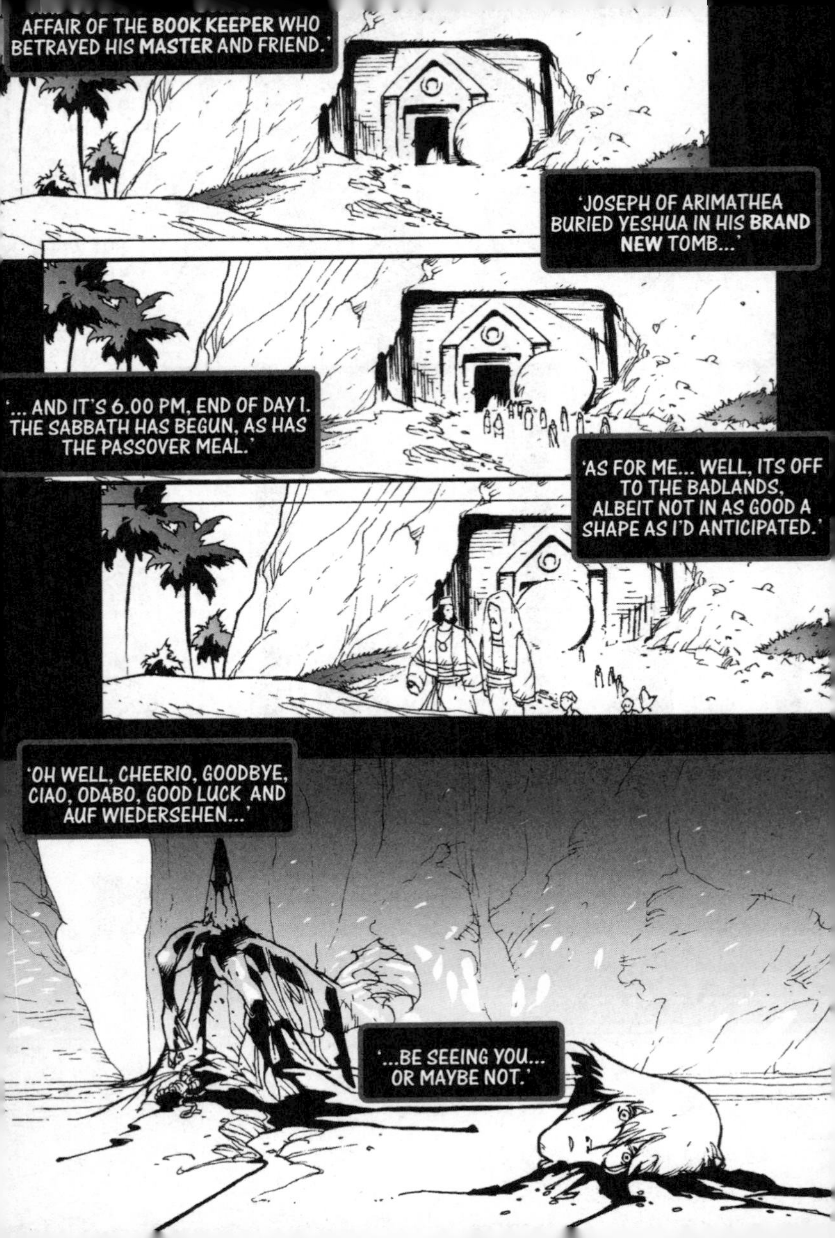
AFFAIR OF THE BOOK KEEPER WHO BETRAYED HIS MASTER AND FRIEND.'
'JOSEPH OF ARIMATHEA BURIED YESHUA IN HIS BRAND NEW TOMB...'
'... AND IT'S 6.00 PM, END OF DAY 1. THE SABBATH HAS BEGUN, AS HAS THE PASSOVER MEAL.'
'AS FOR ME... WELL, ITS OFF TO THE BADLANDS, ALBEIT NOT IN AS GOOD A SHAPE AS I'D ANTICIPATED.'
'OH WELL, CHEERIO, GOODBYE, CIAO, ODABO, GOOD LUCK AND AUF WIEDERSEHEN...'
'...BE SEEING YOU... OR MAYBE NOT.'

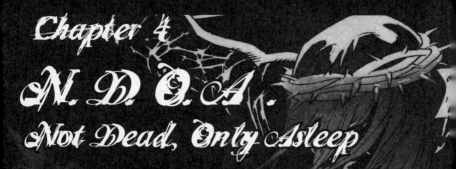

Chapter 4

N. D. O. A.

Not Dead, Only Asleep

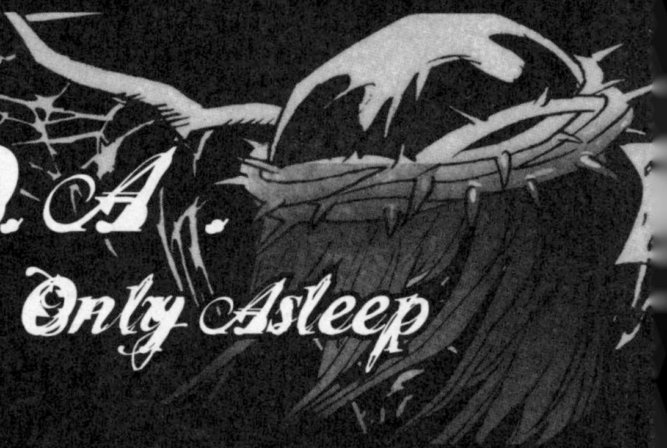

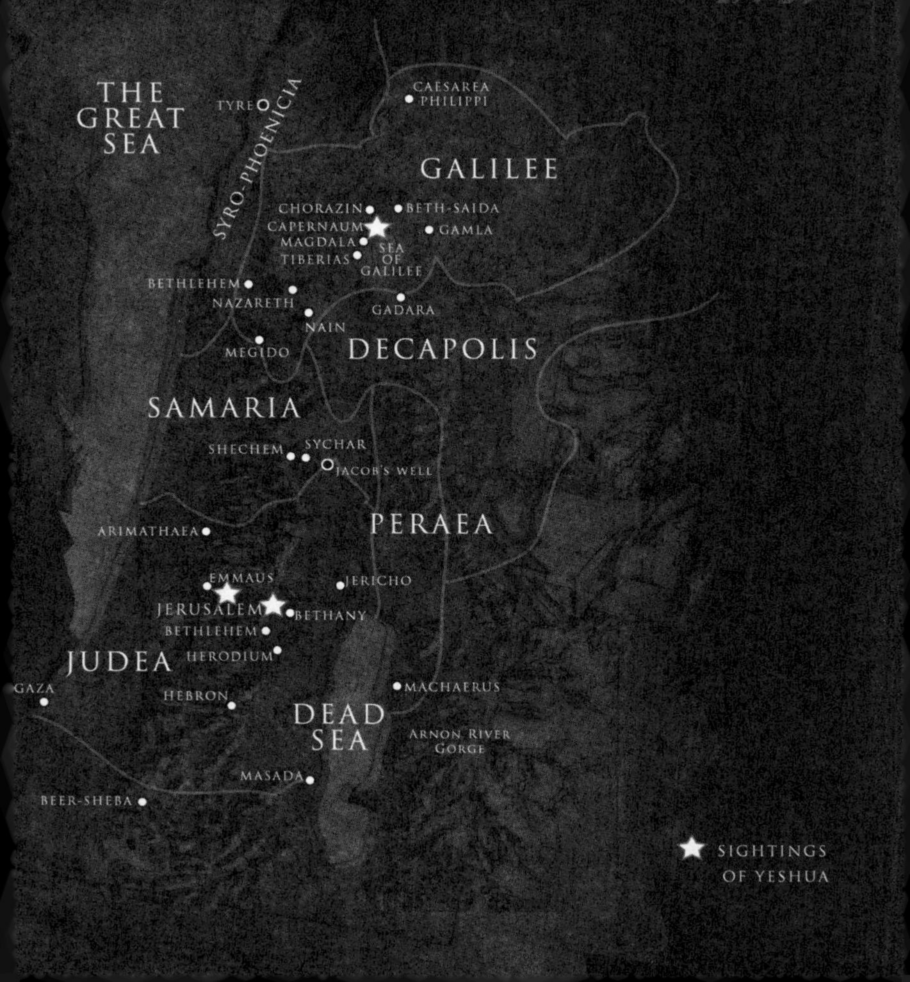
THE GREAT SEA
TYRE
SYRO-PHOENICIA
CAESAREA PHILIPPI
GALILEE
CHORAZIN
BETH-SAIDA
CAPERNAUM
GAMLA
MAGDALA
SEA OF GALILEE
TIBERIAS
BETHLEHEM
NAZARETH
GADARA
NAIN
MEGIDO
DECAPOLIS
SAMARIA
SHECHEM
SYCHAR
JACOB'S WELL
PERAEA
ARIMATHAEA
EMMAUS
JERICHO
JERUSALEM
BETHANY
BETHLEHEM
HERODIUM
JUDEA
GAZA
HEBRON
MACHAERUS
DEAD SEA
ARNON RIVER GORGE
MASADA
BEER-SHEBA
SIGHTINGS OF YESHUA

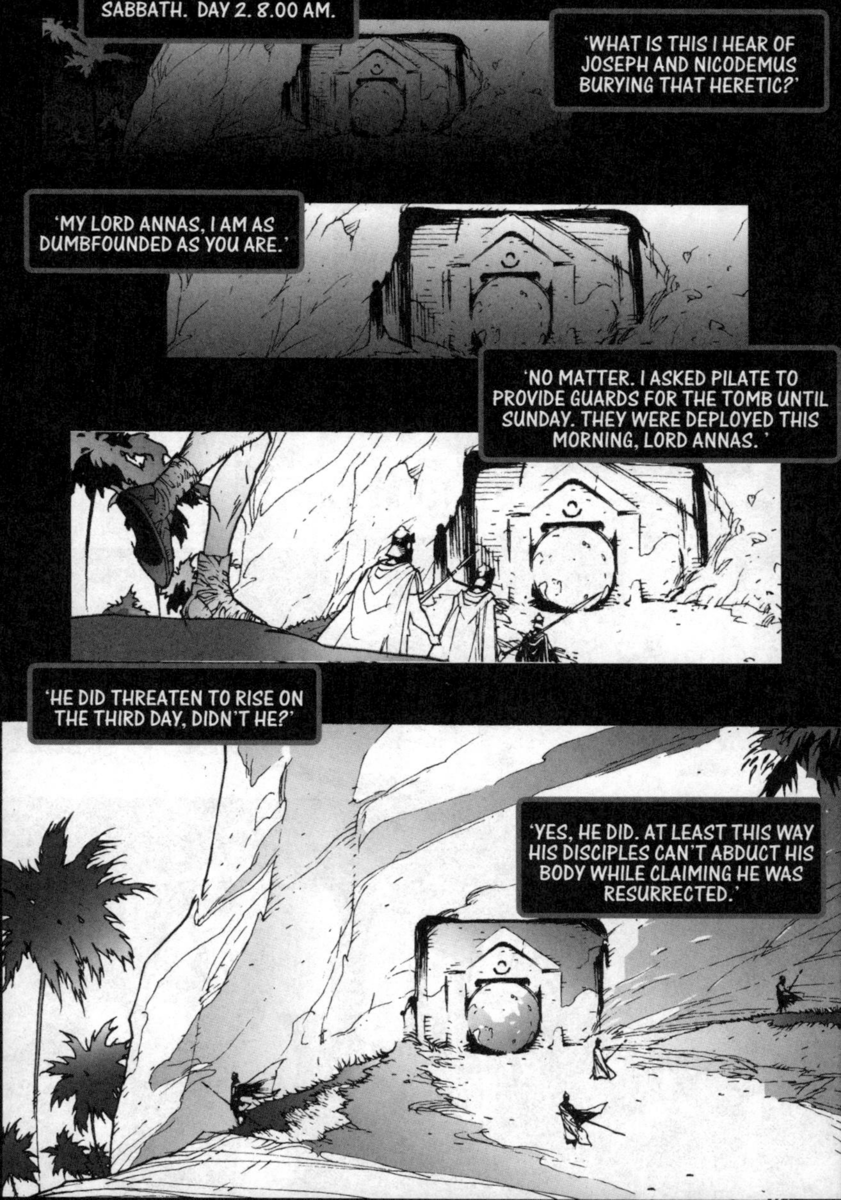
SABBATH. DAY 2. 8.00 AM.
'WHAT IS THIS I HEAR OF JOSEPH AND NICODEMUS BURYING THAT HERETIC?'
'MY LORD ANNAS, I AM AS DUMBFOUNDED AS YOU ARE.'
'NO MATTER. I ASKED PILATE TO PROVIDE GUARDS FOR THE TOMB UNTIL SUNDAY. THEY WERE DEPLOYED THIS MORNING, LORD ANNAS.'
'HE DID THREATEN TO RISE ON THE THIRD DAY, DIDN'T HE?'
'YES, HE DID. AT LEAST THIS WAY HIS DISCIPLES CAN'T ABDUCT HIS BODY WHILE CLAIMING HE WAS RESURRECTED.'

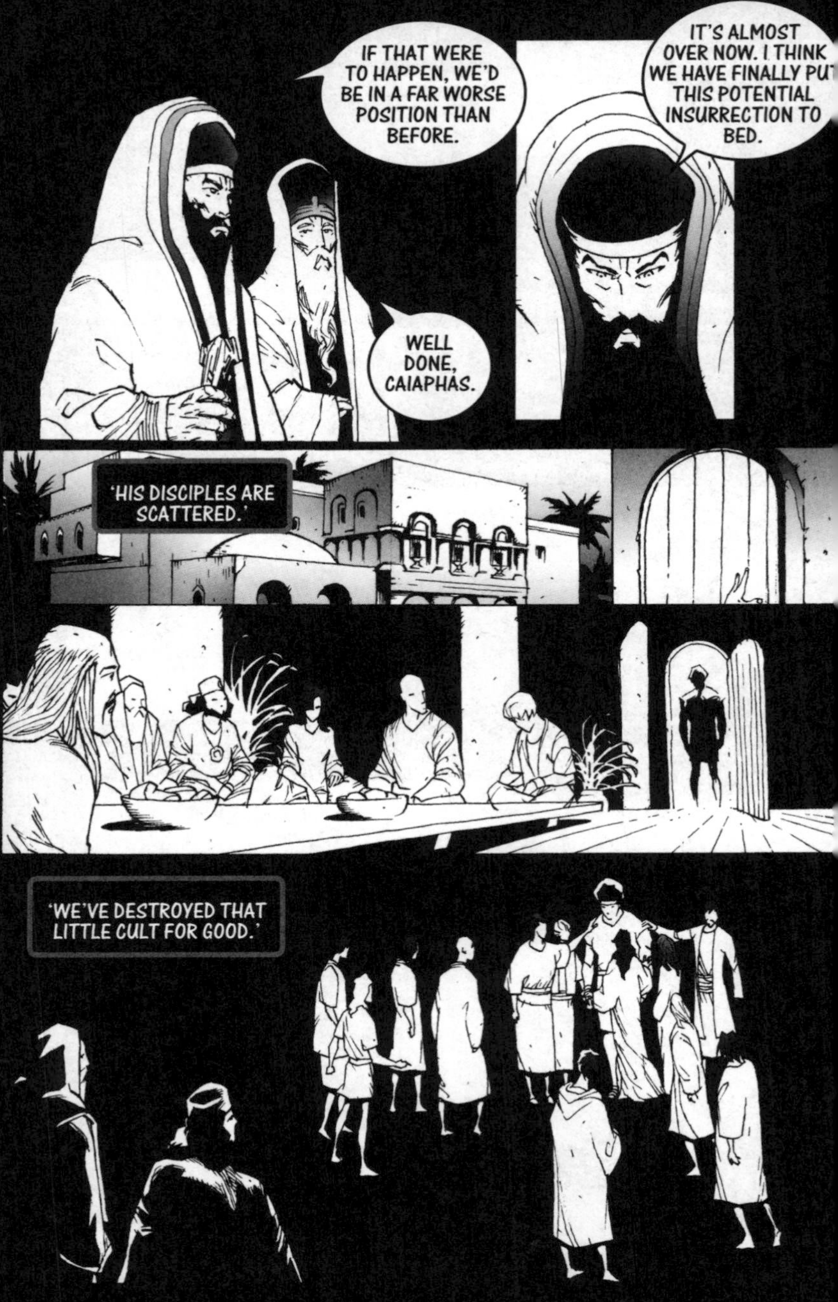
IF THAT WERE TO HAPPEN, WE'D BE IN A FAR WORSE POSITION THAN BEFORE.
WELL DONE, CAIAPHAS.
IT'S ALMOST OVER NOW. I THINK WE HAVE FINALLY PUT THIS POTENTIAL INSURRECTION TO BED.
'HIS DISCIPLES ARE SCATTERED.'
'WE'VE DESTROYED THAT LITTLE CULT FOR GOOD.'

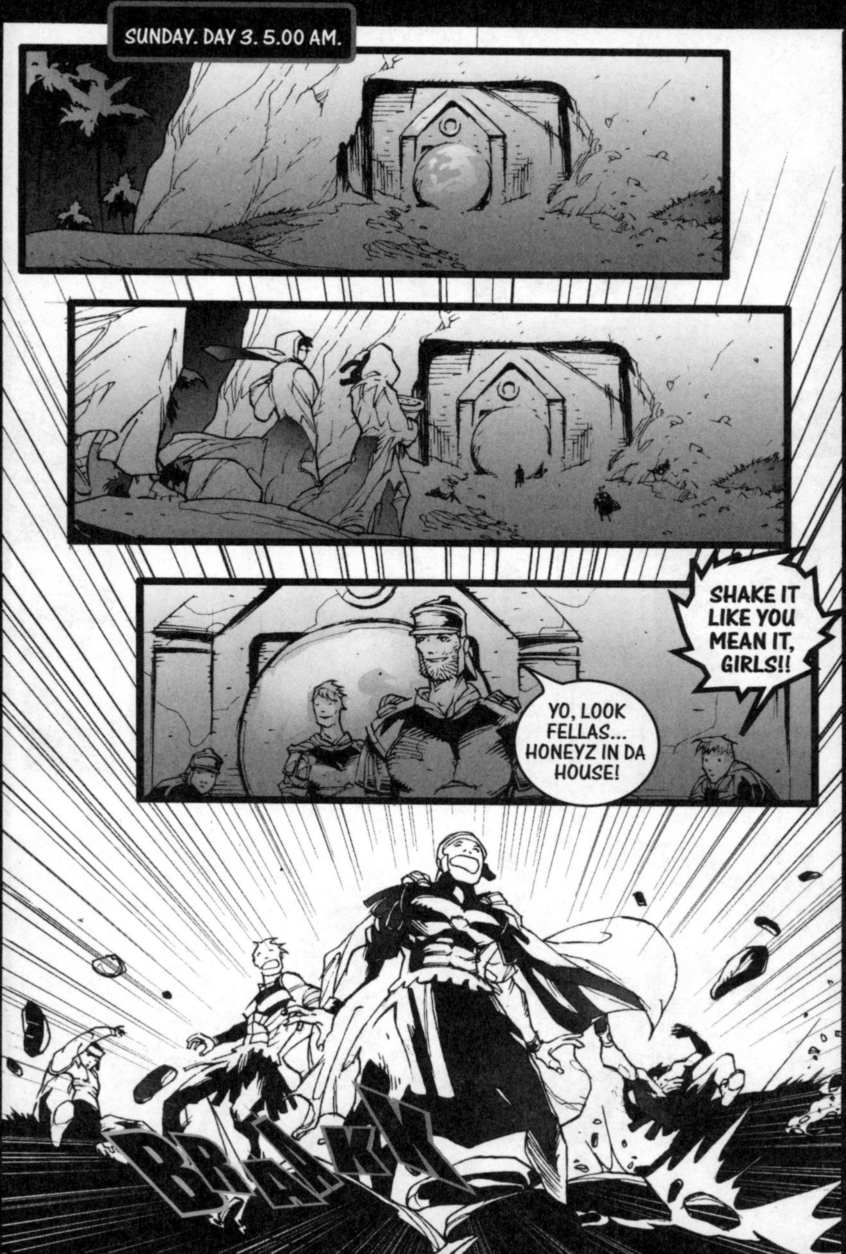
SUNDAY. DAY 3. 5.00 AM.
YO, LOOK FELLAS... HONEYZ IN DA HOUSE!
SHAKE IT LIKE YOU MEAN IT, GIRLS!!
BRAKK

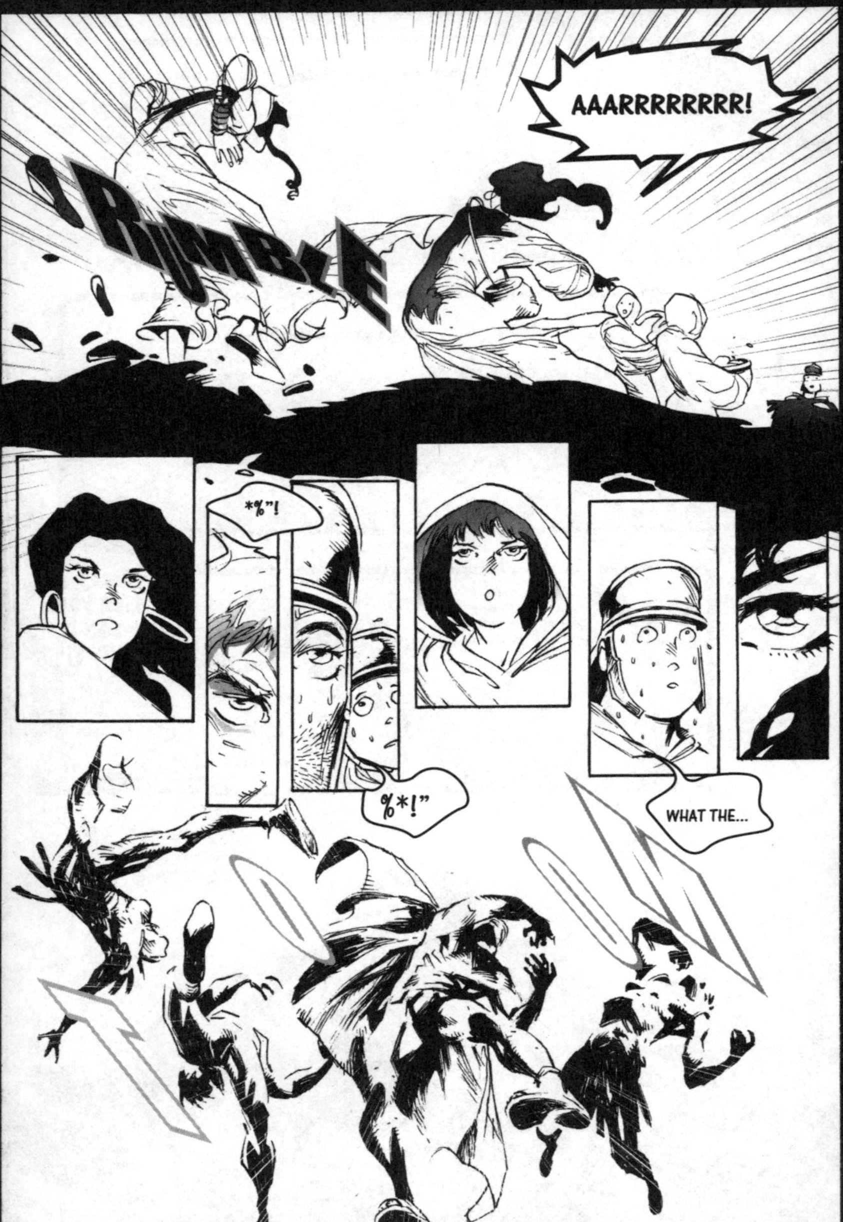
AAARRRRRRRR!
RUMBLE
*%"!
%*!"
WHAT THE...

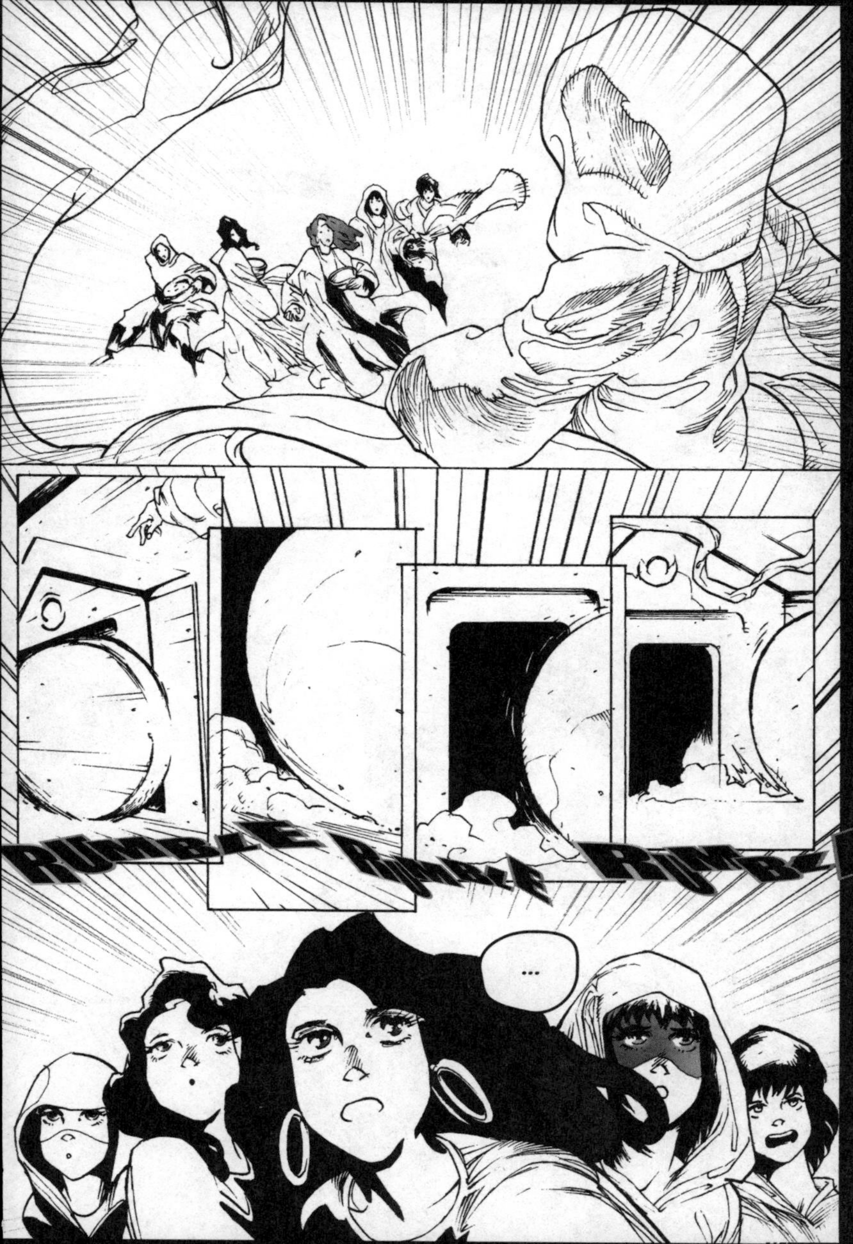
RUMBLE
RUMBLE
RUMBLE
...

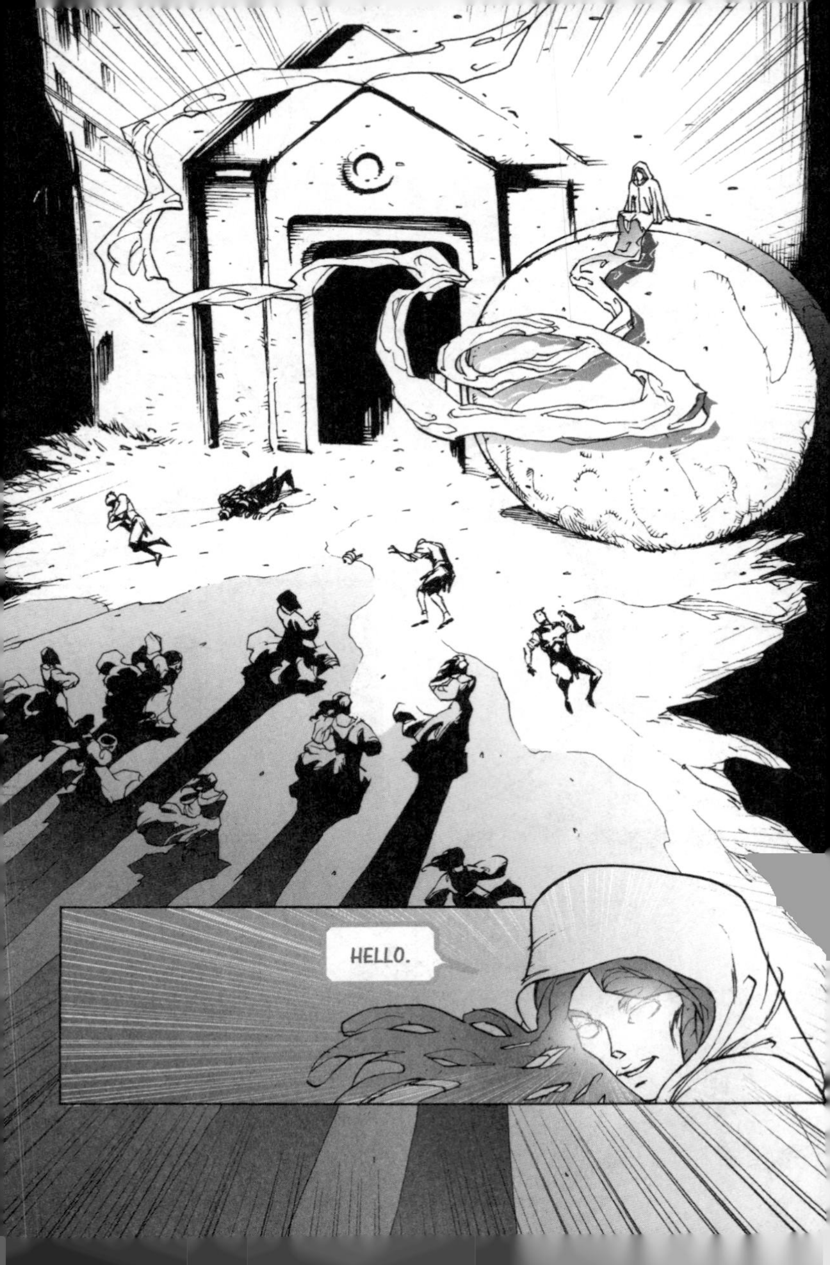
HELLO.

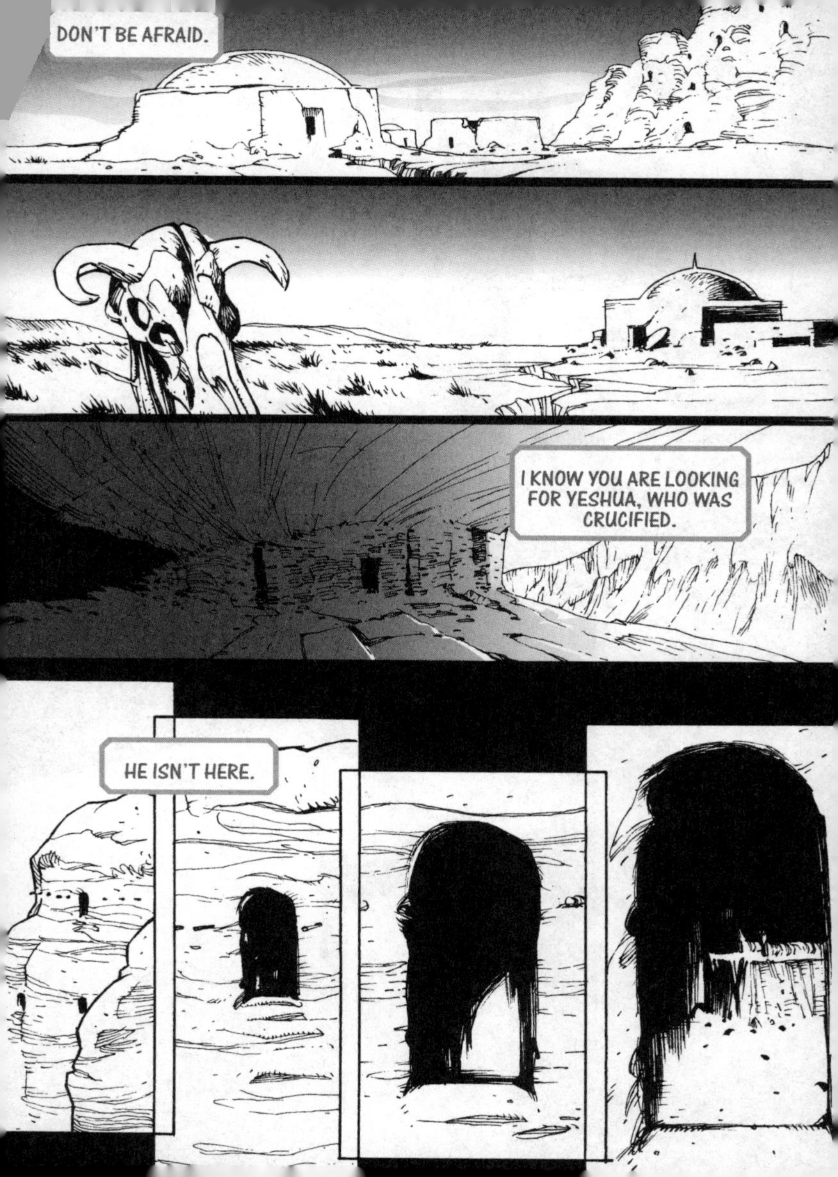
DON'T BE AFRAID.
I KNOW YOU ARE LOOKING FOR YESHUA, WHO WAS CRUCIFIED.
HE ISN'T HERE.

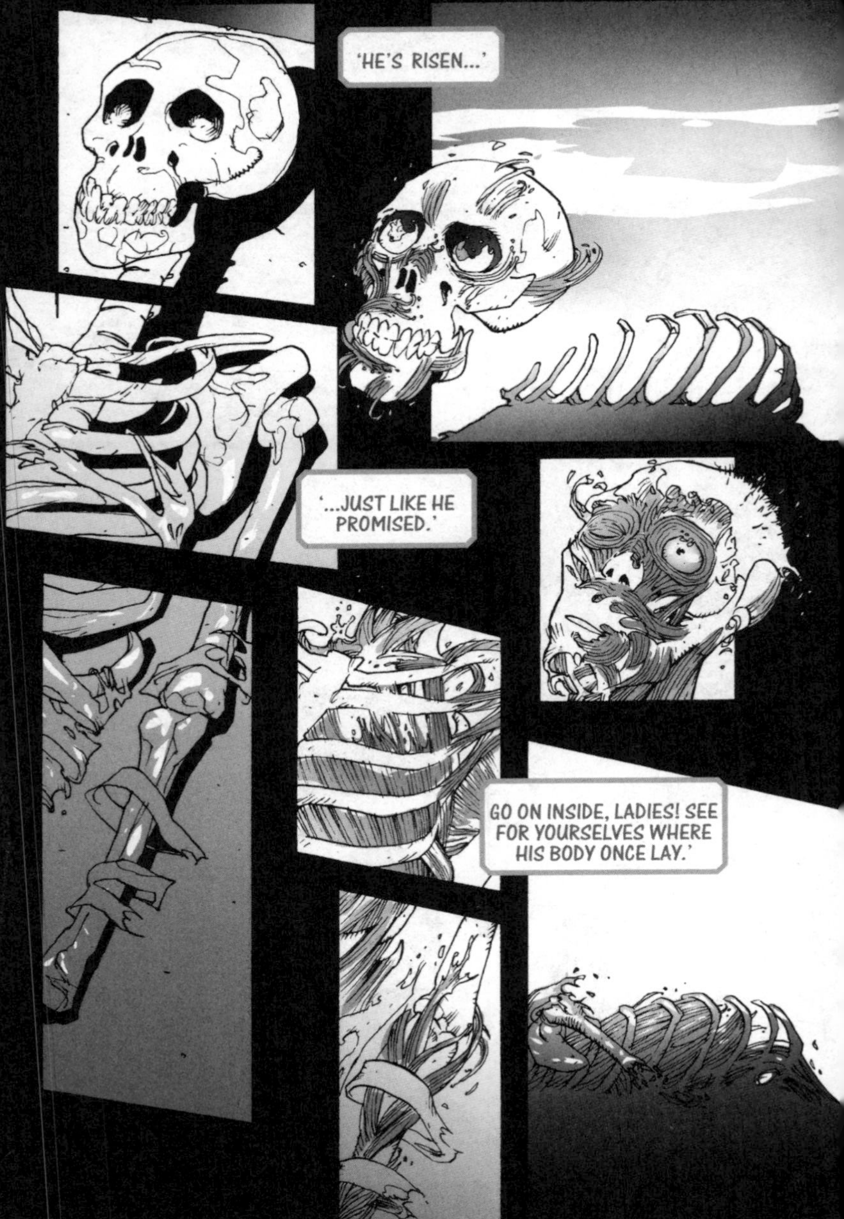
'HE'S RISEN...'
'...JUST LIKE HE PROMISED.'
GO ON INSIDE, LADIES! SEE FOR YOURSELVES WHERE HIS BODY ONCE LAY.'

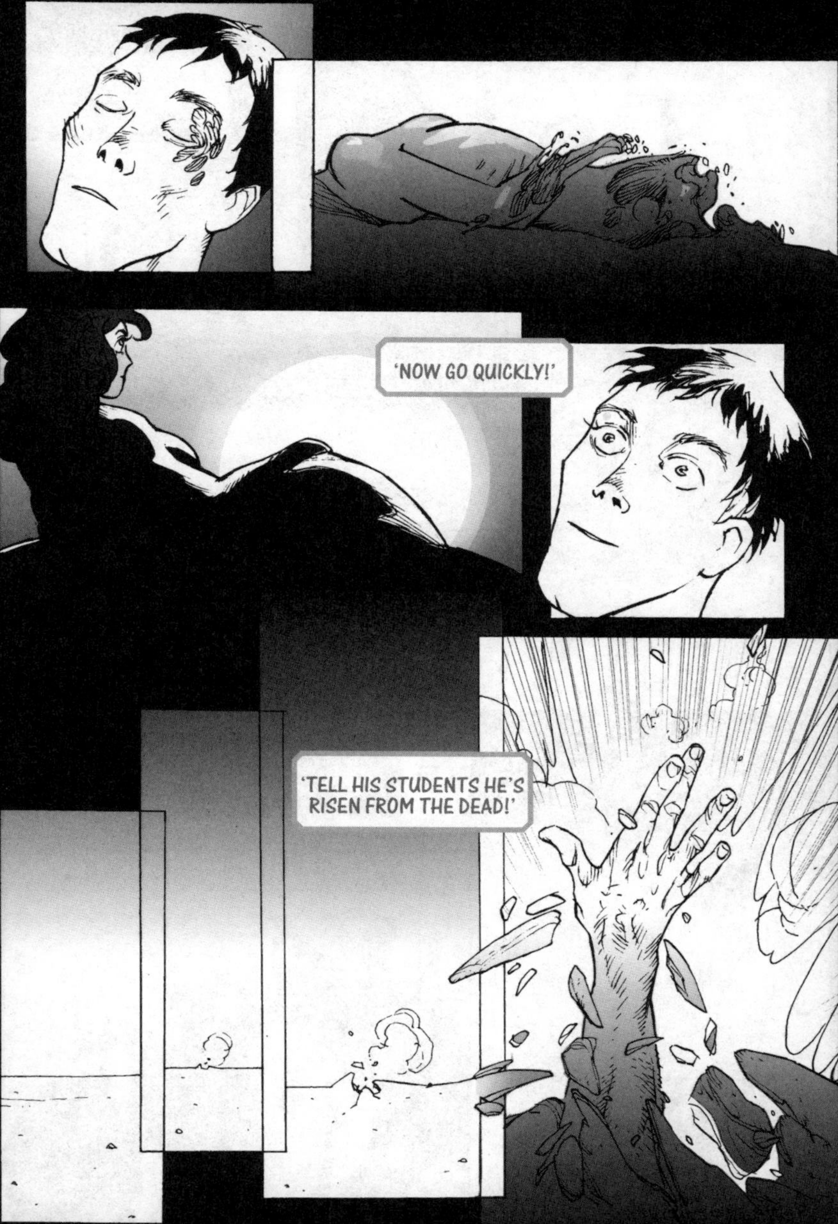
'NOW GO QUICKLY!'
'TELL HIS STUDENTS HE'S RISEN FROM THE DEAD!'

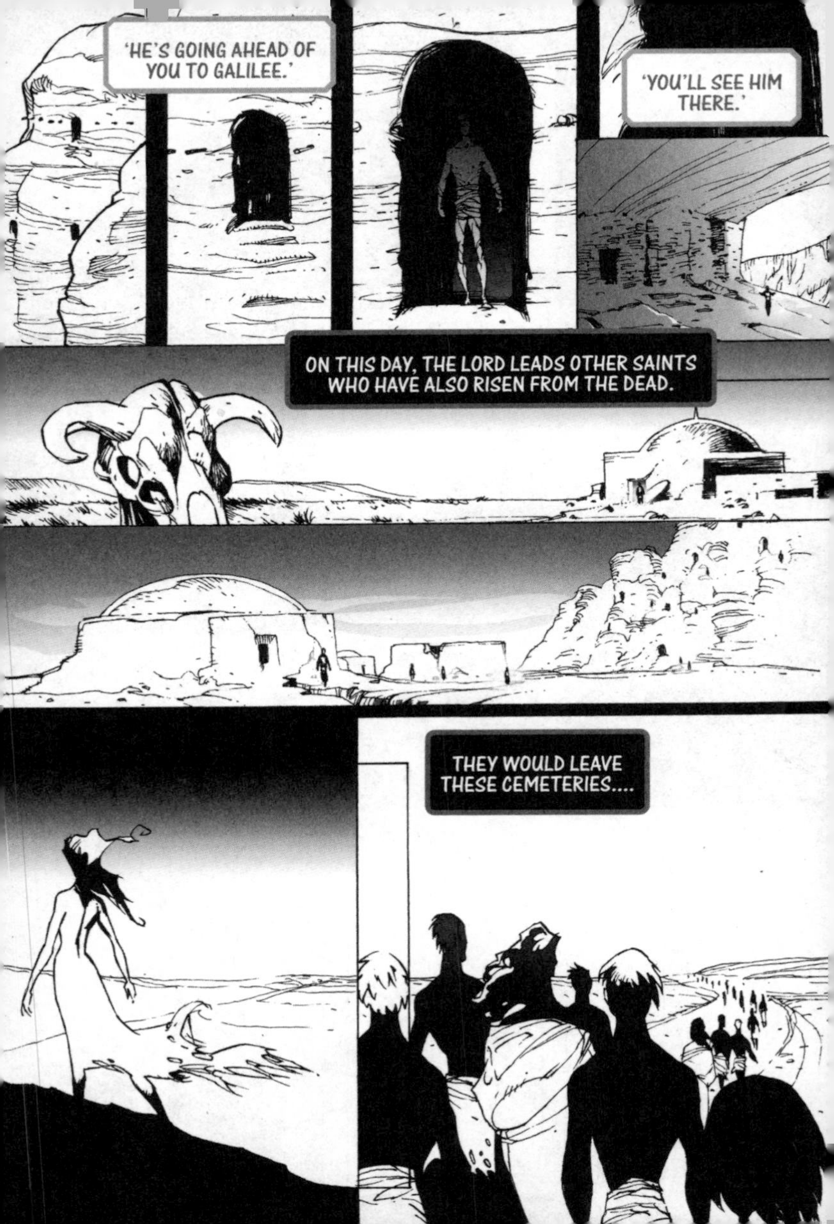
'HE'S GOING AHEAD OF YOU TO GALILEE.'
'YOU'LL SEE HIM THERE.'
ON THIS DAY, THE LORD LEADS OTHER SAINTS WHO HAVE ALSO RISEN FROM THE DEAD.
THEY WOULD LEAVE THESE CEMETERIES....

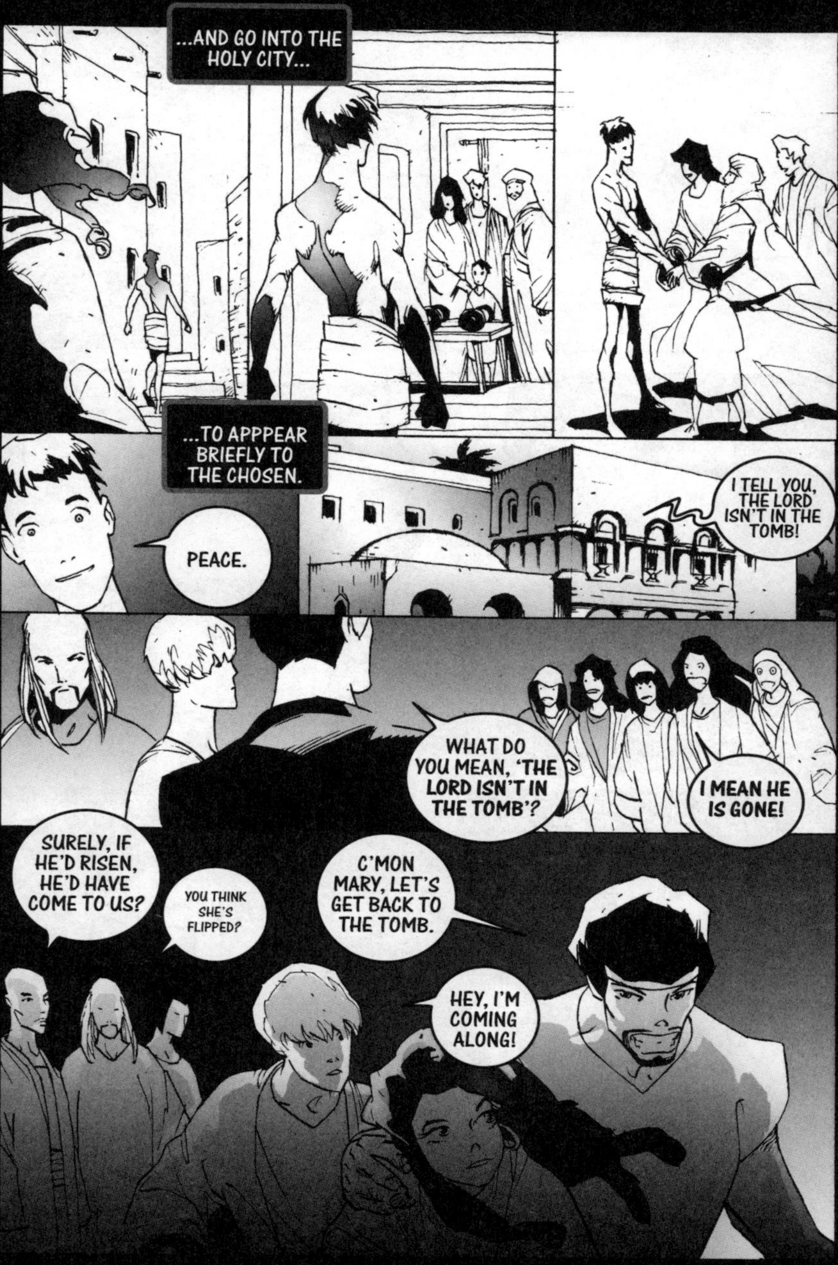
...AND GO INTO THE HOLY CITY...
...TO APPPEAR BRIEFLY TO THE CHOSEN.
PEACE.
I TELL YOU, THE LORD ISN'T IN THE TOMB!
WHAT DO YOU MEAN, 'THE LORD ISN'T IN THE TOMB'?
I MEAN HE IS GONE!
SURELY, IF HE'D RISEN, HE'D HAVE COME TO US?
YOU THINK SHE'S FLIPPED?
C'MON MARY, LET'S GET BACK TO THE TOMB.
HEY, I'M COMING ALONG!

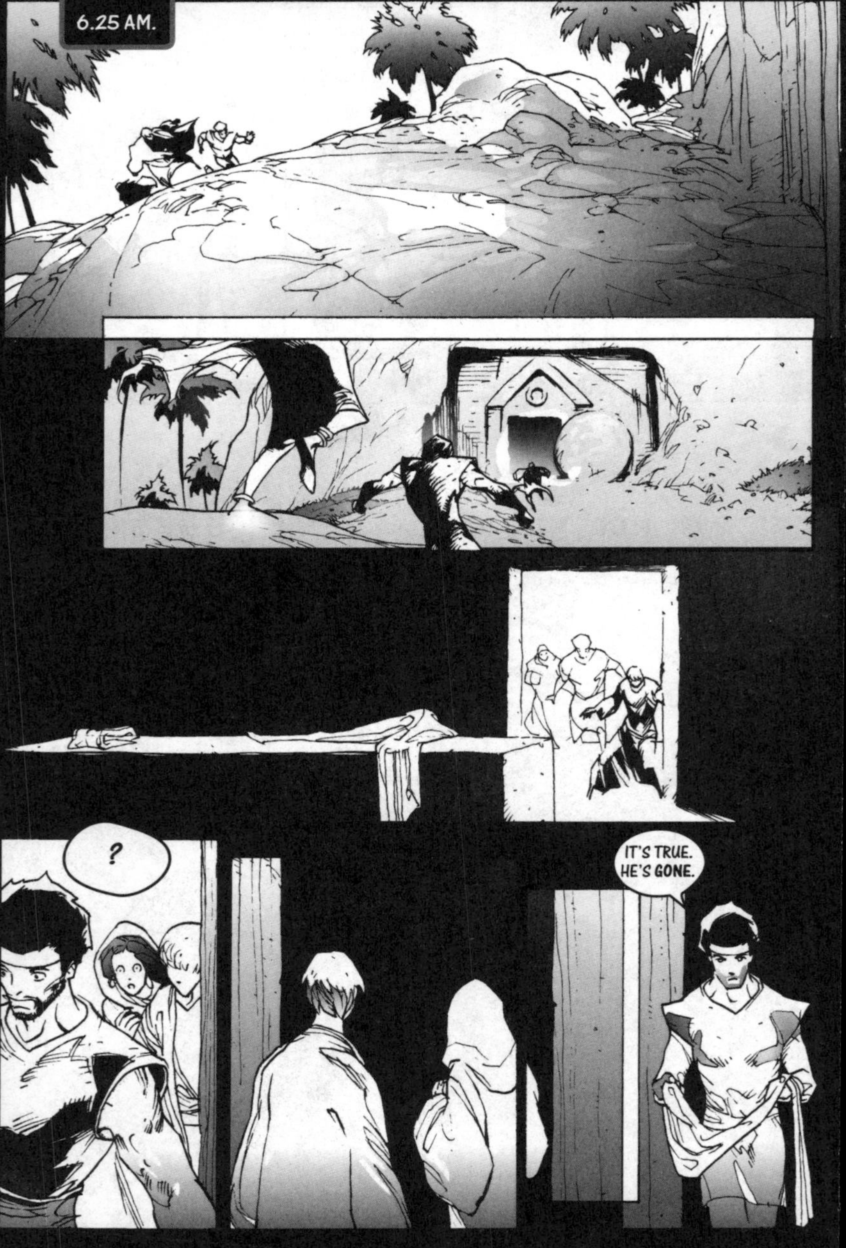
6.25 AM.
?
IT'S TRUE. HE'S GONE.

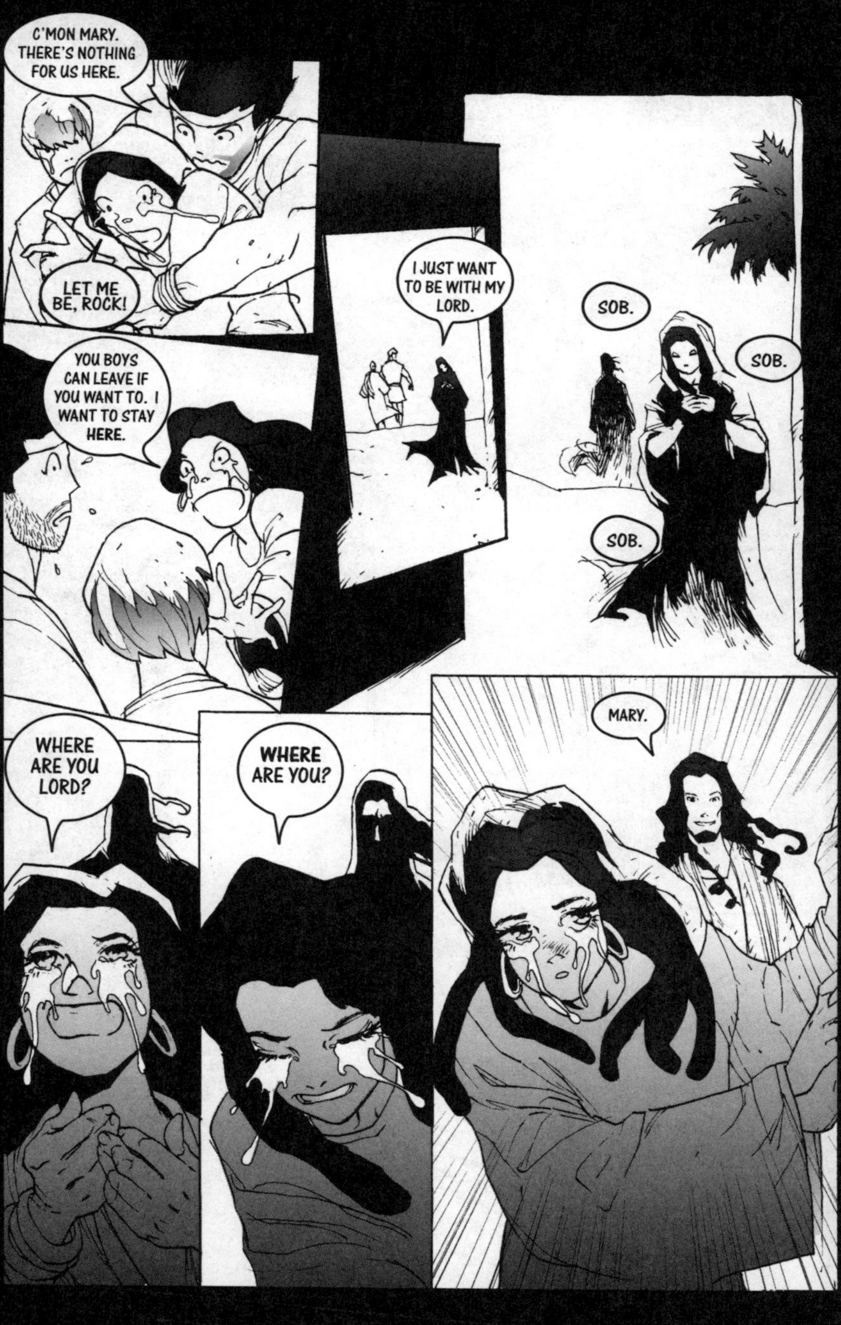
C'MON MARY. THERE'S NOTHING FOR US HERE.
LET ME BE, ROCK!
YOU BOYS CAN LEAVE IF YOU WANT TO. I WANT TO STAY HERE.
I JUST WANT TO BE WITH MY LORD.
SOB.
SOB.
SOB.
WHERE ARE YOU LORD?
WHERE ARE YOU?
MARY.

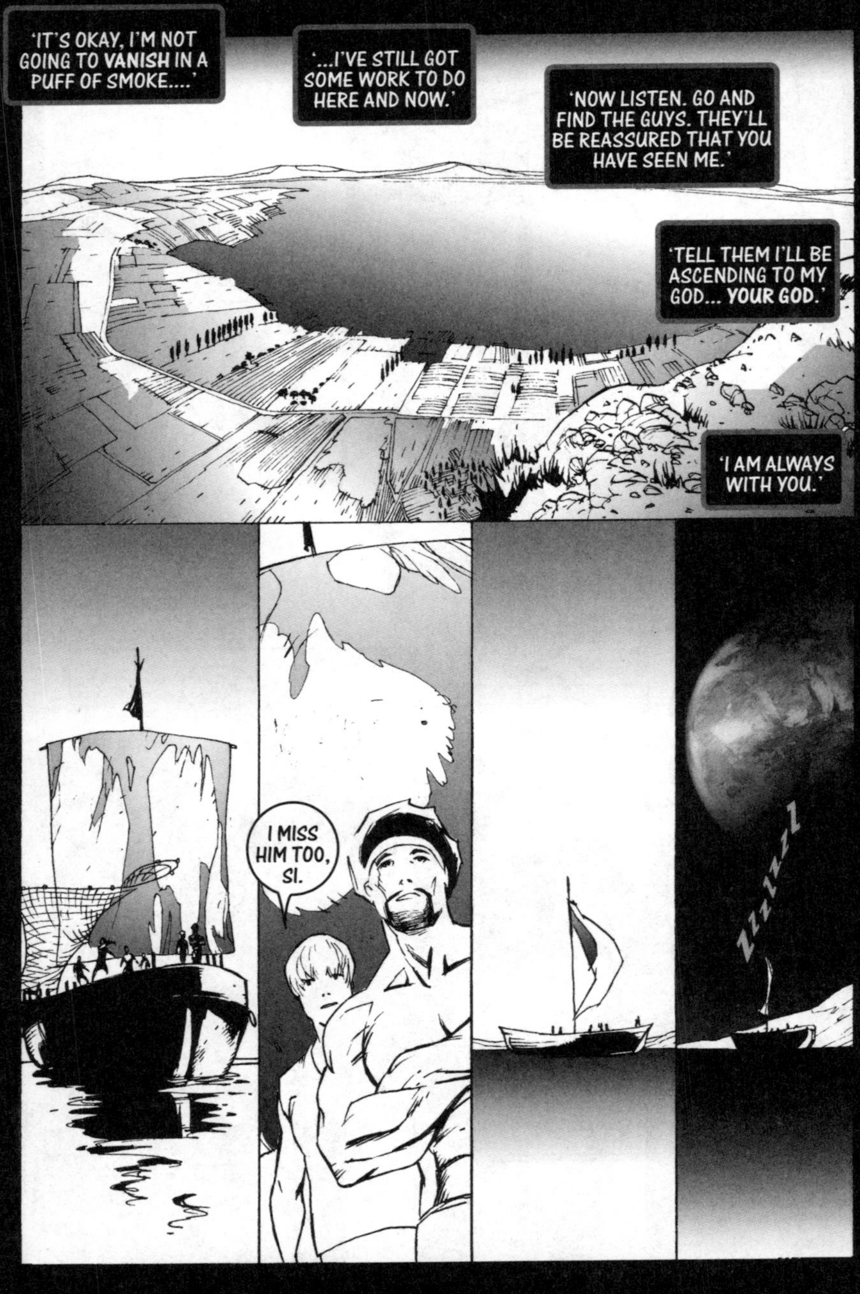
'IT'S OKAY, I'M NOT GOING TO VANISH IN A PUFF OF SMOKE....'
'...I'VE STILL GOT SOME WORK TO DO HERE AND NOW.'
'NOW LISTEN. GO AND FIND THE GUYS. THEY'LL BE REASSURED THAT YOU HAVE SEEN ME.'
'TELL THEM I'LL BE ASCENDING TO MY GOD... YOUR GOD.'
'I AM ALWAYS WITH YOU.'
I MISS HIM TOO, SI.
ZZZZZZZ

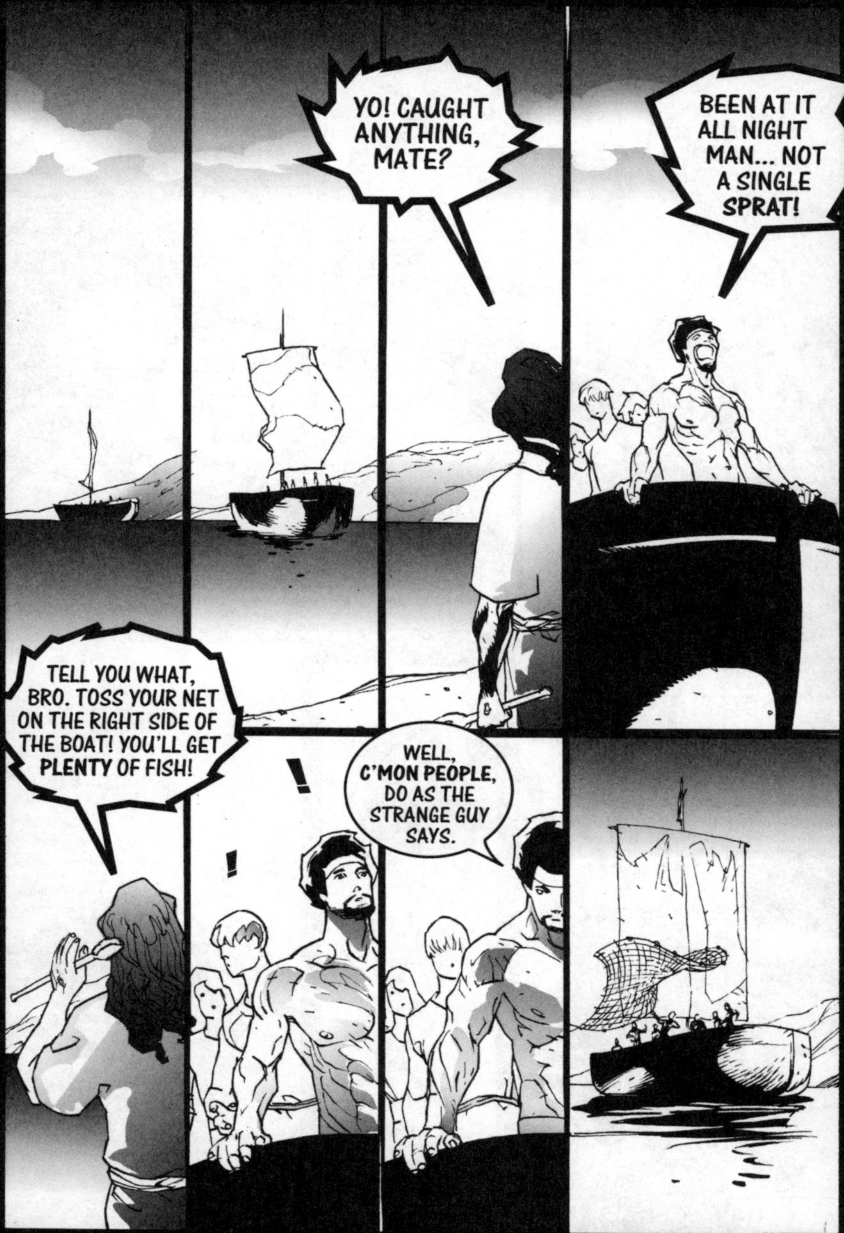
YO! CAUGHT ANYTHING, MATE?
BEEN AT IT ALL NIGHT MAN... NOT A SINGLE SPRAT!
TELL YOU WHAT, BRO. TOSS YOUR NET ON THE RIGHT SIDE OF THE BOAT! YOU'LL GET PLENTY OF FISH!
!
!
WELL, C'MON PEOPLE, DO AS THE STRANGE GUY SAYS.

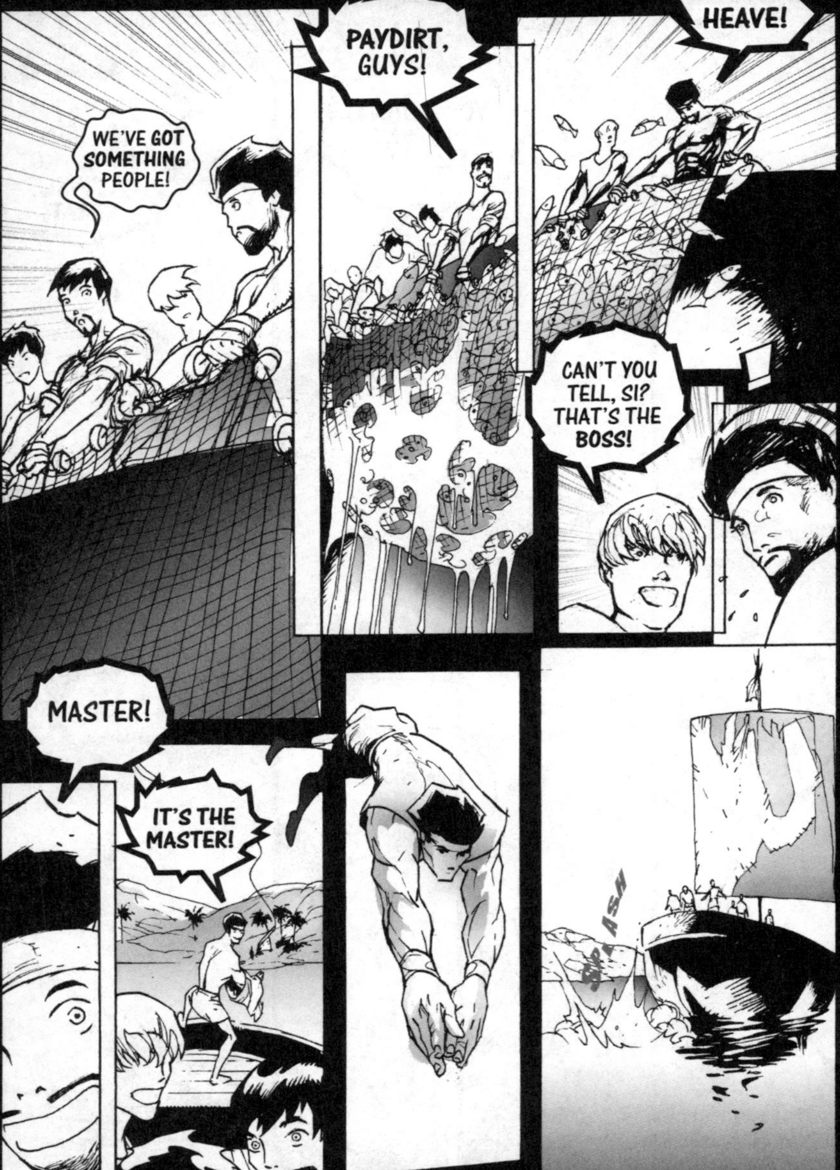
WE'VE GOT SOMETHING PEOPLE!
PAYDIRT, GUYS!
HEAVE!
CAN'T YOU TELL, SI? THAT'S THE BOSS!
MASTER!
IT'S THE MASTER!
SPLASH

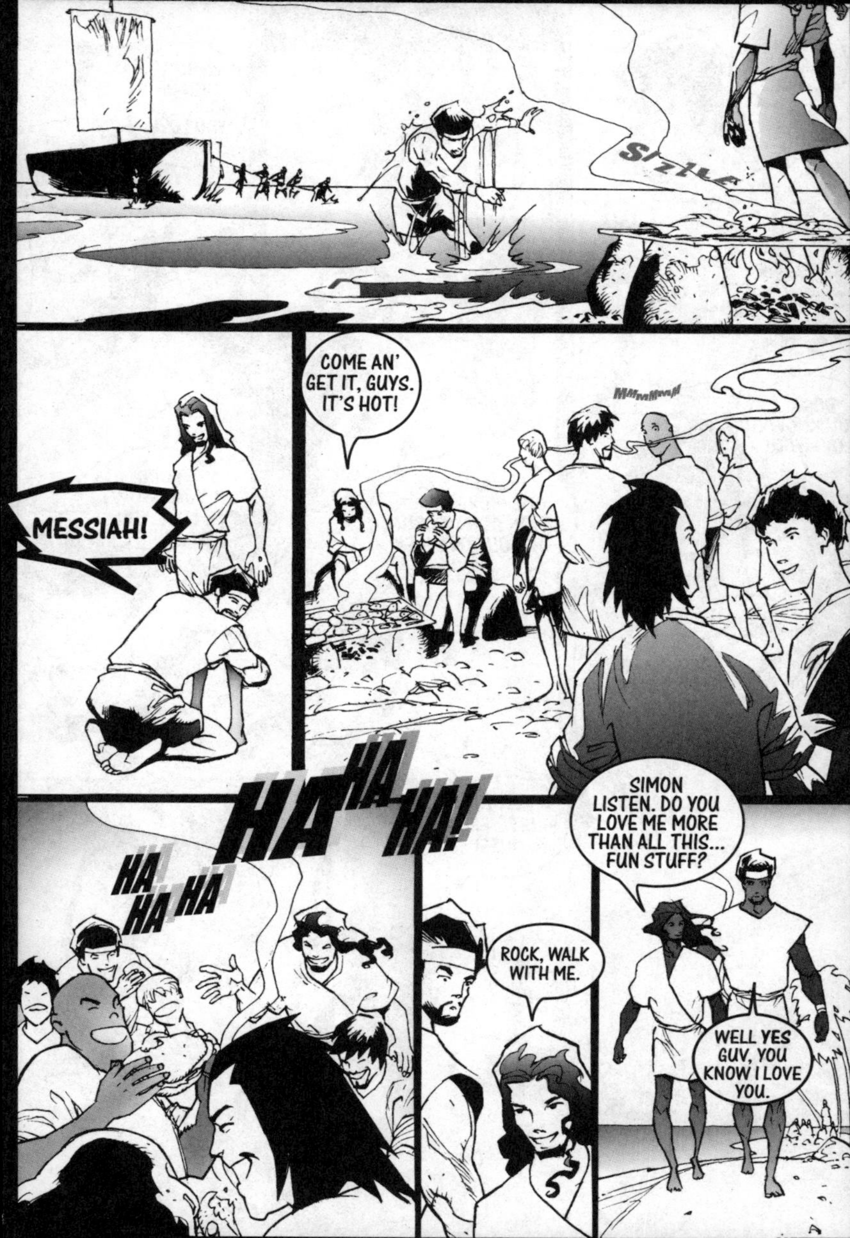
SIZZLE
MESSIAH!
COME AN' GET IT, GUYS. IT'S HOT!
MMMMMMM
HA HA HA HA HA HA!
SIMON LISTEN. DO YOU LOVE ME MORE THAN ALL THIS... FUN STUFF?
ROCK, WALK WITH ME.
WELL YES GUV, YOU KNOW I LOVE YOU.

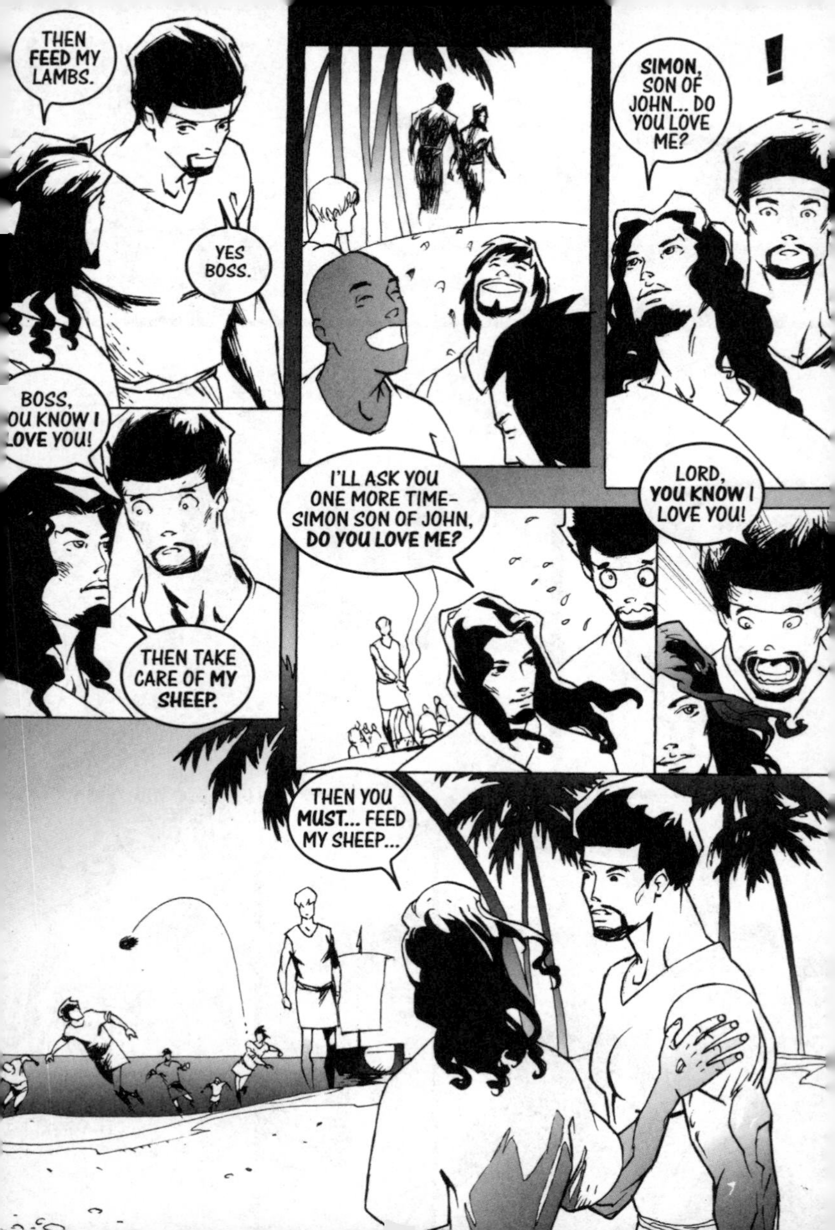
THEN FEED MY LAMBS.
YES BOSS.
SIMON, SON OF JOHN... DO YOU LOVE ME?
!
BOSS, YOU KNOW I LOVE YOU!
THEN TAKE CARE OF MY SHEEP.
I'LL ASK YOU ONE MORE TIME- SIMON SON OF JOHN, DO YOU LOVE ME?
LORD, YOU KNOW I LOVE YOU!
THEN YOU MUST... FEED MY SHEEP...

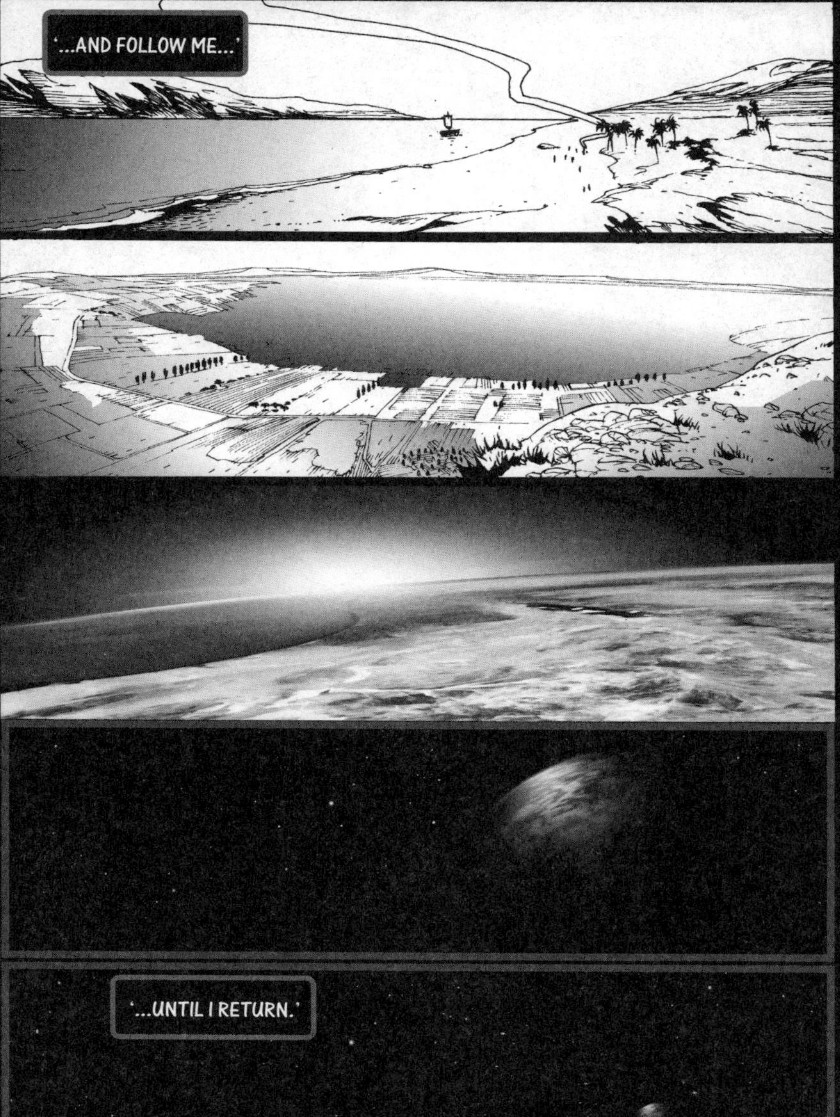
'...AND FOLLOW ME...'
'...UNTIL I RETURN.'

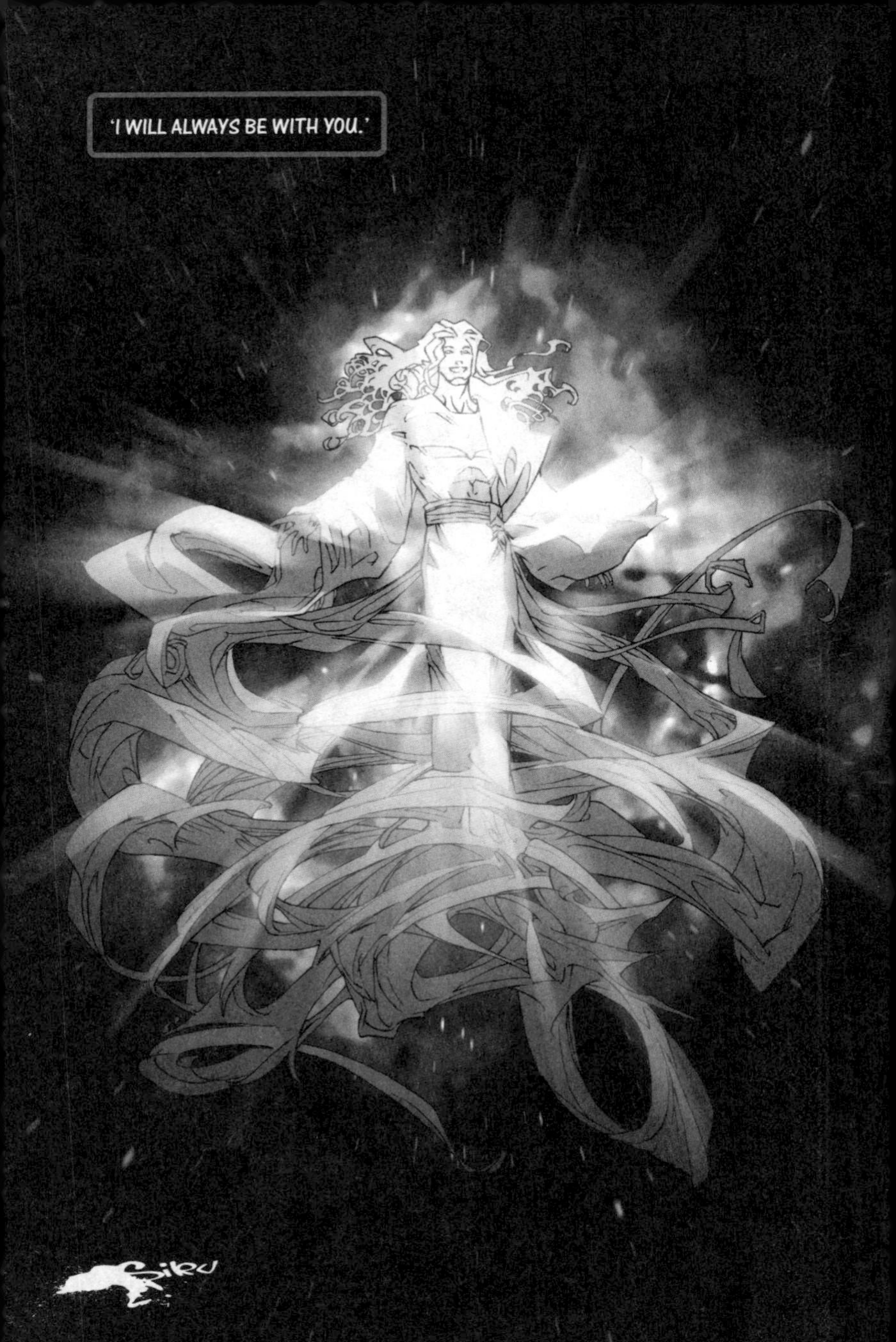
'I WILL ALWAYS BE WITH YOU.'

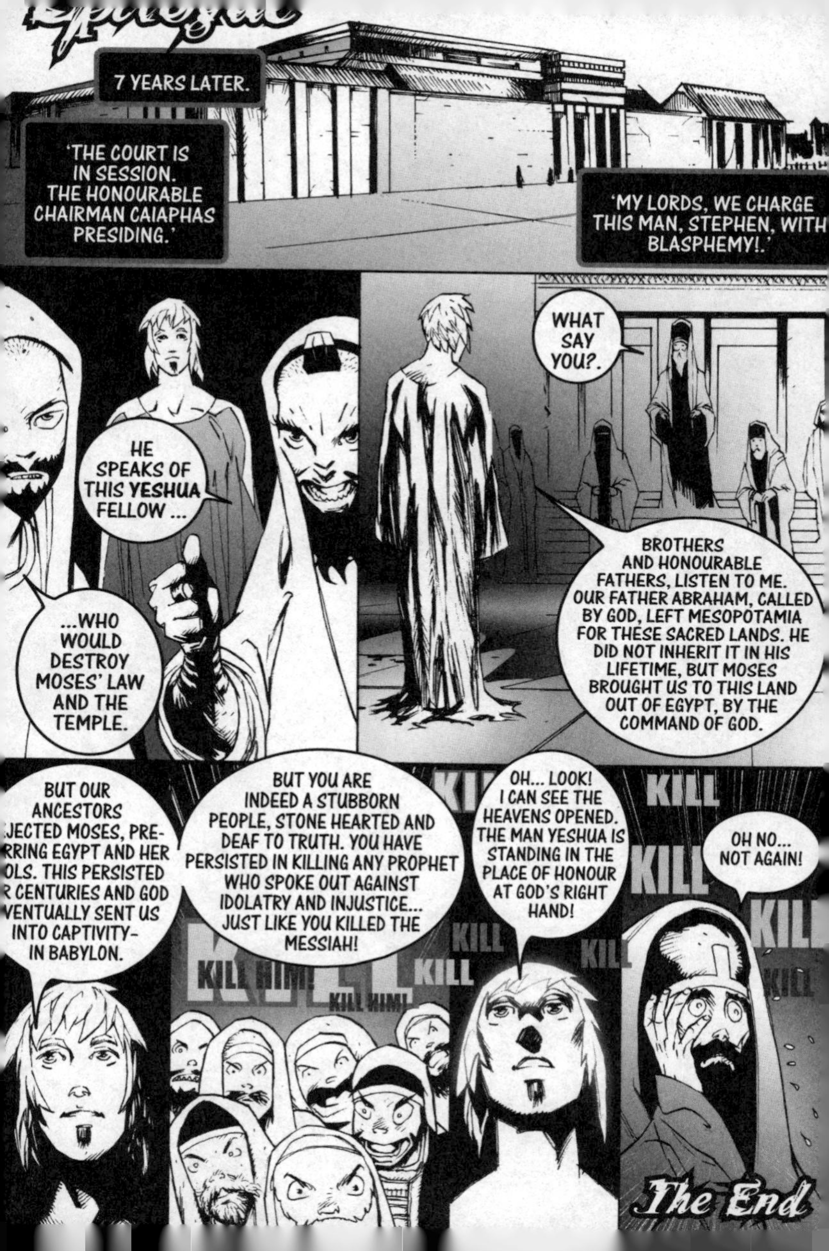
7 YEARS LATER.
'THE COURT IS IN SESSION. THE HONOURABLE CHAIRMAN CAIAPHAS PRESIDING.'
'MY LORDS, WE CHARGE THIS MAN, STEPHEN, WITH BLASPHEMY!.'
HE SPEAKS OF THIS YESHUA FELLOW ...
...WHO WOULD DESTROY MOSES' LAW AND THE TEMPLE.
WHAT SAY YOU?.
BROTHERS AND HONOURABLE FATHERS, LISTEN TO ME. OUR FATHER ABRAHAM, CALLED BY GOD, LEFT MESOPOTAMIA FOR THESE SACRED LANDS. HE DID NOT INHERIT IT IN HIS LIFETIME, BUT MOSES BROUGHT US TO THIS LAND OUT OF EGYPT, BY THE COMMAND OF GOD.
BUT OUR ANCESTORS JECTED MOSES, PRE- RRING EGYPT AND HER OLS. THIS PERSISTED R CENTURIES AND GOD VENTUALLY SENT US INTO CAPTIVITY- IN BABYLON.
BUT YOU ARE INDEED A STUBBORN PEOPLE, STONE HEARTED AND DEAF TO TRUTH. YOU HAVE PERSISTED IN KILLING ANY PROPHET WHO SPOKE OUT AGAINST IDOLATRY AND INJUSTICE... JUST LIKE YOU KILLED THE MESSIAH!
KILL HIM!
KILL HIM!
KILL
KILL
KILL
OH... LOOK! I CAN SEE THE HEAVENS OPENED. THE MAN YESHUA IS STANDING IN THE PLACE OF HONOUR AT GOD'S RIGHT HAND!
KILL
KILL
OH NO... NOT AGAIN!
The End

SKETCHES

These next few pages show the development of characters, storyboards and layouts.

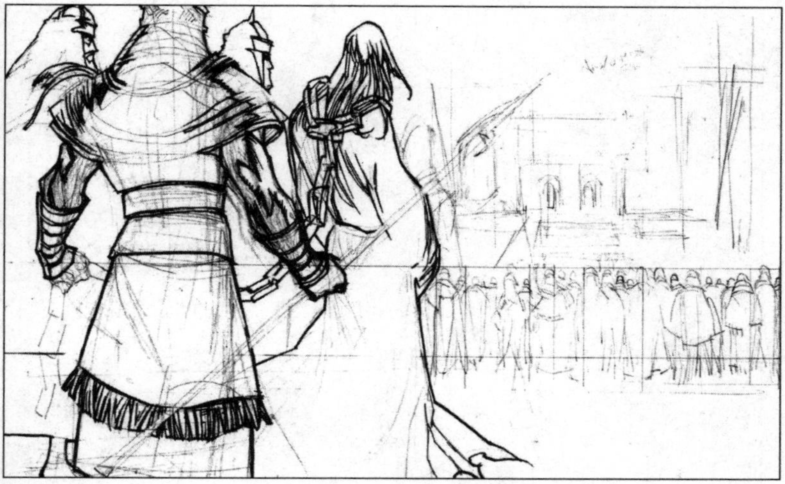

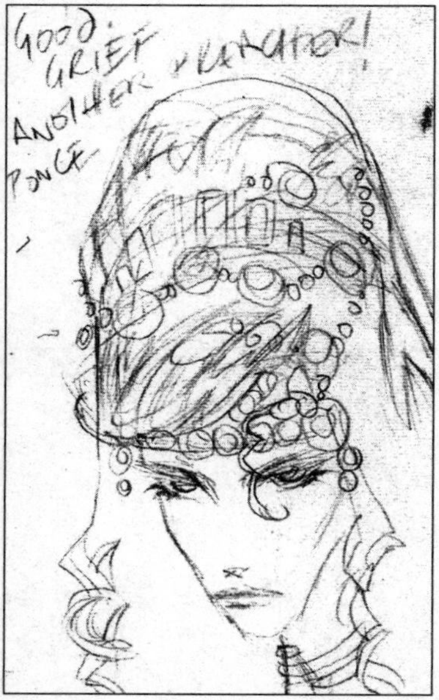
GOOD GRIEF
ANOTHER
PONCE

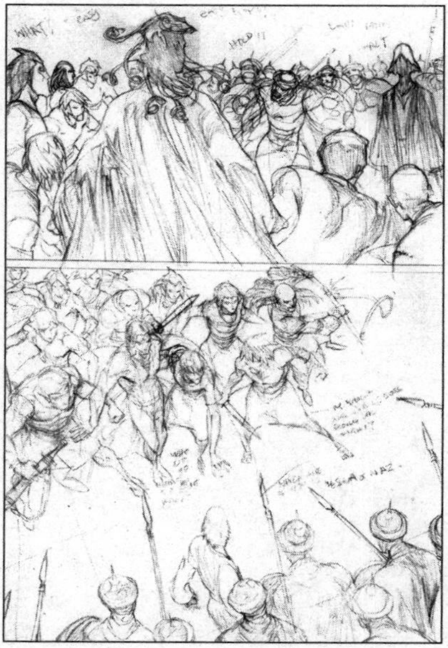

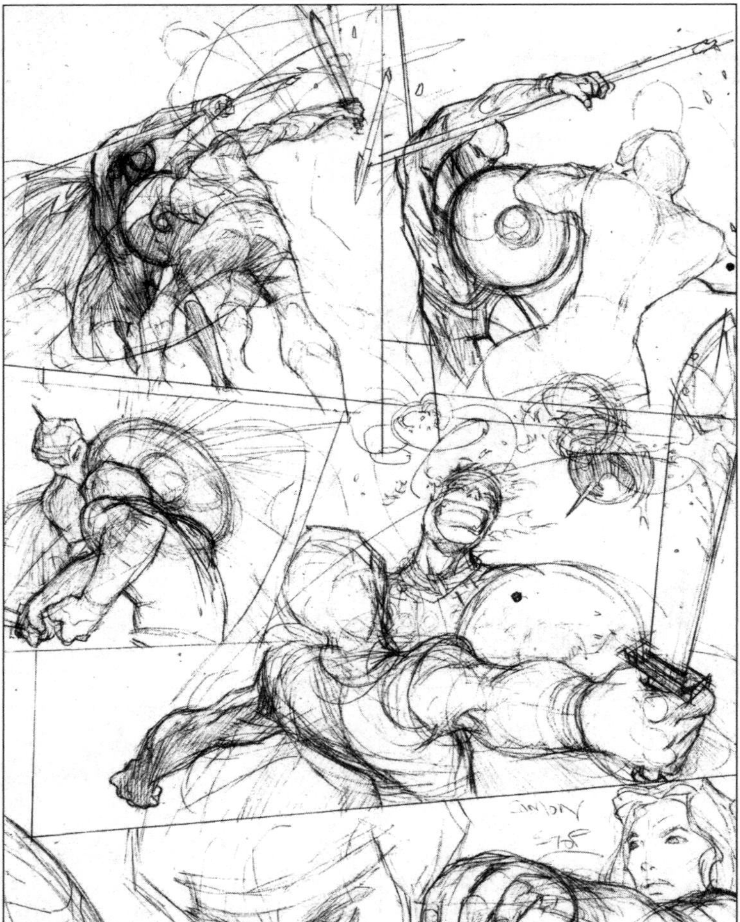

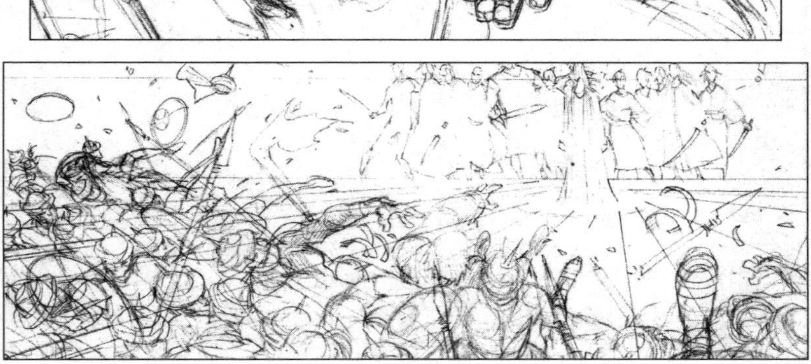

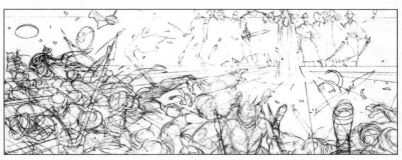

Abraham
The father of the Hebrews. Christians claim him as their spiritual father.

Annas
Otherwise known as Ananus, son of Seth. High Priest between AD 6 to AD 15. He remained influential and was regarded as 'the power behind the throne' with several members of his family succeeding him as High Priest, including Caiaphas who married his daughter.

Antonia fortress
A military garrison built by Herod the Great in honour of Mark Antony. Adjacent to the north west corner of the Temple, it later became a praetorium. It is thought to be the place of Yeshua's trial by Pilate.

Battalion
Translated from the Roman legion military unit known as 'cohort', it is a sub unit consisting of 470 – 480 legionaries.

Caesarea
The north western coastal pagan city rebuilt by Herod the Great in honour of the Emperor Caesar. Pilate's official residence and home to the greatest deep-sea harbour of the ancient world.

Caiaphas
High priest and chairman of the Sanhedrin between AD 18 and AD 37.

Chanuth, the
The market place on the Mount of Olives, across the Kidron Valley from the Temple.

Christ, the
From the Greek, literally meaning 'the Anointed'. Its Hebrew origin is 'the Messiah'. In the Old Testament the title implied little more than 'set apart to perform a particular task'.

Contubernia, the
Otherwise called 'the tent group'. Comprised of only eight legionaries, it was the smallest organised unit in the Roman army.

David, King
Military leader, prophet, musician/ song writer and poet, he was the second king of the united kingdom of Israel. He rose to prominence after killing the Philistine giant warrior Goliath, while he was only a teenager.

Elijah
Considered one of the greatest of the prophets, Elijah lived in the 9th century BC. Jews expect his return as a precursor to the coming of the Messiah.

Ethnarch
A ruler of an ethnic group as designated by Roman power. While this office is higher than the title 'tetrarch', it is not quite as high as the title 'king'. An example of an ethnarch who sought the higher office of king

within the Roman Empire was Herod Archelaus, who ruled over Samaria, Judea and Idumea.

Galilee
The largest and furthest north of the three provinces (with Judea and Samaria) that comprised Israel in Roman times. It also was the most troublesome politically.

Gentiles
Non-Jews and non-followers of the Jewish faith.

Hasmonaean palace
Originally built by the Hasmonaean (Maccabean) kings, it was later refurbished by the Herods. It was probably in use during springtime which coincided with Passover celebrations. Standing on the edge of the western hill, it provided a splendid view of the Temple activities (on the western side). Some scholars believe Yeshua was interrogated here by Herod Antipas.

Herod
Name used of the kings and rulers in the centuries just before and after Jesus, descended from Herod the Great (and his father, Antipater).

Herod the Great
Otherwise known as Herod the Builder, born 73 BC, died 4 BC. Brutal and paranoid client king of Judea and father of Archelaus, Antipas and Philip. He was famous for his many great buildings including the second temple in Jerusalem. His slaughter of the Bethlehem babies and toddlers in his hunt for Yeshua is well known.

Hosanna
It means, 'save now' in Hebrew.

Jacob
Grandson of father Abraham, son of Isaac and brother of Esau. His twelve sons were forefathers of the twelve tribes of Israel — they were — Reuben, Simeon, Levi, Judah, Dan, Naphtali, Gad, Asher, Issachar, Zebulun, Joseph and Benjamin.

Jeremiah
Jeremiah was one of Israel's greatest prophets. He made use of performance art and props as illustrations of his prophetic warnings to Israel.

Jerusalem
The sacred capital of Israel and the Jewish faith. The seat of the temple of God.

Jews
Descendants of Abraham.

Levites
A priestly tribe — descendants of Levi, one of Jacob's sons. As priests, they offered sacrifices, pronounced blessings, provided Temple music, policed the Temple boundaries, blowing trumpets announcing festive occasions and conducted general maintenance of the Temple. They